Preface

About 20 years ago, when both of us were working as mental health professionals in agencies that served a large Asian American client population, we were struck by the gap between the actual therapeutic strategies we used with our Asian American clients and the therapeutic methods and techniques we had learned in graduate school. Throughout the last two decades, this gap has continued to be evident to us both as clinicians and as university faculty. From discussions with other mental health professionals working with Asian Americans, we have learned that they also share our observation.

Even though the availability of literature on Asian American mental health services has significantly increased in recent years, there are still relatively few publications that systematically describe culturally syntonic clinical practices developed by practitioners working with Asian American clients. A major concern in Asian American communities is that clinicians and clinicians-in-training do not have sufficient practitioner-focused literature to prepare them for working with this population. Our colleagues working in the communities have even said to us, "Hopefully, one day you will write about what we are doing. We want other clinicians to build on what we have done rather than keep reinventing the wheel." Comments like these planted the seed for this book.

Our intention for writing this book was to provide a practical and culturally relevant treatment guide for psychotherapy and counseling with Asian American clients. This book takes the commonalities among Asian American groups and uses them to create a bridge between Western therapeutic approaches and Asian cultural practices. In this process, we have taken particular precautions against stereotyping Asian American perspectives and behaviors. The discussions in the book are based on our own clinical experiences and observations, as well as those of our colleagues who work in Asian American communities. This book is intended to be a practical guide for clinicians, clinicians-in training, and students to use as a foundation for providing mental health services to Asian American clients.

Acknowledgments

We want to acknowledge and thank our friends and colleagues who have contributed to this book. Their insightful comments and suggestions and the enlightening examples from their clinical practices were invaluable. Alphabetically, these individuals include Stephen Cheung, PhD, clinical psychologist and administrator at Asian Pacific Treatment and Counseling Centers in Los Angeles, who provided information on that agency's impressive work in serving the Asian American population in Greater Los Angeles and on his extensive experience in group therapy with its clients; Richard Kim, PhD, clinical psychologist, formerly at Coastal Asian Pacific Mental Health Services, Los Angeles County Department of Mental Health, who provided information on Coastal's Community Living Program, which offers culturally appropriate services to Vietnamese American trauma victims, and on his insightful experience in group therapy with its clients; Daniel Lam, EdD, director of the Family and Behavioral Health Division of South Cove Community Health Center in Boston, who provided information on that center's exemplary work in the Asian American communities of Greater Boston and vicinity; and Yoshi Matsushima, LCSW, Program Manager of Coastal Asian Pacific Mental Health Services, Los Angeles County Department of Mental Health, who shared with us his most informative case example in Chapter 6 demonstrating strategies for engaging Asian American clients.

We also wish to thank our graduate assistants who helped us in various aspects of this book. Stephen Woda, MS, and Caroline Tran, MS, now graduated from California State University at Los Angeles, were meticulous in their literature search and most resourceful in locating hard-to-find materials. Darcey Sullivan, at the University of Massachusetts Boston, contributed her excellent administrative and computer skills to our endeavor by compiling and formatting the references for the final draft of the book.

Finally, we appreciate our friends and family who willingly encouraged and supported our endeavor.

1

Introduction

This book is focused on the practical aspects of providing culturally appropriate psychotherapy and counseling for Asian American clients. It systematically examines the issues that mental health professionals need to understand in order to serve this population adequately. This is a book with an applied orientation, and case examples are used extensively as illustrations. It is intended to be used as a map, a practical guide, for directing mental health professionals in their clinical work with Asian American clients.

Because our concern is the provision of culturally appropriate psychotherapy and counseling, we will be focusing primarily on working with Asian American clients who are identified with Asian cultures and who embrace Asian cultural values, norms, and worldviews. This is the population whose cultural orientation requires mental health professionals to adapt and modify their clinical approaches that are developed in the context of Western culture. This book is intended for all mental health professionals, such as psychologists, clinical social workers, counselors, therapists, psychiatrists, psychiatric nurses, and others, as well as students, interns, and trainees. For convenience, we will use the word *clinicians* as a general term to include all these mental health providers and providers-in-training. Likewise, *mental health services, therapy,* and *treatment* will be used as general terms to include both psychotherapy and counseling.

The topics of this book are based mainly on the "frequently asked questions" posed to us by clinicians seeking to develop their cultural proficiency in providing mental health services to Asian American clients. These include questions such as: Are the various Asian American groups very similar or very different from one another? What do you do differently, as an Asian American clinician working with an Asian American client, as compared to what you do when you are working with a mainstream European American client? Why did my Asian American client agree to a second appointment and then never show up or call to cancel? What aspects of Asian cultures or of Asian Americans' social environmental experiences are salient for consideration in mental health services? How are these cultural and social environmental factors manifested in diagnostic and therapeutic encounters, and how should clinicians address them? What are culturally congruent service delivery models? How do you prepare clinicians to work with Asian Americans? Our answers to these questions are based on the literature and in particular on our own clinical experience in the Asian American communities. We also rely on the collective experience of our colleagues working in the community clinics with whom we have ongoing interactions and discussions concerning services for Asian American clients. Case examples, including examples of model service programs, are described throughout this book to illustrate the issues and clinical strategies.

This book begins with general, but important, background information about Asian Americans. Chapter 2 examines the commonality and diversity among Asian Americans and clarifies the use of the term *Asian Americans* in different contexts. Recognizing the diversity among Asian American groups, the chapter explains the rationale of this book in focusing on Chinese Americans, Japanese Americans, Korean Americans, Vietnamese Americans, and Filipino Americans. These groups share many cultural elements due to the historical interactions among their countries of origin. The chapter provides a review of the core culture heritage of these Asian American groups, namely Confucianism, Buddhism, and Taoism, the three philosophies that are fundamental to East Asian and some Southeast Asian cultures. The chapter also examines the historical and contemporary aspects of Asian immigration to the United States and the current demographics. This background information is aimed at helping mental health professionals develop a better appreciation of the cultural heritage and the common life experience of Asian Americans.

Chapter 3 presents a Cultural And Social Environmental (CASE) framework for conceptualizing salient issues in these two areas that are relevant to mental health services for Asian American clients. Clinicians must be aware that individual Asian Americans may differ in their identification with Asian versus mainstream American culture, as well as in the social environmental problems they encounter. This chapter examines specific issues in these areas, including the concepts of accommodation, assimilation, and acculturation, as well as biculturalism. The discussion also covers the issues of biracialism and racial/cultural identification.

Because the majority of Asian Americans are immigrants or from immigrant families, Chapter 4 gives special attention to the dynamics and clinical implications of immigration and refugee experience. Premigration, migration, and postmigration issues are discussed in the context of general systems theory. This chapter also reviews the impact of migration on the family life cycle, the cultural gap within the immigrant family, and the clinical issues concerning particular family situations, such as split households, "astronauts," and "parachute kids." In terms of refugee experience, the traumas encountered by Southeast Asian refugees in their premigration and migration stages are additional stressors that typically further complicate their postmigration adaptation process. Mental health professionals must have an empathic understanding of these immigration and refugee issues to develop their sociocultural sensitivity in working with Asian American clients.

Chapter 5 is focused on specific Asian American cultural and social environmental issues that may be manifested in diagnostic assessments, which are an important component of psychotherapy and counseling. This chapter reviews the major cultural formulations for diagnostic assessments proposed in the literature and examines how cultural and social environmental factors may affect diagnostic assessments for Asian American clients. Included in this discussion are the client's perception of the presenting problem, symptom manifestation, and readiness to disclose issues to the clinician. Precautions in the use of formal psychological tests are discussed as well. Because the application of cultural issues is contingent on a client's cultural orientation, this chapter also examines the assessment of cultural identification for Asian American clients. Practical suggestions for addressing cultural and social environmental factors in diagnostic assessments are made throughout the chapter.

Continuing with the discourse on cultural and social environmental factors, Chapter 6 examines these factors in the context of engaging Asian American clients in psychotherapy and counseling. These factors may affect the therapeutic relationship between clinicians and clients and, in turn, may affect clients' willingness to seek or to continue treatment. Engaging clients in treatment is a critical aspect of the therapeutic process regardless of a clinician's theoretical orientation, for there is little a clinician can do if a client does not return for further sessions. This chapter is focused particularly on Asian American clients who are less assimilated into mainstream American culture, such as many immigrants and refugees who are not familiar with the Western concept of psychotherapy and counseling. The chapter offers many practical suggestions for addressing these issues on the individual clinician-client level and on the institutional level. Asian American clients do seek and benefit from mental health services when these services are provided in the appropriate cultural and social environmental contexts.

Chapter 7 examines the application of major therapeutic approaches of psychotherapy and counseling (psychoanalytic, person-centered, cognitive behavioral) in working with Asian American clients. Although all of these approaches can be used with this population, clinicians must be responsive to their clients' cultural and social environmental contexts and must apply the concepts and techniques judiciously and sensitively. Clinicians need to be aware of the differences in the worldviews and values of these therapeutic approaches, which are based on Western cultures, and the worldviews and values of Asian cultures. Practical guidelines for applying these therapeutic approaches are included along with case examples.

Chapter 8 continues to examine the application of therapeutic approaches to Asian American clients. However, the focus is shifted from individual treatment modalities to two relational treatment modalities: family therapy and group therapy. Again, techniques and strategies that are congruent with the cultural and social environmental contexts of Asian American clients are discussed. Pitfalls in applying these relational treatment modalities are identified. The chapter includes case examples and practical guidelines for clinicians.

Chapter 9 is focused on the institutional and systemic issues of mental health service delivery. This chapter examines models for providing mental health services that are sensitive to the cultural and social environmental contexts of Asian Americans and reviews currently existing exemplary service programs. The chapter also discusses emerging practices, such as the general practitioner approach and the school-based or school-linked family services approach. Because primary prevention is a crucial component of a comprehensive mental health service program, the chapter highlights strategies for addressing the cultural gaps between the home and external mainstream environment and between parents and children at home. These cultural gaps are major risk factors for many Asian Americans. The role of mental health professionals as agents of institutional change is emphasized throughout this chapter. Clinicians need to assume this challenging role to overcome the cultural and social environmental barriers that impede services to Asian American clients.

This book concludes, in Chapter 10, with an examination of the critical curriculum and training issues in preparing clinicians to provide mental health services to Asian American clients that are appropriate to their cultural and social environments. The discussion includes practical suggestions for developing proficiency in the cultural competency domains of awareness, knowledge, and skills. In conclusion, this chapter provides a synopsis of the major issues covered in this book and summarizes these issues with the acronym *ASIAN AMERICAN*.

2

Asian American Cultures and Demographics

This chapter provides an overview of the demographic trends and the core cultural heritage shared by many Asian American groups. It examines the commonalities and diversities among Asian Americans in terms of both their cultural traditions and their migration experience. This general background information is aimed at helping mental health professionals develop an appreciation of the cultural commonalities and other similar life experiences of Asians living in the United States. In subsequent chapters, we will examine the relationship between specific cultural and social environmental issues and psychotherapy and counseling, including diagnostic assessment and service delivery models.

Terminology Concerning Asian Americans

Asian American is a general term referring to Americans who originated from many different Asian countries. We will start by clarifying some of the common terminology used to denote them.

Asian Americans and Pacific Islanders

Traditionally, the U.S. Census Bureau has been grouping Asian Americans together with Pacific Islanders under the general term *Asian and Pacific Islanders.* This single category includes over 51 groups of people (U.S.

Bureau of the Census, 1993b). Among them, 30 groups are Asians and 21 groups are Pacific Islanders. Ten major Asian groups are identified in the census. As ranked from most to least numerous, they are Chinese, Filipino, Japanese, Indian, Korean, Vietnamese, Laotian, Cambodian, Thai, and Hmong. Twenty other Asian groups are listed under the term *other Asian.* Alphabetically, they are Bangladeshi, Bhutanese, Borneo, Burmese, Celebesin, Ceram, Indochinese, Indonesian, Iwo-Jiman, Javanese, Malayan, Maldavian, Nepali, Okinawan, Pakistani, Sikkim, Singaporean, Sri Lankan, Sumatran, and Asian-not specified. Three major Pacific Islander groups are identified in the census: Hawaiian, Samoan, and Guamian. Eighteen other Pacific Islander groups are listed as "other Pacific Islanders." Overall, Asian Americans constitute about 95% of the Asian/Pacific Islander population, and Pacific Islanders constitute the remaining 5%. Interestingly, not all the different groups were recognized as distinct categories in the census data collected at different times. For example, in the 1970 census, Asian Indians were counted as "white," whereas Vietnamese and many other smaller Asian groups were grouped together in a general "other" race category (Gardner, Robey, & Smith, 1985; Min, 1995c). Koreans were added as a category in the 1970 census. Asian Indians, Vietnamese, and others were added in the 1980 census. It is expected that the 2000 census will categorize Asian Americans as one racial group and Pacific Islanders as another rather than continuing to group them together.

Asian Americans *Versus* Orientals

As noted in the fourth edition of the *Publication Manual of the American Psychological Association* (American Psychological Association, 1994), preferences for terms used to denote specific ethnic and racial groups may change over time. Currently, *Asian Americans* is the proper term for denoting Americans of Asian descent and immigrants from Asia, and specific subgroups should be identified as *Chinese Americans, Filipino Americans,* and so on. However, before the 1960s, *Orientals* was a common term used by both Asian Americans and non-Asian Americans to denote Asians. In the late 1960s, with the heightened racial/ethnic awareness of the civil rights movement in the United States, Asian American activists rejected the term *Orientals* in favor of *Asian Americans* (Baron & Gall, 1996; Cao & Novas, 1996; Espiritu, 1992). They regarded *Orientals* as a pejorative term associated with the negative stereotypes of Asians, such as being "inscrutable," "mysterious," "exotic," "passive," and "despotic" (Cao & Novas, 1996; Espiritu, 1992). The word *Orientals* also connoted an imperialistic, colonialist, and Eurocentric relationship imposed on Asians, as the word *Orient* denotes the "East," which is the position of

Asia in relation to Europe (Cao & Novas, 1996; Espiritu, 1992; Ham, 1999). In addition, being called *Orientals* implied that Asian Americans were "foreign" because the term did not distinguish them from people living in Asia (Cao & Novas, 1996). Hence, as an act of self-determination and empowerment, Asian American activists chose *Asian Americans* as the general term to denote all Americans of Asian descent.

The spearhead of this "Asian American" movement was in California, the state with the largest Asian American population (Baron & Gall, 1996; Espiritu, 1992). In 1968-1969, Asian American students along with other minority students at San Francisco State College (currently San Francisco State University) and the University of California at Berkeley demonstrated for the establishment of ethnic studies programs (Baron & Gall, 1996; Kim, 1986; Ng, 1995). The chapters of the Asian American Political Alliance established at both campuses also started promoting the use of the term *Asian American* in place of *Oriental* (Baron & Gall, 1996). This change was soon adopted by student activists at the University of California at Los Angeles (Espiritu, 1992). Throughout the 1970s and the 1980s, use of the term *Asian American* gradually spread beyond California and beyond academia. By the late 1980s, the word *Oriental* had become a dated term. Calling an Asian American an *Oriental* may be seen as insulting, insensitive, or, at best, socioculturally uninformed. However, the preference for using *Asian American* instead of *Oriental* is strictly a U.S. phenomenon, with its roots in the civil rights movement. Many people in Asia do not think there is anything wrong with the term *Oriental*. New Asian immigrants may not always be aware of the negative connotations of this term in the United States and may identify themselves to others as "Orientals." Similarly, English-language publications in Asia may also use the term *Orientals*. Though this discrepancy can be confusing, mental health professionals in the United States should adhere to the term *Asian Americans,* which is the preference of the Asian American community.

Growth of Asian American Population

In recent decades, the numbers of Asian Americans or Asian/Pacific Islander Americans have doubled at every census. From a mere 0.60 million in 1950, the Asian/Pacific Islander population grew to a total of 7.27 million in the 1990 census, an increase of over 12 times (Gardner et al., 1985; Hing, 1993). In 1997, their numbers reached 10.03 million (Table 2.1) (U.S. Bureau of the Census, 1998d). This growth trend is expected to continue into the 21st century, with the projected numbers being 11.25 million, 24.34 million, and 34.35 million for the years 2000, 2030, and 2050 respectively (U.S. Bureau of the Census, 1998d). This is a 4.7-fold in-

crease from 1990 to 2050. This growth rate is the highest among all eth-
nic/racial groups identified in the census and is matched only by the
4.3-fold increase of the Hispanic-origin group (note that persons of Hispanic origin can be of any race), which is projected to increase from 22.35
million in 1990 (U.S. Bureau of the Census, 1992) to 96.51 million in 2050
(U.S. Bureau of the Census, 1998d). To look at these statistics in another
way, Asian/Pacific Islanders will increase from 2.9% of the total U.S. population in 1990 to 8.7% of the total population by the year 2050. In fact,
these numbers are just a middle-range projection. The highest series projection puts the Asian/Pacific Islander population dramatically higher at
11.85 million, 32.30 million, and 50.20 million in the years 2000, 2030,
and 2050 respectively (U.S. Bureau of the Census, 1998d).

Asian Americans as a Group

Currently, although there is a significant presence of Asian Americans
in many parts of the United States, their actual numbers are still relatively small in comparison to the total U.S. population. As of 1997, Asian
and Pacific Islanders constituted only 3.7% of the general population.
Grouping them under a single category was simply a matter of convenience for census data collection and reporting. However, in terms of public services planning and delivery, professionals need to be aware of the
diverse cultures and needs of these different groups of people. Fortunately, the growth of the Asian American population in many localities
and the projected growth in the coming decades have made this issue clear
to many public policy makers as well as mental health professionals. Yet
we must also avoid the other extreme position that Asian Americans can
never be discussed as a unified group (Hong, 2000; Hong, Garcia, &
Soriano, 2000; Hong & Ham, 1994). Our challenge is to recognize the differences among many Asian American groups while acknowledging their
commonalities as unifying contributions to the generic term *Asian Americans*. Any polarizing position is misleading and often counterproductive.
The field of Asian American mental health services will become confusing and fragmented by a multiplicity of dichotomous classifications. The
emphasis on diversity among Asian Americans sometimes makes the design and provision of culturally syntonic services seem like an insurmountable hurdle. A more unifying approach is conducive to the development of cultural competence in mental health professionals and the
planning of culturally appropriate therapeutic interventions. No doubt,
recognizing the differences among the various Asian groups is important.
In fact, as we will discuss later in this chapter, one should go even further

Table 2.1 U.S. Population by Race, 1993-2050 (Actual and Projected, in Thousands and as Percentage of Total Population)

Year	Total U.S. Population	White	Black	American Indian, Eskimo, Aleut	Asian/Pacific Islander	Hispanic Origin[a]
1993	257,753	214,715 (83.3%)	32,180 (12.5%)	2,184 (0.8%)	8,675 (3.4%)	25,334 (9.8%)
1995	262,761	218,066 (83.0%)	33,093 (12.6%)	2,252 (0.9%)	9,349 (3.6%)	27,274 (10.4%)
1997	267,636	221,334 (82.7%)	33,947 (12.7%)	2,322 (0.9%)	10,033 (3.7%)	29,348 (11.0%)
2000[b]	274,634	225,532 (82.1%)	35,454 (12.9%)	2,402 (0.9%)	11,245 (4.1%)	31,366 (11.4%)
2030[b]	346,899	269,046 (77.6%)	50,001 (14.4%)	3,515 (1.0%)	24,337 (7.0%)	65,570 (18.9%)
2050[b]	393,931	294,615 (74.8%)	60,592 (15.4%)	4,371 (1.1%)	34,352 (8.7%)	96,508 (24.5%)

SOURCE: U.S. Bureau of the Census (1998d).
a. Persons of Hispanic origin may be of any race; numbers overlap with counts in the other four racial categories.
b. Middle-series projections.

9

to recognize the regional differences within a single country (Hong & Ham, 1994). However, mental health professionals also need to acknowledge that there are enough commonalities among Asian Americans for them to be considered as a group in comparison to other ethnic groups in the United States (Hong, 1993a; Hong & Ham, 1994; Min, 1995c). As Min (1995c) has stated succinctly, despite their interethnic and intraethnic differences, Asian Americans have enough common cultural values as well as common life experiences in the United States to have a pan-Asian identity.

Keeping in mind the commonalities as well as the differences among Asian Americans, our subsequent discussion in this book will focus on the larger subgroups that share a similar cultural heritage. Historically, two centers of cultural influence existed in Asia (McCasland, Cairns, & Yu, 1969). China was the predominant power in East Asia, and India was the predominant power in South Asia. Countries in Southeast Asia were influenced by one or both of them, depending on their geographical proximity and ease of communication and travel in premodern times. In this book, we are concentrating on cultures that share the Chinese influence. Other Asian cultural groups, such as Asian Indian Americans and Pakistani Americans, are beyond the scope of our present work. Specifically, we will be focusing on Chinese Americans, Japanese Americans, Korean Americans, Vietnamese Americans, and, to a certain extent, Filipino Americans. Given that there are also important similarities between the cultures of these countries and other Asian countries, as well as the common experience of Asian Americans in the United States, many of the issues discussed in this book are often applicable, with caution, to other Asian Americans in general.

Historical Interrelationship of Asian Cultures

To better appreciate the common cultural heritage of the Asian American groups, an overview of the historical relationships among their countries of origin is essential.

Historical, Political, and Cultural Relationships

Since early historical times, China was a center of civilization as well as political power in Asia. Its influence was analogous to that of Rome or Greece in Europe (Cotterell, 1993). Its philosophies, religions, system of government, writing system, art, and technology were basically followed by all the neighboring countries.

China's cultural influence started to flow gradually into Korea as early as the first millennium B.C. (Fairbank, Reischauer, & Craig, 1973). In the first century B.C., China extended direct rule over Korea and created Chinese settlements there. This further established Chinese cultural and political influence in the area. Even after Chinese rule and the Chinese colonies in Korea dissolved during the fourth century A.D., the Chinese influence persisted. For most of its history, Korea maintained a tributary relationship with China. It looked toward China as the model of civilization and absorbed most of the core elements of Chinese culture as well as the Chinese political system (Cotterell, 1993; Fairbank et al., 1973).

China's historical relationship with Vietnam was similar to that with Korea. At about the same time that China extended its rule over Korea, it also annexed the area of what was later known as North Vietnam. Chinese rule here lasted for a full thousand years, from 111 B.C. to 939 A.D. (Fairbank et al., 1973). Thus, the Chinese system of government and most of the literate culture of ancient China were firmly established in this country. Even after gaining independence from China, Vietnam continued to follow the Chinese cultural and political models. Like Korea, Vietnam maintained a tributary relationship with China well into the 19th century and assimilated its cultural influence (Cotterell, 1993; Fairbank et al., 1973).

Early Chinese influence came to Japan by way of Korea, which was geographically in between China and Japan. Unlike Korea and Vietnam, Japan was never occupied by China, even though at various times in history its rulers were regarded by Chinese emperors as subordinate princes (Cotterell, 1993; Fairbank et al., 1973). In the beginning, the flow of Chinese cultural influence into Japan was basically a gradual and unconscious process. But after Buddhism was firmly established in the Japanese court in 587, the Japanese government began to make a deliberate effort to import Chinese culture (Fairbank et al., 1973). Prince Shotoku (574-662), a major political figure at that time, was credited with formally adopting major elements of Chinese culture, including Buddhism and Confucianism, as well as the system of government and calendar. After that, Japan continued to use Chinese civilization as a model (Cotterell, 1993; Fairbank et al., 1973).

Direct contact between China and the Philippines was established from at least the Sung Dynasty of China (960-1279) (Wickberg, 1965). Instead of political control or dominance, China's early cultural influence over the Philippines came mainly by means of seafaring traders and settlers who had established a significant presence there. By the time of the Ming Dynasty of China (1368-1644), Chinese traders had established their eastern seafaring route that passed through the Philippines en route from South China to other parts of Southeast Asia (Wickberg, 1965). Also, long before the arrival of the Spanish in the 16th century, native rulers in Luzon, the largest of the over 7,000 islands constituting the Philippines, had been sending emissaries and tribute to China (Pan, 1990). In 1405, the Chinese Emperor Yung Lo of the Ming Dynasty even sent an official to govern Luzon, and it was briefly brought under direct Chinese political authority (Pan, 1990). However, China did not maintain imperialistic interest in the island for long. Thus, when the Spanish arrived in Luzon and founded the city of Manila in 1575, the major resistance was not from the official Chinese government but from the Chinese settlers there (Pan, 1990). Major conflicts with the powerful local community of Chinese traders and Chinese from abroad continued at various times throughout Spanish colonial rule. Despite efforts by the Spanish to limit their influence and to expel them, the Chinese were able to maintain a powerful presence. Over the years, as a result of both coercion and inducement from the Spanish colonial rulers, as well as other social factors, a significant number of Chinese were converted to Catholicism and married converted *Indias* (native Filipinas). Their offspring, known as *Chinese mestizos* or simply as *mestizos,* often showed a combination of the cultural attributes of the Spanish, Indio, and Chinese (Wickberg, 1965). Although their numbers relative to the total Filipino population were small, by the 19th century Chinese mestizos made up a third or more of the population in six provinces and accounted for 5% to 16% of the population in another six provinces (Wickberg, 1965). At present, there are many Filipinos with *mestizos* in their ancestry.

The Philippines was ceded to the United States by Spain after the Spanish-American War in 1898 and became independent in 1946. As a result of the long history of Spanish rule and the subsequent rule by the United States, the Philippines is the most westernized of the Asian countries. For example, due to Spanish influence, the Philippines is the only Asian country where Christianity is the majority religion, with over 80% of the people being Roman Catholics (Agbayani-Siewert & Revilla, 1995; Min, 1995c). Its cultural heritage is dominated by Christianity rather than by Confucianism or Buddhism, which were prominent forces in other East Asian countries (Min, 1995c; Root, 1997). In addition, the current political, economic, and educational systems of the Philippines have been strongly influenced by the United States. In a sense, Filipino culture reflects a mixture of Western and Eastern cultures. It clearly shows the historical influence of Spanish culture and the more recent socioeconomic and political influence of the United States. However, the culture of the Philippines still shares many characteristics with the cultures of its neighboring Asian countries because of its geographical location and historical interactions with them (Araneta, 1993). Among the common cultural characteristics that have significant implications for mental health services, the most prominent are the emphasis on familism and the importance of "smooth interpersonal relationships" (Agbayani-Siewert & Revilla, 1995). Like the other Asian countries discussed earlier, Filipino culture is family oriented. It focuses on the reciprocal obligations among family members in both the nuclear and extended family, as opposed to the individualism in Western cultures. In interpersonal interactions, open display of anger, direct criticisms of others, conflict, and confrontation are discouraged. Harmony or "going along with others" is valued.

In sum, this overview of the historical relationships among these Asian countries shows that, in cultural terms, they can be discussed as a composite group. No doubt, there are national differences among these countries, as well as regional differences within each country. However, as a group, they generally have more commonalities with one another than with European or mainstream American culture (Hong, 1993a; Min, 1995c). This is similar to the case of U.S. culture. Regional differences exist throughout the United States: the East Coast, the West Coast, the Midwest, and the South. However, there are enough commonalities for us to talk generally about a U.S. culture or a mainstream American culture. In a similar way, we can also talk about these Asian cultures as a group.

Philosophical and Religious Traditions

Having examined the historical relationship among the five countries, we will now turn to the common foundation of their traditional cultures. In general, the worldviews of these Asian cultures, with the partial exception of the Philippines, are based on the philosophies and religions of Confucianism, Taoism, and Buddhism (Hong, 1993a; Hong & Friedman, 1998). This orientation distinguishes them, as a group, from Western or European cultures, whose worldviews are based on the Judaeo-Christian legacy. It is important for clinicians to understand the core teachings of these Asian religions and philosophies to develop an empathic appreciation of the values, norms, and other elements of Asian cultures. Here we will give an overview of Confucianism, Taoism, and Buddhism, focusing on their basic teachings with regard to interpersonal relationships and a person's way of life, both of which are crucial factors to consider in psychotherapy and counseling. In subsequent chapters of this book, we will discuss how the values, norms, and other elements of worldviews identified here may be manifested in the context of mental health services for Asian Americans. Clinicians interested in learning more about these philosophies and religions are encouraged to read the references cited here, especially the concise but in-depth discussion in Huston Smith's (1991) book.

Confucianism

Confucius (c. 551-479 B.C.), is the westernized name of Kong Fu Zi (Kung Fu Tzu), which means Master Kong or Teacher Kong. He was the most prominent Chinese philosopher, whose teachings were deeply embedded in the cultures in many Asian countries for more than 2,000 years. Over the centuries, many well-known philosophers and scholars promoted and expounded on the original teachings of Confucius. One of them was Mencius (c. 371-289 B.C.), the westernized name of Meng Zi (Men Tzu), whose teachings were regarded as among the classics of Confucianism.

Confucius lived and taught at a time when China was politically disintegrating into a system of semi-independent states ruled by regional lords who paid only nominal allegiance to the central ruler of the Chou Dynasty. Confucius felt that the social and political turmoil in his time was a result of the moral deterioration of the ruling class, which in turn led to the moral deterioration of the common people (McCasland et al., 1969). He sought to revive the "traditional culture," under which rulers would cultivate virtue and inspire their subjects to follow their example. He established what was likely to be the first school for commoners, departing from the practice of that period, in which only aristocrats could receive education. By the time of his death at age 72, some of his disciples had become government officials in different states, and others had established schools to promote his ideas. In the first century A.D., Confucianism was officially instituted as a state philosophy of a unified China.

Confucianism was a comprehensive philosophical system of ethics and government encompassing all aspects of life, including interpersonal relationships, religion, and education (McCasland et al., 1969; Smith, 1991). Central to it was the concept of the "virtuous" or "righteous" person (*Jun Zi* or *Chun Tzu*). This was a person who possessed and practiced the virtues of inner integrity, righteousness, loyalty, altruism, and, above all, love, benevolence, or human-heartedness (*Jen* or *Ren*) (Fairbank et al., 1973). The foundation of *Jen* (*Ren*) was empathy, putting oneself in the other person's position. This concept is best illustrated by two sayings in the *Analects of Confucius* as cited by McCasland et al. (1969). Passively, *Jen* (*Ren*) means "Do not do to others what you would not like yourself" (p. 618). Actively, it means "[If] you yourself desire rank and standing, then help others to get rank and standing" (p. 618). Confucianism emphasized mutual responsibility and the relationship of a person with society and, especially, with the family. This established the foundation of collectivism in Asian cultures, with the focus on the family and the community, as opposed to the individualism of the West. Social life consisted of five basic relationships: parent-child, older-younger siblings, husband-wife, friend-friend, and ruler-subject. The social codes stated that parents should be loving and children should practice filial piety; older siblings should be gentle and younger siblings should be respectful; husbands should be good and wives should listen; elder friends should be considerate and younger friends should be deferential; rulers should be benevolent and subjects should be loyal (Smith, 1991). Confucianism also emphasized the role of education in helping one to develop into a righteous or virtuous person who will practice benevolence or *Jen (Ren)*. Later, Mencius went further to specify that human nature is innately good. Evil in a person is the result of a detrimental environment that obstructs the person's ability and effort to develop his or her innate goodness (McCasland et al., 1969). It is interesting to note how this position resonates with the premises of humanistic psychology. Although Confucius was later venerated as a holy man, with temples built in his honor, Confucianism is basically a philosophy, a way of life, and a worldview rather than a religion.

Taoism

Taoism is the second most important school of Chinese thought, second only to Confucianism (Fairbank et al., 1973). Its basic ideas are deeply ingrained in the culture. As Fairbank et al. (1973) put it, Chinese artists and poets, no matter how closely they were identified with Confucianism, have usually been Taoist at heart.

Lao Zi (Lao Tzu) is generally regarded as the founder of Taoism. Very little is known about his life. In fact, there are even questions about whether he was a historical person or merely a legendary figure. It is believed that he was born around 604 B.C., about 50 years earlier than Confucius (McCasland et al., 1969; Smith, 1991). The basic text of Taoism is *Dao De Jing (Tao Te Ching)* or *The Way and Its Power,* a book attributed to Lao Zi. This is a small book of about 5,000 words, written in a cryptic style. There are many different interpretations of its contents (Fairbank et al., 1973; McCasland et al., 1969). Like Confucianism, over the centuries, the teachings of Lao Zi had been expounded and developed by many other scholars and philosophers. Among them was Zhuang Zi (Chuang Tzu) (c. 369-286 B.C.), whose metaphor of the "butterfly dream"—"Was I a man dreaming that I was a butterfly, or a butterfly dreaming that I was a man"—is well known in the West.

Lao Zi emphasized *wu wei,* which literally means "doing nothing" or inaction. It could be expressed as passivity, absence of ambition for power or gain, simplicity, modesty, and nonviolence in government as well as in everyday life (McCasland et al., 1969). He advocated a "minimal government interference" or laissez-faire approach in government and a simple, peaceful lifestyle in harmony with fellow human beings and with nature. After Lao Zi, Taoism slowly developed into three basic schools: philosophical or scholastic Taoism, religious Taoism, and the hygiene school (Smith, 1991). Philosophical or scholastic Taoism continued to develop as a philosophy, whereas the other two schools took a more drastic turn.

Religious Taoism emerged in the middle part of the second century A.D. It instituted elaborate rituals and elevated Lao Zi to the status of a deity (McCasland et al., 1969; Smith, 1991). It was a pantheistic religion that incorporated many of the beliefs and practices of folk religion. Early Taoist monks often practiced alchemy, emphasizing the cultivation of elixirs or potions for immortality. The hygiene school, which also sought to promote health and long life, became influential during the first century A.D. But instead of magic and elixirs, it focused on the balance of *Qi* (*Chi*), a force or energy. Its followers sought to enhance physical health and mental peace through exercises aimed at normalizing or balancing the *Qi* (*Chi*) or forces in one's body. *Qi Qong* (*Chi Kung*), a form of meditation in conjunction with controlled breathing, and *Tai Ji Quan* (*Tai Chi Chuan*), a form of martial arts that combines calisthenics, dance, meditation, and breathing (Smith, 1991), are two traditional exercises that are commonly practiced today. They are considered to be health practices rather than religious rituals and are practiced by Taoist and non-Taoist alike. As we will discuss in Chapter 9, some Asian American mental health clinics actually include *Tai Ji* (*Tai Chi*) and other similar forms of exercises as a component of their programs, or as a way to engage clients. Interestingly, *Qi-Qong* psychotic reaction is one of the culture-bound syndromes listed in the fourth edition of the *Diagnostic and Statistical Manual of Mental Disorders* (*DSM-IV*) (American Psychiatric Association, 1994). Although this is regarded as a psychiatric disorder by mental health professionals in the West, in Asian folk belief the symptoms are considered to be the result of practicing *Qi Qong* (*Chi Kung*) improperly.

Buddhism

Buddhism was founded in India by Siddhartha Gautama (c. 560-480 B.C.). He was a prince who abandoned a life of comfort and luxury to seek enlightenment as an ascetic. Later he became known as the Buddha or the Enlightened One (McCasland et al., 1969; Smith, 1991). Buddhism developed from Hinduism and spread to become a major religion in Asia. However, within India, it eventually reintegrated with Hinduism and diminished as a distinct major religion (McCasland et al., 1969).

The basic tenets of Buddhism can be found in the Four Noble Truths (McCasland et al., 1969; Smith, 1991). Stated simply, life is suffering (*dukkha*), and desire (*tanha*) is the cause of suffering. Suffering can be eliminated by ending desire, and the way to achieve this is through the Eightfold Path. The Eightfold Path can be considered as the rules of proper living, which consist of right knowledge, right thought, right speech, right conduct, right livelihood, right efforts, right mindfulness, and right concentration. In brief, the Eightfold Path involves a life free of evil or vain thoughts, desires, speech, or conduct. It requires a person to hold the proper occupation and refrain from taking any life or harming others. It also prescribes continuous self-examination, meditation, and learning about the principles of Buddhism (McCasland et al., 1969; Smith, 1991).

During the first century A.D., Buddhism spread from India into China and, in the next few centuries, grew into a major religion. This new religion was particularly appealing to the Taoist monks who found many commonalities between religious Taoism and Buddhism (McCasland et al., 1969). From China, Buddhism spread to Japan and Korea. The Tang Dynasty (618-906) was generally regarded as the heyday of Buddhism in China. Buddhism was very adaptable to the cultural milieu of the different host countries. In China, over the years, Buddhism developed into various schools by incorporating many elements of Chinese culture and thought adapted from Confucianism and Taoism. Similarly in Japan, some schools of Buddhism incorporated elements of Shintoism, an indigenous Japanese religion (McCasland et al., 1969). Today, Buddhism continues to be a major religion in Asia. Although there are different schools or sects of Buddhism, they are not mutually exclusive. The average lay follower often may not even be mindful of such distinctions (Hong & Friedman, 1998). Many followers may also practice other folk religions along with Buddhism.

Overall Influence

Confucianism, Taoism, and Buddhism are deeply embedded in the worldviews of many Asian cultures (Hong, 1993a; Hong & Friedman, 1998). Looking at the common themes among these three philosophies or religions, we can see their imprint on many core Asian cultural values, such as the emphasis on interpersonal harmony, moderation, compromise, mutual respect, modesty, nonassertiveness, nonaggression, respect for life and for nature, and acceptance of one's fate. Specific values and norms of Asian cultures discussed in later chapters can often be traced to one or all of these philosophies and beliefs. It should be noted that Asians do not have to identify themselves as, say, Confucian, in order to practice the teachings of Confucius. The Asian family system is based on Confucianism. Being raised as a child in an Asian family is enough to socialize one, consciously or unconsciously, into the ideals of this philosophy. In other words, the prescriptions of these philosophies and religions are often synonymous with Asian cultural norms and values. An Asian who is identified with traditional culture will inadvertently be following their teachings.

Asian Immigration to the United States

Having examined the common roots of Asian cultures, we can now turn our attention to the shared experiences of Asian Americans as immigrants in the United States. A good way to develop an empathic understanding of these experiences is to take a historical look at Asian immigration and U.S. legislative policies affecting Asian immigrants. Asian immigration to the United States can be roughly divided into two periods: pre-World War II and post-World War II. Between these two periods was a moratorium on Asian immigration due to discriminatory U.S. policies.

Pre-World War II Asian Immigration

The pre-World War II period mainly involved Asian immigrants who came to the United States in the 1800s to early 1900s. The majority of these early immigrants were laborers, although there were also small numbers of skilled or educated immigrants, such as merchants and college students.

Among the various groups of Asians, the Chinese were the first to arrive in large numbers. Many of them came in the 1850s to build the transcontinental railroad or work in the gold mines of California (Hing, 1993; Hong & Friedman, 1998; Wong, 1995), and some came to work in the plantations of Hawaii (Tsai, 1986). By 1880, close to 106,000 Chinese immigrants lived in the mainland United States, and another 10,000 lived in Hawaii (Kim, 1986; Wong, 1998). The second group of Asians to arrive in significant numbers was the Japanese, followed by the Koreans, and then by the Filipinos, all of whom were mainly recruited to work in the sugarcane plantations of Hawaii (Hong & Friedman, 1998; Min, 1995b). Japanese workers started arriving there in the 1890s, and by 1900, they had become the largest ethnic group on the islands, numbering 61,000 (Nishi, 1995). In the early 1900s, these workers started to get restive over the poor work conditions on the plantations and organized a number of strikes. To dilute their power, the plantation owners started to recruit Korean workers, about 7,000 of whom arrived between 1903 and 1905 (Min, 1995a). In addition, they began recruiting Filipino workers around 1906, with over 100,000 Filipinos coming in the following two decades (Agbayani-Siewert & Revilla, 1995; Uba, 1994).

Asian Indians also started coming to the United States in relatively large numbers in the early 1900s. Many of them intended to immigrate to Canada but eventually entered the United States when they were turned away by the Canadian government (Sheth, 1995). These early immigrants were mostly farmers and laborers, with a small number of middle-class students, elites, and political refugees. Vietnamese and other Southeast Asian immigrants did not come in significant numbers until the late 1970s, when many of them had to flee their countries in the aftermath of the Vietnam War.

Moratorium on Asian Immigration

As the number of Asian immigrants increased from the late 19th century to the early 20th century, anti-Asian sentiments began to develop (Hing,

1993; Hong & Friedman, 1998; Min, 1995b). Chinese immigrants, who were the largest and most visible Asian group in the United States at that time, were the first targets of discrimination. Anti-Chinese sentiments became particularly intense and malicious when their labor was no longer in high demand on the U.S. mainland, with the completion of the transcontinental railroad and the end of the California gold rush. A series of laws on both federal and state levels were enacted to discourage and limit Chinese immigration. The most infamous of these was the Chinese Exclusion Act passed by Congress in 1882. It was the first and only immigration act to exclude a specific nationality group. It made Chinese ineligible for American citizenship and severely restricted their immigration (Uba, 1994; Wong, 1995, 1998). Another example was the antimiscegenation laws prohibiting intermarriage between whites and Chinese or "Mongolians," which were passed by 14 states: Arizona, California, Georgia, Idaho, Mississippi, Missouri, Montana, Nebraska, Nevada, Oregon, South Dakota, Utah, Virginia, and Wyoming (Lyman, 1974; Spickard, 1989). These were in addition to laws in other states prohibiting intermarriage between whites and "colored people" which, of course, included Asians (Kim, 1986). Eventually, immigration restrictions on the Chinese were extended to all Asians, and additional discriminatory legislation and policies made it practically impossible for them to immigrate to the United States. Thus, Asian immigration to the United States almost came to a halt in the few decades preceding World War II.

Post-World War II Asian Immigration

The exclusion of Asian immigrants and the legislative discrimination against them started to relax during World War II (Hing, 1993; Hong & Friedman, 1998; Min, 1995c). This was partly due to the alliance between the United States and China during the war and partly due to the need to counteract Japanese wartime propaganda about the anti-Asian policies of the United States. In 1943, Congress passed what was known as the "Chinese Repealer," which again allowed Chinese to naturalize and become U.S. citizens, and removed most of the Chinese exclusion laws (Hing, 1993). However, it still restricted Chinese immigration to a quota of 105 immigrants per year. These changes were extended to other Asian groups in subsequent legislation. In other areas of legislative racism, California repealed its antimiscegenation law in 1948, and in 1967, the U.S. Supreme Court finally nullified all laws forbidding interracial marriage (Kim, 1986; Root, 1992; Spickard, 1989). Another significant change was the Immigration and Naturalization Act of 1965, which became effective in 1968 (Hing, 1993; Min, 1995b). This act instituted a relatively fairer immigration system by assigning equal quotas to most countries, regardless of race or ethnicity. It also allowed Asian immigrants who were already in the United States to sponsor their family members living abroad to join them. Persons with specific professional or technical skills could also apply for immigration along with their nuclear families. Together with the post-World War II sociopolitical factors in Asia, the Immigration and Naturalization Act of 1965 contributed significantly to the rapid growth of the Asian American population in recent decades (Hong & Friedman, 1998; Min, 1995c). According to 1997 census estimates, about 61% of the Asian American population are foreign born (U.S. Bureau of the Census, 1998c).

The Immigration and Naturalization Act of 1965 gave preference to professional and technical workers as well as to family reunification. Thus, Asian immigrants entering the United States after this legislation tend to be more educated as a group, in contrast to those who came during the pre-World War II period, when the majority were uneducated laborers. For example, about 30% to 40% of Asian immigrants who entered the United States from 1970 to 1990 were college graduates (Min, 1995c).

The numbers of Asian Americans belonging to the various groups are shown in Table 2.2. These numbers are based on the 1990 census data (U.S. Bureau of the Census, 1992), the latest available data for specific groups. As can be seen in this table, the rate of increase has been dramatic for all Asian American groups, with the exception of Japanese Americans. Before the change in immigration regulations in 1965, Japanese Americans were the largest group of Asian Americans. However, in the 1970 census, Chinese Americans became the largest group, and in the 1980 census, Filipino Americans also surpassed Japanese Americans and became the second largest group (Hong & Friedman, 1998; Min, 1995c). The relatively slow increase in Japanese American population was mainly due to the smaller number of Japanese nationals immigrating to the United States. Most of the current Japanese Americans are descendants of immigrants who came before 1924, unlike other Asian American groups, among whom most members are foreign born (Hong & Friedman, 1998; Nishi, 1995; Uba, 1994). According to the 1990 census, whereas 63% of all Asian Americans are foreign born, only 32% of Japanese Americans are foreign born (Min, 1995c; U.S. Bureau of the Census, 1993a). The relatively slow rate of Japanese immigration to the United States is probably the result of several factors. In the immediate years after World War II, the postwar sentiments between two countries formerly at war made it unlikely for the Japanese to emigrate to the United States. Also, the U.S. government's internment of Japanese Americans during World War II doubtless had a chilling effect on Japanese nationals considering immigration (Hing, 1993). The internment was a major upheaval for Japanese Americans and raised the issue of whether, even as American citizens, they could feel secure living in the United States. Another possible factor is the political stability of Japan and its rapid development into a world economic power in recent decades (Hing, 1993). This made it unnecessary for the Japanese to leave their country for either political or economic reasons.

Major social and political turmoil after World War II, including the communist takeover of mainland China, the Korean War, and the Vietnam War, affected immigration from many Asian countries. These sociopolitical conflicts and their aftermath were the primary reason for people of these countries to emigrate (Hong & Friedman, 1998). Many of them came for the social and political security of the United States, as well as for the freedom and the economic and educational opportunities available here (Hing, 1993).

Shortly after World War II, in 1949, mainland China was taken over by the communist government, with the nationalist government retreating to Taiwan. The official tension between the two governments is still an ongoing issue that threatens the stability of East Asia and is a driving force behind postwar Chinese immigration to the United States. In the 1980s, both mainland China and Taiwan relaxed their tight emigration policies (Hong & Friedman, 1998). At the same time, modifications in U.S. immigration regulations treated mainland China, Taiwan, Hong Kong, and Macau as separate entities and allotted each of these places its own quota for immigration to the United States. Together, these quotas increased the total number of Chinese immigrants allowed into the United States each year. All these changes further contributed to the rapid growth of the Chinese American population in recent years. Of the 1.6 million Chinese Americans reported in the 1990 census, about 69% are foreign born (Min, 1995c; U.S. Bureau of the Census, 1993a).

Much as China experienced the trauma of a civil war, Korea experienced the trauma of the Korean War (1950-1953) that split the country into North and South Korea. The tension between the two Koreas still persists today. Thus, despite South Korea's strong economy in recent years, this political issue is still a major reason for Koreans to emigrate (Hong & Friedman, 1998). Although there were only about 8,000 Korean immigrants in the United States before 1950 (Gardner et al., 1985), their numbers increased to over 69,000 by the 1970 census and, as shown in Table 2.2, have increased even more drastically since then. Of the close to 8 million Korean Americans reported in the 1990 census, about 73% are foreign born (Min, 1995c; U.S. Bureau of the Census, 1993a).

The Vietnam War, which ended in 1975 with the fall of South Vietnam, was a major upheaval that sent large numbers of Vietnamese, most of them as refugees, to the United States. The turmoil in the region also caused many Cambodians, Laotians, and Hmongs to flee their countries. Together, these groups were called Southeast Asian refugees or Indochinese refugees. They started arriving in the United States from the late 1970s to the 1980s, with Vietnamese refugees being the largest group (Hong &

Table 2.2 Asian Americans in the United States, 1950-1990

	1950	1960	1970	1980	1990
Total U.S. Population	151,325,798	179,323,175	203,211,926	226,545,805	248,709,873
Asian/Pacific Islander	599,091	877,934	1,429,562	3,550,439	7,273,662
Chinese	150,005	237,292	436,062	806,040	1,645,472
Filipino	122,707	176,310	343,060	774,652	1,406,770
Japanese	326,379	464,332	591,290	700,974	847,562
Indian				361,531	815,447
Korean			69,150	354,593	798,849
Vietnamese				261,729	614,547
Laotian					149,014
Cambodian					147,411
Thai					91,275
Hmong					90,082
Other Asian					302,209

SOURCE: 1950 to 1970 data from Gardner et al. (1985); 1980 to 1990 data from Min (1995c) and U.S. Bureau of the Census (1983, 1992).

Friedman, 1998; Min, 1995c; Rumbaut, 1995; Tran, 1988; Uba, 1994).
Thus, the Vietnamese American population increased by 2.3-fold between
the 1980 census and the 1990 census. This is the highest growth rate
among the major Asian American groups. Over 600,000 Vietnamese
Americans were reported in the 1990 census, and about 80% of them were
foreign born (Min, 1995c; U.S. Bureau of the Census, 1993a).

The Philippines became independent in 1946, but it has continued to
maintain close economic, political, and educational ties with the United
States. Because the Philippines is the most westernized and the most
Americanized of the Asian countries, Filipinos generally find it easier
than other Asian immigrants to accommodate to American culture and
life, and many of them are fluent in English (Agbayani-Siewert & Revilla,
1995; Hong & Friedman, 1998; Uba, 1994). As seen in Table 2.2, the number of Filipino Americans has almost doubled at every census since the
1960 census. Currently they are the second largest group of Asian Americans. Of the 1.4 million Filipino Americans reported in the 1990 census,
about 64% are foreign born (Min, 1995c; U.S. Bureau of the Census,
1993a).

Most Asian Indian immigrants came to the United States when immigration restrictions were relaxed after the Immigration and Naturalization
Act of 1965. A large group also came by way of Africa when they were ex-
pelled by the Ugandan government in the early 1970s (Sheth, 1995). Asian
Indian Americans are the fourth largest group among Asian Americans,
numbering over 800,000 in the 1990 census. About 75.4% of them are foreign born (Min, 1995c; U.S. Bureau of the Census, 1993a).

Distribution of Asians in the United States

According to 1997 census estimates, about 95% of the Asian and Pacific
Islander American population reside in metropolitan areas, and about
55% of them live on the West Coast (U.S. Bureau of the Census, 1999).
California is the state with the highest number of Asian/Pacific Islanders,
with approximately 3.8 million (U.S. Bureau of the Census, 1998b). This
is close to 40% of the total Asian/Pacific Islander population in the United
States. They make up about 12% of California's population. Los Angeles
County and Orange County, both in southern California, are the areas in
California with the highest number of Asian/Pacific Islanders (U.S. Bu-
reau of the Census, 1998b).

New York and Hawaii, respectively, are the states having the second and
third largest Asian/Pacific Islander populations. New York has about
953,000 Asian/Pacific Islanders, or around 9.5% of the total U.S.
Asian/Pacific Islander population (U.S. Bureau of the Census, 1998b).

They make up about 5% of the state's population. Many of them reside in the Greater New York City metropolitan area (Gall & Gall, 1993). Hawaii has about 749,000 Asian/Pacific Islanders, or around 8% of the total U.S. Asian/Pacific Islander population (U.S. Bureau of the Census, 1998b). Because Hawaii is a much less populous state than California or New York, the Asian/Pacific American presence there is more evident. They make up about 63% of Hawaii's population, a percentage that dwarfs California's. Honolulu County is the region with the highest number of Asian/Pacific Islanders.

Texas, New Jersey, Illinois, and Washington are the next four states with large Asian/Pacific Islander populations, with their numbers at about 524,000, 424,000, 383,000, and 311,000 respectively (U.S. Bureau of the Census, 1998b). Many of them reside in the metropolitan areas of Houston, New Jersey-Philadelphia, Chicago, and Seattle (Gall & Gall, 1993; Gall & Natividad, 1995). Florida, Virginia, and Massachusetts make up the rest of the top 10 states in Asian/Pacific Islander population, with their numbers at approximately 253,000, 233,000, and 210,000 respectively (U.S. Bureau of the Census, 1998b).

Economic Attainment

As a group, Asian/Pacific Americans have a median family income that is higher than that of other major ethnic groups counted in the census data. In 1997, the median family income of Asian/Pacific Americans was $45,249, as compared to $38,972 for white Americans, $26,628 for Hispanic Americans, and $25,050 for African Americans (U.S. Bureau of the Census, 1998a). However, these data are somewhat misleading. The same data also showed that 14.0% of Asian/Pacific American families lived at the poverty level, in comparison to 11.0% of white American families, 27.1% of Hispanic American families, and 26.5% of African American families (U.S. Bureau of the Census, 1998a). This is reflective of the wide range of income among Asian Americans. Most importantly, these census data have to be interpreted with caution, as Asian American families tend to be larger and have more income earners per family than white families (Hing, 1993; U.S. Bureau of the Census, 1998a). Also, a large percentage of Asian Americans live in metropolitan areas and states with a high cost of living; this skews the income level of Asian Americans upwards when compared to the white population nationally (Kitano & Daniels, 1988). Keeping these cautions in mind, we will examine the financial situation of various Asian American groups.

There are major variations in the economic attainment of the different Asian American groups. Here we will refer to the 1990 census data (U.S.

Bureau of the Census, 1993a, 1994), the latest available data set with breakdown for different Asian American groups. According to these data, the relative median incomes of the major ethnic groups (Asian Americans, white Americans, Hispanic Americans, and African Americans), as compared to one another, are similar to those in the 1997 data. As for comparisons among the various Asian American groups, Japanese Americans, Asian Indian Americans, and Filipino Americans are the most affluent, with median family incomes at $51,550, $49,309, and $46,698 respectively (Hing, 1993; Hong & Friedman, 1998; Min, 1995c). These incomes are all higher than that of white Americans. Only 3.4% of Japanese American families and 5.2% of Filipino American families are at the poverty level. Asian Indian Americans are similar to white Americans, with 7.2% living at the poverty level.

Financially, Chinese Americans are a very polarized population. Their median family income of $41,316 is higher than that of white Americans, according to the 1990 census. However, 11.1% of Chinese American families live at the poverty level (Hong & Friedman, 1998; Min, 1995c). These figures reflect the economic diversity of this community, which has a large professional and business class as well as a significant number of inner-city low-level workers and underemployed immigrants. To a certain extent, Korean Americans are in a similar situation. However, their median family income of $33,909 is lower than that of white Americans, and 14.7% of their families live at the poverty level, according to the 1990 census (Hing, 1993; Hong & Friedman, 1998; Min, 1995c).

Because the majority of Vietnamese Americans are refugees who came to the United States under chaotic circumstances, many of them have had to rebuild their lives. Thus, it is understandable that, financially, they are a distance from the other Asian groups. Their median family income is $30,500, and 23.8% of their families live at the poverty level, according to the 1990 census (Hing, 1993; Hong & Friedman, 1998; Min, 1995c).

Subcultural Variations

As mentioned earlier in this chapter, there are cultural variations within each of the Asian American groups. The difference between the generally more Americanized United States-born population and the new immigrants may be most evident. There are also variations relating to socioeconomic classes within each ethnic group. These issues will be discussed in greater detail later in this book. Here we will discuss two other major sociocultural variations of which mental health professionals need to be aware: differences in religious affiliation and differences in subcultures within a particular Asian country.

Differences in Religious Affiliation

Buddhism is the most common religion in the countries we are discussing, with the exception of the Philippines, where the majority religion is Catholicism. However, it should be noted that there are also followers of Christianity in Asia. In fact, Christian churches, both Protestant and Catholic, may play an important role in the social life of many Asian Americans (Hong & Friedman, 1998; Hong & Ham, 1994). For example, many of the early Korean immigrants came from areas of Korea with a large Christian presence (Min, 1995a). Contact with American missionaries was probably one of the factors contributing to their decision to come to the United States to work. It was estimated that about 40% of these early immigrants were Christians before they came to this country (Min, 1995a). As a result, ethnic Korean churches played an important part as social organizations for their networking, support, and fellowship. Today, Korean churches continue to play a major role in Korean American communities. It is estimated that about 75% of Korean Americans are affiliated with Korean churches (Min, 1997). Ethnic Christian churches are also very active in many Chinese American communities, often serving as social centers where immigrants can network. Though no national numbers are available, Hong and Ham (1994) have reported that, for example, in the San Gabriel Valley area of Los Angeles, which has a large Chinese American population, there are close to 100 Christian churches with Chinese congregations led by Chinese-speaking ministers or priests. Also, there are many Buddhists in the Chinese American population, as Buddhism is the major religion in China. Thus, clinicians must not make assumptions about the religious practice of Chinese American clients. Similarly, in the Vietnamese American community, although the majority religion is Buddhism, there are also many Catholics (Min, 1995c). This is the result of former French colonial rule over Vietnam, which gave the Catholic Church a prominent position in Vietnamese society. Thus, while acknowledging the overarching influence of Confucianism, Buddhism, and Taoism in the formation of Asian worldviews, it is important for the clinician to avoid jumping to conclusions about the religious affiliation of specific Asian American clients, who may belong to different religions or may profess no religion at all (Hong & Friedman, 1998; Hong & Ham, 1994).

Subcultural Differences Within a Country

Clinicians should be aware of subcultural differences within a particular Asian country. The most obvious of these are the differences often found between the rural areas, which tend to be more traditional, and the metropolitan areas, which tend to be more westernized. Regional subcultural variations also exist within a country. This is particularly true for China, which is geographically slightly larger than the United States (Hong & Friedman, 1998; Hong & Ham, 1994). Here we will examine some of the variations in the Chinese American population.

In addition to local customs and practices, an important issue is the different dialects spoken by immigrants from different regions of China. There are dozens of Chinese dialects. They are usually categorized into eight major groups in the literature on Chinese linguistics (Chen, 1996). The dialects are simply named after the areas where they are used. Many of the early Chinese immigrants spoke Toisanese because they were from the Toisan area of the Guangdong (Canton) Province. This dialect continues to be used by many of the long-time residents of the Chinatowns and their family members who may have moved to other areas. Cantonese is spoken in Hong Kong, historically a part of Guangdong (Canton) Province. Thus, Chinese immigrants from Hong Kong or those who came from China via Hong Kong generally speak Cantonese. Many of these immigrants came to the United States in the 1970s and 1980s. Mandarin is the official dialect that has been taught for decades in the schools in both Taiwan and mainland China. With the increase of Chinese immigrants from mainland China and Taiwan in the 1980s, Mandarin has also become a common dialect in the Chinese American communities. In addition to these three commonly spoken dialects in the Chinese American communities, Taiwanese, Fukinese, and Sawtowese are also dialects that mental health providers will encounter from time to time.

In terms of written Chinese, two forms of characters (writing) are used at present. The traditional form is used in Taiwan, Hong Kong, and the Chinese American communities in the United States. A simplified form, which is adapted from the traditional form, has been promoted in mainland China in the past few decades. Both forms follow the same grammatical rules. In general, the language issue, especially the dialects, is a barrier to providing services to Chinese immigrants who are not fluent in English. Community mental health clinics often have a difficult time locating and recruiting Chinese-speaking clinicians who can provide services in the particular dialect or dialects spoken by their clients.

Chinese immigrants may also come to the United States from different areas of Asia. Besides those coming from mainland China, Taiwan, Hong Kong, and Macau, there are ethnic Chinese who lived in various Southeast Asian countries, such as Vietnam, Cambodia, Singapore, Malaysia, the Philippines, or other countries before they came to the United States (Hong & Friedman, 1998; Hong & Ham, 1994). For example, it has been estimated that ethnic Chinese account for up to 25% of Vietnamese refugees/immigrants and up to 15% of Cambodian refugees/immigrants (Rumbaut, 1995). Although they are considered to be former nationals of these countries by the U.S. Immigration and Naturalization Service, many of them identify themselves as Chinese in daily life. Thus, a clinician has to be particularly careful about the ethnicity issue and the sociocultural experience of the different groups of Chinese Americans.

In sum, when providing services to Asian American clients, mental health professionals must be knowledgeable about the commonalities that distinguish Asian Americans, as a group, from mainstream white Americans. However, they must also be alert to the possible social cultural differences among the Asian American groups, as well as the variations within a particular ethnic group.

Summary

In this chapter, we have examined the commonalities and diversities among Asian Americans, as well as the brief immigration history and the demographics of the major Asian groups. We have also reviewed the basic tenets of Confucianism, Buddhism, and Taoism, all of which had a fundamental influence in the cultures of origin of Asian Americans. Keeping in mind that unique cultural values, practices, and social environmental experiences exist among the various Asian American groups, as well as among individuals within a group, this book emphasizes the commonalities of Asian Americans and highlights specific elements of the pan-Asian identity. The information presented in this chapter is intended to provide mental health professionals with a basic orientation to cultural background and historical as well as contemporary demographic information about Asian Americans, with the goal of helping them develop a more empathic understanding of this population. Clinicians are encouraged to expand on this foundation by referring to the references cited in this chapter.

3

Framework for Conceptualizing Cultural and Social Environmental Issues

This chapter presents a conceptual framework that we have developed to serve as a clinical compass for orienting mental health professionals in their work with Asian American clients. We call this framework the *C*ultural *A*nd *S*ocial *E*nvironmental (CASE) model because it is focused on two of the most essential determinants of Asian American client uniqueness: the cultural context and the social environmental context (Hong, 1989). Together, these two determinants establish the core of Asian Americans' cultural self-identity and social behavior (Triandis, 1995). The CASE model is an effective way to organize the vast existing body of knowledge about these determinants into a coherent and systematic approach for clinicians to use with their Asian American clients.

In this chapter, we will examine some of the key concepts concerning the two determinants. In our discussion of the cultural context, we will address the issue of cultural identification, including the concepts of accommodation, assimilation, and acculturation, as well as the current psychological literature on biracial/bicultural identity development. In our discussion of the social environmental context, we will examine the stressors commonly faced by Asian Americans as immigrants or as ethnic minorities in the United States. Clinicians must have a working knowledge of both cultural and social environmental contexts to provide effective mental health services to their Asian American clients (Hong, 1989; Lee & Zane, 1998).

The Cultural and Social Environmental Model

The CASE model is composed of two factors or dimensions: cultural context and social environmental context (Hong, 1989). The first factor, cultural context, pertains to pivotal beliefs, attitudes, and social norms evolving from the worldview and value orientation of Asian American cultures versus mainstream American culture (Hong, 1989). Examples of these issues include collectivism or familism versus individualism and norms and values defining social relationships, interpersonal interactions, and achievement of life goals. To apply cultural issues appropriately in psychotherapy and counseling, a clinician needs to discern a client's cultural orientation: that is, the degree to which the client identifies with Asian cultures and mainstream American culture. Hence, the cultural context of the CASE model can also be considered as the cultural identification dimension. This dimension is a refinement of Hong's (1989) model and is based on the frameworks proposed by a number of authors, such as Kitano and Daniels (1988), Sodowsky, Kwan, and Pannu (1996), and Berry and Sam (1997), all of whom describe acculturation, or development of cultural identity, as a multifaceted process with four general orientations or outcomes. Although the terminology used in these frameworks or models may differ, the basic ideas are similar. In the CASE model, as illustrated in Figure 3.1, the first orientation refers to Asian Americans who are primarily identified with Asian cultures and not identified with mainstream American culture. This group includes, for example, Chinese Americans, Filipino Americans, Japanese Americans, Korean Americans, or Vietnamese Americans who are primarily identified with their respective culture of origin. The second orientation refers to Asian Americans who reject their cultures of origin and are primarily identified with mainstream American culture. The third orientation, adaptive biculturalism, pertains to Asian Americans who embrace both Asian cultures and mainstream American culture without rejecting either one. They are proficient in both cultures and feel comfortable with them. The fourth orientation, maladaptive biculturalism, encompasses Asian Americans who feel marginalized or alienated from both Asian cultures and mainstream American culture. They may feel torn between two worlds, not belonging to either culture. As depicted in Figure 3.1, the arrows along the horizontal plane of the figure emphasize that cultural identification is a continuum rather than a dichotomous state. Individuals may have different degrees of identification with Asian and mainstream American cultures. The high and low categories in the figure are simply used for the convenience of graphically portraying the model. Indeed, an important aspect of the CASE model is the recognition that a person's cultural identification is a process and may change over time, especially in the case of an immigrant living in the context of the mainstream host culture. Consequently, we use the term *cultural identification* rather than *cultural identity,* as *identification* underscores a process and a changeable condition, whereas *identity* implies a static configuration.

The second factor or dimension of the CASE model is the social environmental context or social environmental problems (Hong, 1989). This factor pertains to the life problems and social barriers encountered by clients in daily living as individuals or as a group. Examples of such issues include difficulties created by financial hardship, educational problems, occupational concerns, and family discord. Besides problems on the personal level, there may be stressors on the societal level. These include, for example, socioeconomic disadvantages of inner-city communities, social

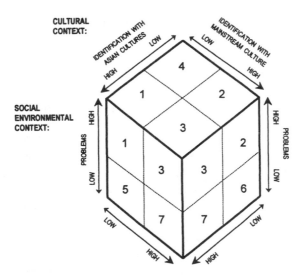

1. Primarily Asian --- High social environmental problems
2. Primarily mainstream --- High social environmental problems
3. Adaptively bicultural ---- High social environmental problems
4. Marginal/maladaptively bicultural --- High social environmental problems
5. Primarily Asian --- Low social environmental problems
6. Primarily mainstream --- Low social environmental problems
7. Adaptively bicultural --- Low social environmental problems
8. Marginal/maladaptively bicultural --- Low social environmental problems (not shown in figure)

Figure 3.1. Cultural and Social Environmental Model (CASE)

SOURCE: Adapted from Berry and Sam (1997), Hong (1989), Kitano and Daniels (1988), and Sodowsky et al. (1995).

barriers to achievement, and racism directed toward Asian Americans as a group. In addition, for the majority of Asian American clients who are immigrants, the impact of migration and the stress related to their resettlement process are crucial social environmental issues to be considered (Hong, 1989; Hong & Ham, 1992). We are using the term *social environmental problems* to describe this dimension of the CASE model, as the issues here include difficulties arising from interpersonal or social situations, such as family discord or racism, as well as challenges relating to the physical environment or other nonsocial situations, such as poor housing conditions or financial hardship. The stressors denoted in this dimension are akin to the psychosocial and environmental problems discussed in the diagnostic system of the fourth edition of the *Diagnostic and Statistical Manual of Mental Disorders (DSM-IV)* (American Psychiatric Association, 1994). These are issues that clinicians must attend to when planning and providing mental health services. As shown in Figure 3.1, social environmental problems are depicted as the vertical dimension of the CASE model. Although the graphic portrayal indicates a high/low dichotomy for this dimension, the degree of social environmental difficulties experienced by an individual actually falls along a continuum, as emphasized by the arrows along the sides of the figure. The high/low distinction is simply used for the convenience of graphically portraying the model.

If we look at the cultural and social environmental dimensions together, the CASE model depicts eight possible categories for describing Asian American clients. For example, the client may be a person who identifies primarily with Asian cultures and is also experiencing a high degree of social environmental adversity, such as a refugee who just arrived in the United States, has limited English proficiency, and is practically penniless. Another client, such as an affluent English-speaking immigrant from a high socioeconomic background, may also identify primarily with Asian culture but experience few social environmental problems. Similarly, differences in social environmental difficulties can be applied to individuals belonging to the other three categories in the cultural dimension, namely those who are primarily identified with mainstream American culture, those who are adaptively bicultural, and those who are marginal or maladaptively bicultural.

By integrating the cultural context and social environmental context into a unified framework, the CASE model provides a unique approach that emphasizes the importance of taking both sets of issues into consideration when working with Asian American clients. The model reminds clinicians not to focus single-mindedly on one area and overlook the other. This is a particular advantage of this model. Furthermore, the CASE model emphasizes that cultural identification and social environmental problems may differ, depending on the individual or the particular community. This emphasis prompts clinicians to recognize their Asian American clients as members of a socially defined group and, at the same time, to be alert to their standings as unique individuals. On the personal level, the CASE model highlights how important it is for clinicians to perceive and respond to each Asian American client as an individual with distinct characteristics and needs rather than as a stereotype of an ethnic group. On the group level, this model can also help mental health providers gauge the needs of a particular Asian American community or neighborhood and plan their services accordingly. In subsequent chapters of this book, we will examine specific cultural and social environmental issues that may affect different aspects of mental health services for Asian Americans. At this point, we want to elaborate further on the CASE model.

Cultural Identification

Cultural identification is a complex process that can be conscious or unconscious, depending on an individual's level of self-awareness. We will begin by examining the motivational forces underlying this process. According to Berry and Sam (1997), when newcomers, such as immigrants, are introduced to a new host or dominant culture, their strategies of acculturation are determined by their responses to two basic issues. The first issue is cultural maintenance: "Is it considered to be of value to maintain one's (original) cultural identity and characteristics?" (p. 269). The second issue is contact and participation: "Is it considered to be of value to maintain relationship with the dominant society?" (p. 296). Four strategies of acculturation are defined by these two issues: assimilation, separation, integration, and marginalization. Assimilation is pursued by those who value contact and participation in the dominant society but do not value maintenance of one's culture of origin. Separation is the choice of those who value maintenance with one's culture of origin but do not value contact and participation in the dominant society. Integration is the strategy pursued by those who value both orientations. Marginalization is the strategy adopted by those who do not value either orientation. In general, these four strategies—assimilation, separation, integration, and marginalization—correspond respectively to the four major orientations of cultural identification in the CASE model: primarily identified with mainstream culture, primarily identified with Asian cultures, adaptively bicultural, and marginal/maladaptively bicultural. We will discuss these strategies in greater detail later in the section on acculturation.

Berry and Sam's (1997) formulation provided a succinct overview of the motivational forces underlying the cultural identification process of an ethnic minority individual or group. The two issues they raised, contact and participation in the dominant society versus cultural maintenance, echoed two major concepts discussed in the cultural identity literature: cultural adaptation and cultural bonding. *Cultural adaptation* refers to the inclination of ethnic minorities or immigrants to adopt elements of the host or mainstream culture. *Cultural bonding,* in contrast, refers to the affinity of ethnic minorities or immigrants for their cultures of origin. Adaptation draws individuals toward mainstream culture, whereas bonding draws them back to the culture of origin. Together, these two sets of forces interact in the development of an individual's cultural identification.

Cultural Adaptation

Cultural adaptation is the process that occurs when two or more cultures come into contact. This contact between cultures may alter some behaviors or attitudes of members from participating cultures or in some cases may lead, through interculturation, to the formation of a new culture that emerges as a distinct entity (Berry & Sam, 1997). In the context of this book, the CASE model is concerned with the cultural identification of Asian American clients and its implications for psychotherapy and counseling. Thus, though acknowledging that the various ethnic minority cultures and mainstream American culture may influence one another, we will be focusing primarily on the factors affecting Asian Americans' adaptation to mainstream culture rather than the possible influence of Asian cultures on mainstream U.S. society. As applied to Asian Americans as ethnic minorities and as immigrants in the United States, cultural adaptation can be conceptualized as a process that partially or wholly transforms them from cultural outsiders to members of the host or mainstream culture. It is an ongoing process continuously evolving over time rather than an event occurring within a discrete moment, and it may involve flux and nondirectional movements (Beiser, 1996; Berry, 1992; LaFromboise, Coleman, & Gerton, 1993; Schmitz, 1994; Searle & Ward, 1990).

Issues of adaptation and assimilation have dominated publications about Asian Americans (Wang, 1991). Some intriguing questions have been raised in the literature: Can Asians be assimilated into the culture of the United States, or are they too different from the prevailing cultural and biological perspectives of "American character?" Even if Asians have achieved educational and socioeconomic successes, can they be totally assimilated into U.S. culture as "Asian Americans?" (Wang, 1991). Several decades ago, these dichotomous questions were essentially resolved by the creation of the metaphor of the "melting pot," which expressed the expectation that assimilation could occur as a melding of cultural, racial, and ethnic differences into an Anglo-American prototype (Alba, 1990). However, "melting pot" assimilation has never become widely accepted, and blurring of ethnic, racial, and cultural identities has not been achieved. Rather, assertiveness among racial, ethnic, and cultural groups has grown, particularly with the impetus of the civil rights movement. Asian Americans, in light of their growing numbers in recent decades, have affirmed their identity as a way to achieve their life goals. Thus, loyalty to one's culture of origin versus adaptation to mainstream American culture continues to be a delicate issue for many.

Cultural adaptation, as a construct applied in the CASE model, encompasses the concepts of accommodation, assimilation, and acculturation. Scholars from different social science disciplines such as anthropology, sociology, and psychology have defined and described each of these concepts from the perspective of their particular field (Bronfenbrenner, 1977; Broom & Selznick, 1963; Falicov, 1988). Here we will provide an integrative approach that will help mental health clinicians understand the complex process of cultural adaptation and its role in cultural identification of Asian Americans.

Accommodation

When used by sociologists in the 1950s, the meaning of the term *accommodation* was influenced by a historical context that defined ethnicity as an important principle of social organization (Alba, 1990). European immigrants to the United States throughout the mid-19th century and first half of the 20th century assumed that they would be retaining their identity and cultural behaviors. With the end of World War II and the restructuring of Europe, ethnic groups sought to reestablish their ethnic identities even though the boundaries of their countries had shifted. Accommodation of immigrant groups to the United States, from this historic context, did not require mutual understanding or even continuous communication between the immigrant group and the majority cultural groups. Rather, recognition of the essential qualities of each group was crucial. Stable accommodation was reflected when major differences of life goals, vital to a group's continued existence, were acknowledged (Broom & Selznick, 1963). At that time, communication theorists critiqued theoretical explanations of how one group could persuade another group to accept or alter its perspective (Lin, 1973). Implicitly, these critiques became paradigms for influencing change and for evaluating the adaptability of individuals within groups to adopt the values and norms of another group.

More recently, in discussions of cross-cultural interpersonal communication from a general systems theoretical perspective, the adaptability of an individual in altering personal existing attributes and internal structures contributes to that individual's management of intercultural challenges and accommodation of environmental demands (Kim, 1991). Accommodation is crucial when an ethnic minority person or newcomer interacts with the host culture. In accommodation, an immigrant may practice elements of the new host culture without actually embracing or internalizing them. These cultural elements are adopted as a convenience or a means of survival in the new environment of the host country. In the context of the CASE model, even Asian Americans who are strongly identified with their ethnic cultures will show some degree of accommodation to mainstream American culture, as this is essential for day-to-day living. For example, a woman who is strongly identified with traditional Asian culture may be very socially graceful in following American etiquette at a party in a mainstream setting. However, privately she may have a strong dislike of the hugging or kissing when others warmly greet her. Rather, she would prefer the more traditional Asian greeting of a bow or nod, or at most a light handshake. Other common examples of accommodation include celebration of certain mainstream American holidays, such as Thanksgiving, with little appreciation of their actual significance, especially in the affective domain. Conversely, accommodation may also mean that individuals are willing to go to work or school on Asian holidays, such as the Lunar New Year, and to limit the scope of celebrations or even move the celebrations to weekends, as is often done in many Asian American communities.

Assimilation

From a historical sociological level of analysis, assimilation requires a breakdown of communication barriers so that the identity of groups can be fused (Broom & Selznick, 1963). From a perspective studied by psychologists, assimilation defines the extent that immigrants are accepted into their new culture, the dominant and powerful social institutions, without prejudice or discrimination (Gordon, 1964; Patel, Power, & Bhavnagri, 1996). Assimilation sometimes may imply abandonment of the immigrants' heritage, culture, and language (Abu-Rabia, 1996), and the price of assimilation for immigrants may be the transformation, even the disappearance, of their original cultural values and traditions (Alba, 1990; Gordon, 1964; Patel et al., 1996). The "English-only" movement in schools is often suggested as a method for hastening the assimilation process for immigrants coming to the United States.

In everyday usage and in the mass media, *assimilation* is often employed as a generic term that encompasses *adaptation, accommodation,* and *acculturation.* At times, these terms are used interchangeably. In the professional literature, *assimilation* is sometimes defined broadly to include acculturation, with acculturation considered to be a form of assimilation (Gordon, 1964; Atkinson, Morten, & Sue, 1993). Conversely, others have used *acculturation* as the more general term and have considered assimilation to be a particular form of acculturation (Berry & Sam, 1997). This variation in terminology can be very confusing. In the context of the CASE model, we will follow Berry and Sam's (1997) framework and view assimilation as a coping strategy by minority groups and newcomers to interact with the dominant culture. Individuals or groups who assimilate are those who give high value to participating in the dominant culture and do not wish to maintain their original cultural identity. This refers to Asian Americans who identify strongly with mainstream American culture to the exclusion of their Asian cultural heritage. These individuals internalize the values, norms, and worldview of mainstream American culture and have little affinity for Asian cultures. Assimilated Asian Americans think, feel, and behave as if they were members of the mainstream culture. Typically, assimilation is a lifelong process that often takes more than one generation to achieve. However, as Atkinson, Morten, and Sue (1998) cautioned, total assimilation requires acceptance by the dominant society. As such, even though some immigrants or their descendants may wish to assimilate, this goal is not completely under their control.

Acculturation

Early use of the term *acculturation* derived from scholarly writings of sociologists who were interested in processes in which one group appropriated values, social norms, and behavioral and attitudinal characteristics of another group. Often, in this early literature, the terms *acculturation* and *socialization* were used synonymously because both constructs were considered to be learned cultural acquisitions such as behaviors and values (Broom & Selznick, 1963). By interchanging these constructs, scholars acknowledged that change occurred when individuals of different cultures were in continuous contact (Redfield, Linton, & Herskovits, 1936). These early scholars focused on acculturation as a group-level phenomenon. More recently, acculturation has been studied by psychologists as an individual-level variable that can be viewed as a state or a process (Graves, 1967; Ward, 1996). Both state and process acculturation are defined and measured in terms of change. State acculturation is the amount of acculturation in relationship to culture-specific indicators such as demonstrated behaviors, expression of feelings, and ways of thinking. Process acculturation is the degree of change over time and is assessed by identifying antecedents and consequences of cultural contact (Ward, 1996). Early research on acculturation often centered on occurrences of psychiatric phenomena such as refugee neurosis (Pedersen, 1994), anxiety (Oberg, 1960), loss and mourning (Knight, Bernal, Garza, & Cota, 1993), and anxiety, depression, and hostility (Arredondo, 1985). More recent research has been influenced by studies on stress and coping (Lazarus & Folkman, 1984), social learning and skills acquisition (Lin, Tazuma, & Masuda, 1979), social cognition (Chataway & Berry, 1989), and intergroup perceptions (Ward, 1996). Another current research focus is on acculturation as a psychological phenomenon affecting identity formation (Berry, 1995; Joiner & Kashubeck, 1996; Yeh & Huang, 1996).

As mentioned earlier, the CASE model reflects Berry and Sam's (1997) definition of acculturation and its four component strategies of coping with intercultural contact: assimilation, separation, integration, and marginalization. *Assimilation* is primary identification with mainstream culture. *Separation* is primary identification with one's culture of origin. However, when separation is imposed by the dominant group on a minority group, the appropriate term will be *segregation* (Berry & Sam, 1997). *Integration* is both the maintenance of one's own culture of origin and, at the same time, participation as an integral part of the dominant culture and society (Berry & Sam, 1997). In the CASE model, this strategy describes Asian Americans who are adaptively bicultural. Typically, integration or adaptive biculturalism is the result of a gradual process of commingling between cultures, and it eventually leads to an expanded set of traditions, values, and norms taken from Asian cultures as well as the host American culture. It involves retaining elements of Asian cultures and simultaneously adopting and embracing elements of mainstream American culture. Through this process, individuals develop an expanded cultural repertoire that they can live with comfortably. *Marginalization* is the situation of individuals or groups who have little interest in maintaining their culture of origin or in integrating with mainstream culture (Berry & Sam, 1997). These individuals experience conflict and confusion or are discouraged in their attempts to integrate two cultures. Their situation is referred to as *maladaptive biculturalism* in the CASE model. Consistent with Berry and Sam's (1997) formulation, the term *acculturation,* when used in this book, refers to all four strategies of responding to cultural contact.

Cultural adaptation is a complex, individual process. The pace and intensity of accommodation and assimilation and the choice of acculturation strategies are different among individuals. A person may move back and forth between culture of origin and host culture and among accommodation, assimilation, and the various strategies of acculturation. An individual may also employ various aspects of these constructs simultaneously. For example, an Asian American woman may accommodate to mainstream culture by sending Christmas cards and giving Christmas presents to her European American friends even if she is practicing Buddhism in her home. At the same time she may be assimilating into her host culture by internalizing the mainstream social norms or definitions of "fashionable appearance" by following trend-setting Western style fashions in dressing, applying makeup, and setting her hair. In another area of her life, she may be acculturating by using the strategy of integration: that is, being adaptively bicultural. For instance, though embracing the Western value of personal autonomy, she may also accept her role as a wife and mother according to the prescriptions of Asian culture. She may conduct herself as an assertive professional in her mainstream job setting but at home choose to put the collective welfare of her family above her own, devoting herself to her husband and children.

In sum, cultural adaptation is a multifaceted phenomenon that incorporates accommodation, assimilation, and other strategies of acculturation. This phenomenon is a set of motivational forces underlying the cultural identification dimension of the CASE model. As applied to clinical services, it gives an overall picture of where the person stands on pertinent cultural issues at the time of seeking mental health services.

Cultural Bonding: Cultural Roots and Evolving Identities

Cultural bonding, the second set of forces underlying the cultural identification process, refers to the affinity of immigrants for their cultures of origin. In a sense, it counteracts the forces of cultural adaptation.

One primary concern of any immigrant group is the maintenance of a link to the motherland and the affirmation of loyalty to their "roots." This is especially evident in diaspora Asians such as the Chinese, who historically have professed the inseparable attachment of those living abroad to their cultural roots in China (Wang, 1991). For any immigrant, bonding with the homeland culture exists in many domains, such as maintaining the language of origin, traditional foods, holidays and festivals, music and dance, friendship patterns, and cultural values, rituals, and norms. The term *roots* includes several meanings: biological-racial-genetic, birthplace of either the individual or the ancestors of the individual, and source of an individual's personal identity (Wang, 1991). Whatever meaning is given to *roots,* the attachment to one's roots is unique and often sacred and everlasting. These unique qualities of "bonding to roots" and loyalty to the motherland may have strong influences on individual identity (Alba, 1990).

Wang (1991) has suggested five types of identity among diaspora Asians: the sojourner, the assimilator, the accommodator, the ethnically proud, and the uprooted. For Asian Americans, all five types of identity are possible and historically have not always been a choice. For example, the sojourner identity was to some extent historically imposed on many Chinese Americans, and later on other Asian Americans. Even if they had decided to settle in their host country, the early Asian immigrants could not plan on becoming assimilated as citizens of their host country because of the hostile sociopolitical climate toward Asians that existed in the United States from the second half of the 19th century up to the onset of World War II. Another contributor to a sojourner identity for early Chinese Americans was the traditional bond to one's ancestral home. A person who went away to make a living was expected to return when his or her goals were accomplished, like "a leaf, which must eventually fall and return to its roots," as poignantly portrayed in a Chinese saying.

In sum, cultural bonding is a process that preserves the sacred connection to one's cultural roots. This process is shaped and transformed by conditions of society and must often be viewed in a historical and social context. We will now examine the major factors that influence cultural bonding and adaptation.

Factors Influencing Cultural Adaptation and Bonding

The mental health literature has identified a number of factors that affect the strength of Asian Americans' bonding with their cultures and countries of origin and their adaptation to their host culture and country (Giordano & Carni-Giordano, 1995; Harwood, 1981; Ho, 1987; Lee, 1997c; McGoldrick, 1982; Sue & Morishima, 1982; Tseng & McDermott, 1981). These factors can be grouped in four main areas: immigration history, language, rituals and norms, and global politics.

Immigration History

Immigration history for individuals, families, and groups involves premigration, migration, and postmigration experiences (Ho, 1987; Hong, 1989). The premigration experiences may include social, political, and economic circumstances that lead to a desire or necessity to leave one's homeland. The migration experiences and the transitional journey from one country and culture to another may include hardships and trauma. This is particularly true for refugees. Postmigration experiences may include positive or negative reception by the new host country, positive or negative psychological and physical adjustment to one's relocation, feelings of similarity to or difference from residents of the new community or neighborhood, congruity or incongruity between previous and present cultural practices, and possible changes in social status and role definitions. We will elaborate on these issues in the next chapter. In this chapter, we will focus on the relationship between migration and bonding. The experiences of immigrant Asian Americans at each stage of the migration process will affect their bonding with their cultures of origin, as well as their desire to assimilate into their host American culture.

Language

Differences in language structures and communication patterns exist between East Asian societies and the United States (Hong, 1989; Lee, 1997c). The linguistic structure of any language affects an individual's worldview. In fact, language shapes the meanings people give to their experiences and leads to formulations of a social context where the linguistic text has meaning (Watson & Seiler, 1992). Structural forms of language also denote standards of conduct and classification systems important to cultural practices (Watson, 1992). Often, individuals who retain their mother tongue are better able to sustain their bond to their culture of origin and to enhance communication with family members across generations. Language goes beyond bonds to an individual's culture of origin; use of a mother tongue signals ethnic-cultural membership and contributes to a sense of solidarity among the members of a cultural group (Alba, 1990). An interesting example of the influence of language can be found in the different Chinese dialects that separate the newer immigrant communities into Cantonese- and Mandarin-speaking subgroups, as well as distinguishing these two subgroups from the Toisanese-speaking Chinese Americans in the older communities. At the same time, the written Chinese language, which is the same across dialects, helps to maintain communication and, along with other common cultural elements, reinforces an overall Chinese identity. Moreover, for immigrants, the mother tongue is a link or a bridge between former and current cultures, as well as across generations. In this regard, to the extent that there is little commonality between the Asian languages and English, the language differences act as a barrier in immigrant Asian Americans' assimilation into mainstream America.

Rituals and Norms for Individuals, Families, Society

In his field research, Cohen (1991) examined the cultural links that bonded immigrant Asian groups deeply to the cultural traditions of their mother countries, regardless of any societal pressures to acculturate into the host country. Cohen's (1991) research and Watson's (1988) scholarly writings have identified the acceptance of standardized rituals as a key element in unifying culture. *Li,* an important part of Confucian thinking, is often translated as "etiquette." It is a concept that includes both "ritual" and "proper behavior" (Cohen, 1991). Rituals involve ceremonial actions based upon beliefs associated with an event itself (Imber-Black, Roberts, & Whiting, 1988). For example, the rituals performed at a wedding are symbolic acts that have evolved and formalized over time. These rituals are reflective of a culture's beliefs and values concerning marriage and the family. Proper behavior, in comparison, comprises the behaviors of everyday living and the actions that regulate daily interactions, such as greeting people. The meaning of *Li* (etiquette) in Confucian thinking is a blend of both ritual and proper behavior. In practical use, an example is the expected behavior for introducing one person to another. Not only would the individuals use the correct gestures and expressions of greeting, but they would keep in mind the traditional values of respect for harmony and regard for hierarchy that underlie the symbolic behaviors of ritual. *Li,* as ritual and as proper behavior, is based upon ethical guidelines and upon teaching ethics as a cultural legacy. These Confucian lessons penetrate, in some way, all Asian Americans from this cultural heritage and convey the elements of a morally good cosmic order. Often, ritual and etiquette are almost indistinguishable. For example, filial piety in daily life is a demonstration of etiquette, such as the proper manner of speaking to one's parents. It can also be a demonstration of ritual as a marking of life cycle events and a part of cultural festivities—for instance, according parents a formal position of honor at weddings or banquets for newborns and at holiday celebrations such as New Year's. Rituals, etiquette, and norms, like language, are the fabrics of interpersonal interaction. They serve as unifying forces within immigrant communities. However, to the extent that they are discordant with mainstream American practices, Asian social rituals, etiquette, and norms act as a barrier to cultural adaptation for Asian Americans.

Global Politics: Similarities and Differences Between Societies

Global consciousness is a dominant theme currently present throughout the world, whether the transition is from Confucianism to Marxist communism, colonialist domination to democratic nationalism, or secular provincialism to participation in global technology. Yet Tu (1991), in his essay about diaspora Chinese, affirmed that

> traditional features of the human condition—ethnicity, mother tongue, ancestral home, gender, class, and religious faith—all seem to be relevant in understanding the worldviews of societies and the need to search for roots despite the pervasiveness of global consciousness. (p. 7)

Maintaining traditional while embracing diverse cultural values and practices is a complex undertaking that often results in confusion and a sense of loss. Polarities, incongruities, antagonism, and exclusionary practices often are the result of individual or societal attempts to create an environment where individuals can coexist within both their culture of origin and their newly adopted culture. Legislation such as immigration laws and exclusionary acts of the legislative bodies and condoned social norms such as racism influences the attitudes and assimilation capability of cultural minorities and newcomers. Over centuries, societies have demonstrated tension, leading to violent animosity, when political, economic, religious, and ethical value differences exist. Tensions also exist for individuals when two different cultures are personally important to them. To lessen this tension, individuals may have to examine the possibilities for bicultural identity formation and to develop visions and life goals that can be consistent with both the new culture and the original culture. This mutuality may be the resolution for many Asian Americans who have to mediate the differences between their cultures of origin and mainstream American culture. Besides personal factors, their success in bridging the cultures is also dependent on the sociopolitical climate they live in. For instance, in a polarized sociopolitical and racial climate, a person trying to reconcile the cultural differences might end up feeling marginalized or being rejected by both groups. The internment of Japanese Americans during World War II is an example of how global politics can affect cultural identification and assimilation or, to put it more succinctly, how global politics and the sociopolitical and racial climate of the United States led to the exclusion of an Asian American group.

In sum, cultural identification is a process of interplay between cultural adaptation and cultural bonding. To fully appreciate the dynamics of cultural identification, mental health professionals need to be informed of the historical as well as contemporary social, political, and cultural context of Asian Americans as immigrants in the United States. A clear understanding of the cultural context or cultural identification dimension of the CASE model will provide guidance to clinicians in determining the degree to which Asian and mainstream American cultural elements should be applied in serving a particular client or a community.

Social Environmental Problems

The second dimension of the CASE model, the social environmental context or social environmental problems, pertains to the social environmental stressors that Asian Americans, as a group or as individuals, may encounter in their lives. These problems may be manifested in different ways in psychotherapy and counseling (Hong, 1989). In some situations, the stress related to social environmental conditions may be the principal presenting problem. For example, a newly immigrated Asian American may present symptoms of an adjustment disorder that is directly related to the stress of migration and resettlement in a new community. In other situations, specific social environmental adversities may be stressors overlaying other mental health or life problems. These stressors are not the specific presenting problems but are issues that clinicians must attend to in providing psychotherapy and counseling. For example, social isolation or loss of employment may be social environmental problems that compound a preexisting family conflict or further aggravate a depressive disorder. On the group level, racism is another common social environmental condition that affects mental health service delivery to Asian American clients. Its prevalence in a particular community or in U.S. society in general may jeopardize the therapeutic relationship between clinicians and clients from different ethnic backgrounds. Institutional racism often limits the alternatives and resources available to Asian American clients in addressing their problems.

The social environmental dimension of the CASE model serves to remind mental health professionals serving Asian Americans to look beyond culture by examining the current and previous life situations and experiences of their clients and to learn about the prevalent social environmental issues relating to their communities in general. Moreover, clinicians must be alert to the specific social environmental difficulties encountered by a particular client. Although those living in a specific neighborhood or community often have common life experiences, additional stressors that are particular to a specific client may also exist. We will identify and elaborate on specific social environmental issues, especially those relating to the migration experience, in later chapters.

Although the cultural context and the social environmental context are conceptually distinct dimensions of the CASE model, their effects on an individual or a community are often interrelated. For example, an Asian immigrant from a lower socioeconomic background working in an ethnic restaurant in the Asian community may be too preoccupied with financial and family responsibilities to have time to learn English or have the opportunity to socialize in mainstream settings. As a result, his or her cultural identification is likely to remain primarily Asian for a long time. Conversely, an Asian American who is primarily identified with mainstream culture and who has mastered the cultural intricacies is less likely to encounter social environmental barriers in daily living as compared to another person who is not knowledgeable about mainstream culture. In this regard, it is important to remember that the cultural and the social environmental dimensions of the CASE model have a complex relationship and may be closely intertwined.

Case Illustration of the CASE Model

The following case provides an illustration of how the CASE model can be applied in the context of clinical work. The clients in this case example, members of an Asian American family, had different life experiences that affected their degrees of identification with Asian and mainstream American cultures. Thus, they each developed their own idiosyncratic strategies for coping with problematic life situations. Yet at the same time they maintained cultural similarities. The clinician must be attuned to both individual difference and commonalities in addressing their problems.

Mr. and Mrs. L. met each other in graduate school when they came to the United States 25 years ago. Mr. L., an ethnic Chinese, was born in Vietnam but fled to Hong Kong at the age of 10. He later came to the United States as a young adult to attend college. Mrs. L. grew up in Taiwan, where her parents had lived for generations. The couple met as graduate students and married. Mrs. L. preferred to live her married life in Taiwan, but Mr. L. did not want to return to Asia because his job opportunities were much better in the United States. Because of Mr. L.'s attitude about employment, the couple decided to remain in the United States. They subsequently had three children, who were 23, 22, and 19 years of age at the time the couple sought therapy from the clinician. All three children were in college and were diligent students. Mr. L. worked as an engineer, and Mrs. L. worked as a laboratory technician. Their friends were primarily Chinese Americans whom they saw frequently at a Chinese social club. They described their life in the United States as comfortable and satisfying. In terms of the CASE model, the L. family members were low in the dimension of social environmental problems until shortly before the couple came for therapy.

The family's satisfying life was interrupted when Mr. L. was suddenly laid off from his job and, for 6 months, Mrs. L. had to be the sole supporter of the family. Later, Mr. L. found another job, but he continued to be anxious and irritable at home. He and Mrs. L. were referred for therapy when his symptoms became more severe and psychotic. Thus, the crisis of being laid off was a social environmental problem that precipitated Mr. L.'s psychiatric condition, but it was no longer a problem at the time of referral. Throughout the progress of therapy, the clinician was aware that she needed to be attuned to the cultural context of the family members, who were different from one another in their degrees of identification with Chinese culture and United States culture. Such differences in cultural identification were related to their distinct premigration and postmigration life experiences and in turn affected their strategies for responding to the family crisis resulting from Mr. L.'s psychiatric condition.

The migration experiences for Mr. and Mrs. L. were markedly different. Mrs. L. was raised in a family of high socioeconomic status. Her parents and extended family were well educated and held professional jobs. She described her upbringing as happy and filled with supportive relatives, friends, and teachers. Chinese traditions were important to her family, and the legacy was passed on to her. Her decision to come to the United States was based upon dreams of adventure, novelty, and excitement. Initially, she came with a sojourner's mentality, planning to return to Taiwan when her studies were completed. Instead, she decided to marry Mr. L. and stay with him in the United States.

Mrs. L.'s adaptation to her new culture offers an example of acculturation through the process of integration. Her pleasant experiences with Chinese culture in Taiwan and her positive outlook on new experiences in the United States led to a sense of confidence that she could embrace two different value systems and incorporate, without fear or distrust, values of her adopted culture. She felt comfortable with both Chinese and mainstream cultures. She was also proficient in her native language and English and in the social etiquette of Taiwan and the United States. In this regard, she fit into the adaptive bicultural category of the CASE model. However, in the face of the family crisis created by Mr. L.'s psychiatric condition, acculturation and integration took another meaning. With the crumbling of the cherished and familiar institution of the Chinese family, she no longer was able to hold two sets of values simultaneously. She began to question her position of acculturation and began to waiver in her choice of integration as a strategy of adaptation to life in the United States. In therapy, Mrs. L. questioned whether her adventure into the New World had been a mistake. She sobbed, "This all happened because I was a bad wife and mother." She was feeling that she had been wrong in adopting many positions about women and motherhood from Western culture rather than adhering to traditional Chinese values and norms by assuming more responsibilities at home. In terms of the CASE model, she was moving from bicultural integration toward a closer identification with Chinese culture. The clinician could surmise that, in a sense, Mrs. L. was wondering whether she should have accommodated, not integrated, to mainstream American culture. In considering possible therapeutic interventions, the clinician recognized the importance of supporting Mrs. L. to reestablish, without guilt, her stance of bicultural integration that, until the time of the family crisis, had provided her a context for feeling secure as an integral member of her host American culture and an active member of her Chinese American social community. An effective intervention was to encourage Mrs. L. to reaffirm her traditional values as a way to create a bond with Mr. L. as well as the children, who were considered by them to be heirs to their Chinese cultural legacy. Following this approach, the clinician was able to gain her confidence to pursue family treatment, an unfamiliar Western approach to healing.

In contrast to Mrs. L., Mr. L. had a very sheltered early childhood. Because of the unstable political situation in Vietnam during his childhood, his parents were secretive about sociopolitical events outside their house. Instead of trying to learn about the world outside his house, he became very knowledgeable about traditional Chinese values and etiquette, which his parents promoted in their household. The sociopolitical reality of the outside world suddenly shattered his sheltered life when he and his family had to escape to Hong Kong to flee impending persecution. From that point on, he felt fearful, confused, suspicious, and lonely. He never liked Hong Kong, where he had only a few friends, whom, as he stated, he never trusted. He came to the United States basically to get away from Hong Kong. After attending graduate school in the United States, he was employed by a major company as an engineer. Throughout his life in the United States, he remained strongly identified with Chinese culture. He was distrustful of foreigners and skeptical of non-Chinese ways of doing things. He was reluctant to seek therapy because it was an unfamiliar Western intervention. He came only when Mrs. L. offered to come with him.

In terms of the CASE model, Mr. L. is an example of an individual who was primarily identified with Chinese culture while taking a position of accommodation to cope with the host culture. He functioned well in his work setting, following mainstream cultural norms and etiquette, but preferred to socialize within the Chinese American community and to follow Chinese cultural practices. His cultural identification was quite different from Mrs. L.'s adaptive biculturalism: that is, her embrace of both Chinese and mainstream cultures. In therapy sessions, the clinician observed that this difference in cultural identification was often a source of tension between the couple. Whether Mr. L. wanted advice or not, Mrs. L. would frequently try to persuade him to be more open-minded to non-Asian ideas so that he could see both Asian and non-Asian approaches to solving problems as helpful. This bicultural position was very difficult for Mr. L. to accept. For example, he agreed to seek therapy, a solution foreign to him, only if the clinician was from his culture and familiar with his traditional Chinese values and norms. During the initial session, when the clinician recommended a medication evaluation by a psychiatrist, Mr. L. was again reluctant, but he eventually agreed on the condition that the psychiatrist would be a Chinese American.

In comparison to the parents, the L. children were more assimilated into mainstream American culture. All three were born and raised in the United States and embraced the mainstream culture imparted to them through public education and the mass media. However, their upbringing also included exposure to their parents' culture of origin. Through daily family living, they had absorbed essential elements of Chinese cultural values, norms, and etiquette. Each of them demonstrated a different degree of loyalty and cultural bonding with Chinese culture while also identifying with mainstream American culture. In this regard, like Mrs. L., they fit the bicultural category of the CASE model, and they demonstrated this in a family session held with Mrs. L. and the children about 2 months after the first meeting with the clinician.

The family session was requested by Mrs. L. to discuss two related events that occurred one day after the couple had their first session with the clinician. Mr. L., in a psychotic rage, violently kicked the family cat, which he blamed for bringing "bad spirits" into the house, and it later died at the veterinarian's office. In response to Mr. L.'s psychotic behavior, Mrs. L. took him to the emergency room of a psychiatric hospital, where he was admitted. After 2 weeks of hospitalization, he was discharged and given medication as an outpatient. At the time the family session was scheduled, Mr. L. had been discharged for about a month. Although his condition was stable, Mrs. L. and the children wanted to discuss his readiness to return to work.

During the family session, all three children were tearful in discussing the death of the cat. Their emotional response was apparently much more intense than one would expect from individuals in traditional Asian cultures grieving the death of a family pet. This was an indication of their assimilation into mainstream American culture. However, the children also demonstrated their understanding of Chinese cultural values and norms and their acceptance of various aspects of Chinese culture—for example, deference to the family hierarchy, as noted in their expressed respect for Mr. L. and their empathy toward his situation.

The oldest son was more observant of Chinese culture than both of his siblings. He was the first one to speak after Mrs. L. made some statements at the beginning of the family session. He spoke in an assured, controlled manner and was dressed formally in a white shirt and tie. He expressed regret about the cat and looked sad and tearful but maintained his composure. He expressed respect for Mr. L. as the head of the family and stated without hesitation that if his father wanted to return to work, his wish should be respected. He discussed his role as the oldest son. His obligation, he stated, was to make up for his father's inability, caused by his illness, to take care of the family. He apologized to his younger siblings for not paying more attention to them when they had been children. Throughout his reflections about his responsibilities, he demonstrated his acceptance and his understanding of his role as the oldest son in traditional Chinese culture.

The daughter, who was dressed fashionably and appeared confident in social interactions, was not willing to talk directly about Mr. L. Instead, she listened attentively and with deference to her older brother's comments about their father. Her statements were focused on their mother's role in the present situation. She emphatically stated that their mother should take her responsibilities as a wife more seriously by monitoring Mr. L.'s behavior more closely and discouraging him from returning to work. She was concerned that Mr. L. might have another psychotic episode and cause embarrassment to himself and the family. She clearly understood the importance of maintaining family reputation, a significant

Asian cultural value. At the same time, she also seemed to be vacillating between certain Asian values and mainstream American values. On one hand, she wanted Mrs. L. to be more of a traditional Chinese wife who would be more concerned with the family reputation; on the other hand, she was critical of Mrs. L.'s frequent deference to the oldest son for advice, a common practice in Asian cultures. Quite a few times in the family session, she expressed frustration and anger at Mrs. L. for not being able to make decisions in the present family crisis. She was hoping that Mrs. L. could function more independently—in a sense, more assertively, in the Western manner. Interestingly, the daughter did not seem to be aware of her contradictory expectations for their mother, which were probably reflective of cultural conflicts within herself. Later on in the session, she stated that she could not confide in their mother about the present family crisis or any crises. She then disclosed that she had been raped in college, an event that she had never before told anybody except a rape counselor at the college to address her concerns about some physical symptoms resulting from the assault. Her response to this crisis was consistent with the traditional Asian perspectives of not shaming the family and of holding feelings within oneself heroically.

The youngest son, dressed in trendy adolescent street clothes, spoke very little and deferred questions that the clinician asked to his older brother, behaving as one would expect for a child who was youngest or lowest in the family hierarchy. He often nodded his head in agreement with his mother and his older brother, conveying his acceptance of their ideas, which reflected traditional Chinese cultural views. He also seemed to have a stronger assimilation to mainstream culture than his older siblings. He cried openly when the family discussed the cat's death.

The members of the L. family are good illustrations of the cultural identification continuum in the CASE model. Mr. L. was primarily identified with Chinese culture but had also accommodated to mainstream American culture. Mrs. L. had accepted many elements of mainstream culture while maintaining her identification with Chinese culture and was adaptively bicultural in this regard. The three children were also bicultural but appeared much more assimilated into mainstream culture than Mrs. L. This family also presents many examples of cultural bonding in terms of remaining rooted to one's culture and its values. Regardless of their differences in adapting to their mainstream American culture, Mr. and Mrs. L. both maintained essential elements of Chinese culture: language, foods, rituals, holidays, and friendship patterns. Their children also were rooted in their parents' cultural heritage while they integrated cultural values of their country of birth.

Interestingly, regardless of their differences in cultural identification, the family members shifted closer to a Chinese cultural perspective in response to the family crisis. Both Mr. and Mrs. L. preferred to have a Chinese American family therapist who would understand their cultural heritage, and they also chose a Chinese American psychiatrist for the medication evaluation. The oldest son assumed responsibility while maintaining respect for the father, a role prescribed by traditional Chinese culture. The younger siblings showed deference to the traditional Chinese family hierarchy, even though the daughter was ambivalent in her views about Mrs. L.'s role. This family also demonstrated the relationship between social environmental problems and cultural identification. A social environmental problem (being laid off) precipitated Mr. L.'s psychiatric condition and led to a family crisis, which in turn disrupted the delicate bicultural positions of some members. Instead of happily accepting both cultures, Mrs. L started to question her position of embracing mainstream American culture. The daughter's expectations for Mrs. L. in relation to the family crisis revealed incongruities in her views of the role of a wife and mother, bringing to the surface a cultural dilemma that she had probably been unaware of before. In working with the L. family, the clinician had to be sensitive to the cultural identification of the members as a family and as individuals, their possible shifts in cultural positions, the emerging cultural conflicts and issues revealed in the process of therapy, and the social environmental problems. In this regard, the clinician found the CASE model very helpful in conceptualizing the family's issues and strategizing effective interventions.

Biracialism: The CASE Model Applied to an Emerging Issue

Biracialism in the United States is an emerging issue that deserves attention in discussions of cultural identification and social environmental issues. Demographic data indicate that American-born Asian Americans are more likely than immigrant Asian Americans to marry out of their ethnic group (Farley, 1996; Lee & Yamanaka, 1990). On the basis of census data on race of spouses for married persons aged 25 to 34, Farley (1996) reported that among American-born Asians, 45.4% of husbands and 54.4% of wives out-married. Among foreign-born Asians, 10.1% of husbands and 23.4% of wives out-married. In all instances, the majority of these out-marriages were to white Americans. If this trend persists, we can expect to see an increasing number of biracial children from intermarriages as the number of second- and third-generation Asian Americans increases in the coming decades.

Though intermarriage between Asian and white Americans may be seen as a positive indication of the social assimilation process of Asian Americans (Lee & Yamanaka, 1990), racial difference between the parents may also contribute to the marginal status of biracial children confronted with their own racial ambivalence (Jacobs, 1992; Kerwin & Ponterotto, 1995;

Root, 1992). Children of biracial marriages often continue to be without a clear racial reference group (Root, 1995). This poses a serious challenge in the development of their ethnic and cultural identity. This relegated marginalization of biracial Asian Americans may often be a presenting problem in psychotherapy and counseling. Besides challenges in their cultural identity development, biracial individuals also face the social environmental stressor imposed by societal biases relating to the hierarchy of color and race in the United States. This hierarchy is most clearly evident for children in Asian-African American intermarriages but is also true for children in Asian-white American intermarriages. However, as Kerwin and Ponterotto (1995) have cautioned, we should be on the guard against overgeneralizing and stereotyping all biracial persons as being marginal and feeling rejected. The process of biracial identity development is an individual process that differs from person to person.

Process of Biracial Identity Development

There are several models describing the process of biracial identity development. Each of these models proposes stages of development that take into consideration an individual's awareness of race integrated with personal and social development. On the basis of his research on black/white biracial children, Jacobs (1992) proposed three distinct stages of biracial identity development:

- *Stage 1.* The biracial child has not categorized people into racial stereotypes but moves freely from one racial color or group to another.
- *Stage 2.* The child begins to internalize a biracial categorization and faces the task of working through racial ambivalence.
- *Stage 3.* The child realizes that racial group membership is determined by one's identification with one's parents and not by one's skin color.

According to Jacobs (1992), with proper parental support and guidance, and positive racial experiences, a child will typically reach Stage 3 by age 8 to 12. However, the process may be longer or different for children who have painful racial experiences. Moreover, developmental issues such as development of sexual identity in adolescence may bring renewed racial ambivalence.

On the basis of his qualitative study of Japanese/white biracial persons, Kich (1992) proposed another three-stage model:

- *Stage 1.* The biracial person develops an awareness of differentness and experiences dissonance.
- *Stage 2.* The person struggles for acceptance from others and at the same time seeks to understand him- or herself. This process may last from age 8 through

late adolescence or late adulthood and may be particularly intense during the high school years.

- *Stage 3.* The person develops a self-acceptance and assertion of interracial identity.

This is a lifelong process, which may be disrupted by developmental events or crises throughout one's life span.

Kerwin and Ponterotto (1995) proposed a six-stage model based on empirical research as well as on integration with other models. They defined their stages according to the identity issues faced by biracial individuals at certain developmental milestones: preschool, entry to school, preadolescence, adolescence, college/young adulthood, and adulthood. They viewed the development of biracial identity as a lifelong process that continues throughout adulthood. At each stage, the resolution of the identity issues is dependent on numerous personal, social, and environmental factors (Kerwin & Ponterotto, 1995).

Although the authors of the various models have proposed time frames or age ranges in which a particular stage usually occurs, there is general agreement that the actual identity development process is personal and individual and is dependent on an individual's situation and experiences. Biracial persons' ability to negotiate conflicts stemming from racial and cultural issues is affected by a host of factors, including parental support, community attitude, acceptance of their extended family, their racial features, and peer feedback (Root, 1995). For example, biracial children growing up in a culturally diverse and harmonious community may find it easier to resolve their identity issue than children growing up in racially polarized or segregated areas. In addition, biracial children's physical/racial features may also affect how they are received by their Asian and non-Asian age peers, which will in turn influence their racial identity development. In this regard, the social environmental aspect of the CASE model plays a crucial role in the racial and cultural identity development of a biracial individual.

Case Illustration of Biracial/Bicultural Identity Development

N. was the daughter of a Korean American mother and a white American father. The family lived in a suburban community with predominantly white residents. Throughout her childhood, N. associated almost exclusively with white friends. She was strongly identified with them and their mainstream American culture. N. was popular in her high school, where she was the only person of Asian American heritage among just a few ethnic minority students. After graduation from high school, N. married her high school sweetheart, a white American. Three years later, N. entered a college with an ethnically diverse student population, where approximately 6% of the students were Asian American. After her first year at this college, N. felt very conflicted. She felt that she had betrayed her Asian heritage. She enrolled in several courses in the Asian American studies program. In her last semester of college, she separated from her husband and sought therapy because of her internal turmoil and anxiety.

In terms of Kerwin and Ponterotto's (1995) model of biracial identity development, N. was experiencing the issues typically faced by biracial persons in the adolescence and college/young adulthood stages. She felt the need to take sides and to choose one culture/race over the other. She felt guilty about ignoring her Korean heritage. According to Kich's (1992) model, she was at Stage 2—struggle for acceptance. Her feelings of confusion and conflict, her need to take sides, and her exploration of her Asian heritage by taking classes in Asian studies were all characteristic of this stage. Although Jacob's (1992) model primarily pertains to children, it can be applied to N.'s reexperiencing of racial ambivalence as a result of life events—in this instance, attending college. Before college, N. resolved whatever racial ambivalence she might have experienced as a child by embracing the racial/cultural identity of her white American father. In high school, she assimilated comfortably with her white peer group. When N. entered the college, she was exposed to a diverse student population from various racial, ethnic, and cultural backgrounds. She now was reexperiencing the racial ambivalence of Stage 2, where a defined racial category was not readily apparent to her. Her own racial ambivalence was reinforced by other students, who noticed her mixed racial features but were not sure of her racial heritage. She was prompted to evaluate whether her identification with her Korean American mother and her new Asian American friends should be greater or less than her identification with her white American father, her white American husband, and her former white American peer group. This was a very painful and stressful situation. Her racial and cultural identity conflict led to her separation from her white American husband. This underscored how life stage issues, such as the race and ethnicity of one's spouse, may become further complications in the racial identity development of a biracial person.

In terms of the CASE model, social environmental issues played a major role in leading N. to the awareness of her biracial issues and conflicts. The move from a suburban community with predominately white residents to a college with a racially/ethnically diverse student population made her cognizant of her biracial status. She questioned her primarily white cultural identification and began to learn and embrace her Asian heritage. Whether she would eventually achieve an adaptive biracial and bicultural identification or identify more with one race and culture than the other was likely to depend on her own self-exploration and development in therapy. She might also be affected by continuing interactions and feedback from her peers and family members, as well as by other social environmental factors, such as the racial climate in her college, future work setting, and residential neighborhood.

Summary

In this chapter, we have introduced the cultural and social environmental (CASE) framework for conceptualizing issues salient for consideration in mental health services for Asian Americans. This model emphasizes that each Asian American client is an individual with a personal position on the continuum of identification with Asian cultures and mainstream American culture and with personal experiences of social environmental difficulties. For some clients, cultural identification issues or specific social environmental stressors may be serious enough to be the sole presenting problems for counseling or psychotherapy. Other clients may seek help for other mental health problems, but even then cultural and social environmental issues are crucial background factors that the clinician must take into consideration. In all situations, mental health professionals must apply interventions that are congruent with the unique cultural and social environmental contexts of each client and must avoid general stereotypes of Asian Americans. The concepts of accommodation, assimilation, and acculturation, as well as biracial/bicultural identification, are reviewed in this chapter.

4

Clinical Implications of Migration

Migration experiences are a major factor for consideration in clinical work with Asian Americans. The majority of this population are immigrants or from immigrant families. As discussed in Chapter 2, approximately 61% of Asian and Pacific Islander Americans are foreign born (U.S. Bureau of the Census, 1998c). If we are considering immigrant families instead of individuals—that is, families with parents who are immigrant and children who are either American born or foreign born—the percentage will be even higher. Therefore, mental health professionals serving Asian Americans need to be knowledgeable about the impact of migration and its implications for clinical work.

In this chapter, we will explore the impact of migration on Asian Americans. Migration is a factor that affects both the cultural and the social environmental dimensions of the CASE model. The term *migration* is used here in a broad sense to include two phenomena: the voluntary emigration of individuals from their home countries to the United States and the flight of refugees from their home countries under the threat of persecution, imprisonment, or death. We will begin by examining the general clinical implications of the migration experience and then discuss the specific cultural and social environmental issues faced by immigrant Asian Americans. Our discussion will conclude with a delineation of the stressors complicating the migration experience of refugee Asian Americans.

Migration and General Systems Theory

We believe that the best way to approach the migration experience is to use a general systems theory perspective because of its concern with change and adaptation (Becvar & Becvar, 1996; Bertalanffy, 1968; Hoffman, 1981). We will use concepts from this theoretical perspective to examine the stressors accompanying migration, both voluntary and involuntary, and their impact upon the functioning of individuals and families.

Stages of the Migration Process

Immigrants, including refugees, undergo three phases of migration: premigration, migration, and postmigration (Ho, 1987). The premigration phase is the period of time before leaving one's country of origin. In this period, prospective immigrants have established a set of values and norms from their existing family and from their developmental history. They have lived together according to rules regarding roles and interaction patterns for behaviors that their culture has set forth for them. In the migration phase, immigrants experience separation from extended family or even nuclear family members and other support networks, as well as societal institutions. Disruption of established life patterns is a common experience. For refugees, trauma, loss, and upheaval are additional adversities in their migration process. The postmigration phase may continue to impose stress upon immigrant families. In the newly adopted country, immigrants are often faced with unpredicted societal and cultural issues brought about by adjustment problems, economic survival, and racial or ethnic prejudice (Florsheim, 1997; Ho, 1987).

General Systems Theory

General systems theory provides a relational framework to examine the migration experience. It offers two key concepts, morphostasis and morphogenesis, that help to clarify the process of coping and adaptation that shapes immigrants' behavioral patterns (Steinglass, 1985). Morphostasis, more commonly known as homeostasis, is a regulatory or equilibrium-seeking mechanism used by a system for maintaining stability, order, and control. In the case of immigrant Asian Americans, homeostasis occurs as a process for maintaining self-organization and self-maintenance by holding tightly to the cultural and social traditions of their homelands. In contrast, morphogenesis, better understood as transformation and change, focuses on growth and development. The morphogenetic process underscores immigrants' intrinsic curiosity to incorporate new experiences with their previously known ways of living their lives. These two processes move concurrently through time, even from one generation to another (Carter & McGoldrick, 1988, 1999). Over time, immigrants struggle to maintain a balance between preserving traditional ways of living and integrating novel experiences into their lifestyle. The process of attaining this balance is often a source of stress and tension for them.

Morphostasis: A Process for Maintaining Tradition

For immigrant Asian Americans, the process of morphostasis includes attempts to cope with changes in the organization of their lives in the new host country and to maintain predictable patterns of behavior within their own culture of origin. Everybody, at one time or another, tends to move toward the stability of homeostasis and to resist change. However, for immigrants, the point of homeostasis may need to shift from a familiar level of stability to a different and new balance point as a way of coping with the new host environment. This new homeostatic calibration may be necessary for survival and for acculturation to occur. Homeostatic calibration is analogous to people's adjustment to different room temperatures. Even though we are accustomed to being comfortable in a room where the temperature has been controlled at, say, 68 degrees Fahrenheit, we can adjust to a norm of either warmer or colder room temperatures. However, if the room is too cold, 32 degrees, or too warm, 100 degrees, we will find ourselves in a crisis situation where we have to seek additional resources or learn new coping skills to find comfort. For immigrants, the external crises brought about by the migration experience are similar to our adjustment to extreme room temperatures. The more stressors immigrants encounter, such as employment problems, housing problems, or racism, the more difficulty they will have in reaching a point of homeostasis or stability. Even in planned migration, when immigrants are generally aware of what is ahead, many of them typically underestimate the difficulties and stressors of settling into a new social cultural environment (Ho, 1987; Hong & Ham, 1992; Lee, 1996; Shon & Ja, 1982). These include the stress of dislocation, or the prolonged separation from their extended family members and friends and from their accustomed lifestyle in their country of origin, the severity of which becomes clear only after they have been in the United States for a while. These difficulties and stressors will interfere with immigrants' pursuit of a new point of homeostasis. However, when the migration experience allows immigrants to maintain enough of their accustomed normative behaviors, homeostasis or stability is more easily achieved. For example, immigrants who choose to live in ethnic enclaves or who have family members already established in the United States are better able to retain patterns of behavior and perspectives from their homeland and thus to maintain a point of homeostasis in their lives (Florsheim, 1997).

Morphogenesis: A Process for Creating Change

Morphogenesis, a process leading to change, is an important systems theory concept for understanding an immigrant's drive toward acculturation. Interactions between a host country and immigrants create the opportunity for transformation and change. Most immigrants display an immense capacity for embracing greater complexity as they incorporate host cultural experiences while holding onto cultural traditions of their country of origin. Acculturation draws upon an immigrant's capability to adopt new life-functioning behaviors and to adapt their own familiar ones. When the regulatory behaviors of an immigrant's experiences, such as family rituals, daily routines, and problem-solving episodes (Steinglass, Bennett, Wolin, & Reiss, 1987), are more congruent with those widely accepted in their new host country, acculturation will be easier for the immigrant. In the process of morphogenesis, immigrants must address three major developmental tasks: (a) defining the boundaries of their relational interactions to determine the extent to which they will integrate unfamiliar values, language, and lifestyles with their familiar traditions; (b) determining allocations of important resources such as money, time, and effort to the process for either transforming or maintaining their traditional life experiences; and (c) deriving an identity that represents the balance between familiar and unfamiliar values, belief systems, and worldviews (Steinglass et al., 1987). Immigrants' response to these developmental tasks is affected by their migration experience and incongruences of cultural dimensions between the country of origin and the new host country, and these effects are idiosyncratically determined. For example, although all immigrants may sense and feel compelled to respond to change agents, individuals may have different migration experiences, different mastery of communication skills, and different awareness of the host country and its cultural norms. Thus, individual immigrants may differ in the extent to which they use the cultural norms of the host country or of their country of origin to grow and develop in response to change agents in their new environment.

Ecological Fit

In examining the relationships between immigrants and their new social cultural environment, Falicov's (1988, 1995) ecological model seems exceptionally relevant. This model, which is modified from Bronfenbrenner's (1977) model, views environmental stressors through layers of contexts: the microsystem, the mesosystem, the exosystem, and the macrosystem. The microsystem consists of relationships among family members. The mesosystem includes interrelations among the community or social settings, such as the extended family, friends, peers, workplace, school, and neighborhood. The exosystem consists of the major institutions of society, such as the mass media and governmental organizations and their policies. The macrosystem involves the values and norms of the culture that determine the context and patterns for interactions to take place. These four levels of the ecosystem are interrelated. Events occurring at one level will affect all other levels. For immigrants, the migration experience is a reciprocal relationship between their familiar culture and their new host culture. The ecological fit or the magnitude of congruence between the immigrants' social cultural environments in their country of origin and in the United States will affect their adaptation to the new culture and will also affect their new adopted community.

In the premigration stage, a stable society typically has a relatively good fit among the levels of the ecosystem. This is graphically depicted by the fit among concentric circles representing the four levels of the system in Figure 4.1. However, we want to emphasize the term *stable society* because some immigrants, such as Southeast Asian refugees, are from war-torn countries that are by no means stable. Even for immigrants from a stable society, the ecological fit among their social cultural environments is typically disrupted in the process of migration. During migration, immigrants experience changes in the microsystem, mesosytem, exosystem, and macrosystem. For example, on the microsystem level, new immigrants may be separated from members of their nuclear families, or family members may have to take on new roles and responsibilities in adaptation to life in the new country. On the mesosystem level, new immigrants are typically cut off from their familiar community, extended family, friends, and acquaintances. They face the challenge of building a new social network and learning to deal with a new exosystem composed of major societal organizations and agencies with their respective functions and regulations. For example, they must learn to deal with the U.S. health care system. Imagine the formidable task facing an immigrant who is trying to sort out the complexity of insurance plans, Medicaid or Medicare regulations, the diversity of medical specialists, or the various disciplines of mental health providers. At the macrosystem level, immigrants learn to function within their new social cultural context. For many immigrants, this is akin to adapting to a whole new way of life. Language is a major issue for those who are not fluent in English. Racism, both overt or covert, and anti-immigrant sentiments are additional stressors. Other aspects of culture, such as values, may affect the lives of immigrants in a more gradual way over time. As an example, Asian American children who either have been born in the United States or have spent their childhood in the United States will customarily become more Americanized than their immigrant parents (Hong, 1989, 1996; Hong & Ham, 1992; Lee, 1996). The resulting incongruity between the individualistic orientation of main-

stream American culture and the familistic orientation of Asian cultures
may eventually produce family discord. In general, the more disruption or
dissonance between immigrants and their new ecosystem, the greater the
adjustment stress and the possibility of dysfunction (Falicov, 1988, 1995).
As illustrated in Figure 4.1, during migration, the microsystem is under
stress (arrows pushing in) and destabilized (indentations) due to misfit
with the new social cultural environment (rectangles), and at the same
time it tries to maintain its original stability (arrows pushing out). The
forces of morphostasis and morphogenesis are at work as immigrants try
to preserve their familiar life patterns but also struggle to adapt to the demands of the new environment. Over time, immigrants generally achieve a
new point of stability or homeostasis, keeping parts of the old familiar patterns of values and behavior as they adapt to the new. As graphically depicted in Figure 4.1, the microsystem stabilizes into an elliptical shape,
maintaining its original circular features while adapting to the rectangles.
Typically, this social and cultural adaptation to life in a host country is a

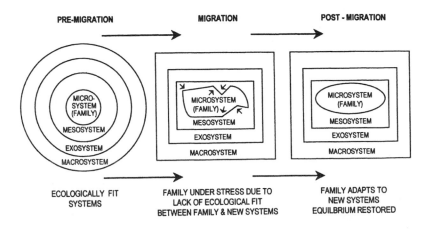

Figure 4.1. Ecological Fit of Immigrant Family at Different Stages of Migration

SOURCE: Adapted from Falicov (1988).

continuous and multigenerational process (Carter & McGoldrick, 1988, 1999; Falicov, 1988, 1995).

The ecosystem model emphasizes reciprocal relationships among the different levels of the system (Bateson, 1972; Falicov, 1988, 1995; Simon, Stierlin, & Wynne, 1985). While immigrants adapt to their new environment, the host society is also affected by the arrival of immigrants. This is particularly observable in areas with a rapid growth of immigrant or refugee Asian American populations. Changes in the host society, for example, may involve accommodating to immigrants' cultural practices such as ethnic foods, consumer goods, and holidays, establishment of ethnic neighborhoods, and development of culturally sensitive business practices, marketing strategies, and public services. But they may also involve ethnic/racial tension between the newcomers and the established residents of the host community and real or imagined competition for jobs and other resources. Anti-immigration movements may result. Although the effects of the reciprocal relationships between immigrants and host communities are important issues, in keeping with the purpose of this book, we are focusing this chapter on the impact of migration on immigrants rather than on the host society.

Clinical Issues Relating to Migration Experience of Immigrant Asian Americans

Having provided a framework for examining the general dynamics of adjustment to migration, we will now turn to specific issues frequently experienced by Asian immigrants in relocating to the United States. Adjusting to a new host society and culture can be a stressful experience that has been described in the literature as "culture shock" (Oberg, 1960), "acculturative stress" (Berry, 1994; Berry & Sam, 1997), and "migration stress" (Beiser, 1996; Kinzie, 1996; Tseng, 1996). This stress can be serious enough to lead to psychological problems, such as clinical depression or anxiety (Beiser, 1996; Berry, 1994; Berry & Sam, 1997; Kinzie, 1996; Tseng, 1996). These problems will be discussed in greater detail in the next chapter. Here we will focus on the major cultural and social environmental issues or stressors facing Asian immigrants when they arrive in the United States.

The major tasks facing immigrants are associated with meeting their physical, material, and emotional needs that are required for settling into the new host society (Hong, 1989; Hong & Ham, 1992; Lee, 1996; Shon & Ja, 1982). Their immediate attention is directed toward taking care of basic physical and economic needs, such as finding new jobs, and, for children in a family, starting new schools. On the family and social levels, adjusting to the new host society involves rebuilding one's support networks and getting used to new family roles or routines. On the psychological level, migration involves a cognitive, structural, and affective transition to the new host culture (Shon & Ja, 1982). Before proceeding to examine these issues in detail, we want to remind clinicians that individual Asian Americans may differ in their migration experiences. Hence, the stressors discussed here must be applied judiciously to specific clients.

Employment Issues

Finding new jobs in the United States is usually not a straightforward procedure for Asian immigrants (Hong, 1989; Hong & Ham, 1992; Lee, 1982, 1996; Shon & Ja, 1982). Employability for immigrants not fluent in English is usually limited to their own ethnic community. Some of these immigrants may eventually broaden their employability by attending English classes. However, this is not always feasible for those who are already busy trying to earn a living and raise a family. Others who have enough financial capital and who are more enterprising may operate small family businesses, such as ethnic restaurants or shops, typically bought from others in their own ethnic group. One noticeable example is Korean immigrants who operate small convenience stores, often in low-income neighborhoods in Los Angeles, or fruit-vegetable stores in New York. They find it is easier to run these businesses because there is an established network of suppliers of merchandise in their ethnic community. This network alleviates the need for them to deal with unfamiliar mainstream suppliers. Many of these immigrants typically see small ethnic businesses as stepping stones. Eventually, they hope to trade up and own shops in better neighborhoods or run other more profitable businesses. Whether they succeed really depends on individual circumstances. Although success stories exist, there are also dismal situations in which immigrants find themselves stuck with a business in a high-crime neighborhood. They survive at subsistence level, with all family members putting their time and energy into a store with limited profitability that they cannot sell to the next investor. Their financial assets are tied up, and this, in turn, prevents them from moving into a more favorable business or neighborhood. Even immigrants who are educated and fluent in English may have difficulty finding new jobs in the United States (Hong, 1989; Lee, 1996). Some may find their premigration work experience discounted by employers. They may also encounter racism manifested through barriers to promotion (i.e., the "glass ceiling"). Others may hold professional credentials unrecognized in the United States. They will have to acquire further education to obtain equivalent professional credentials. Additional examples of underemployment include Southeast Asian refugees who were government workers, officials, or military personnel in their countries of origin and who now have great difficulty finding equivalent jobs in the United States.

Many immigrants came to the United States well aware of such difficulties in employment. They often cite greater freedom, a more stable political environment, or better opportunity for their children as reasons for immigration. However, once settled in the United States, the reality of prolonged low-income employment or underemployment can eventually take its toll. To clinicians, these clients may present a picture of resilience, determination, content, or noble self-sacrifice. Yet underneath such external appearances can be severe stress, doubt, and frustration (Hong, 1989).

School Issues

Adjusting to a new school system is a major stressor for many immigrant Asian families (Hong, 1996). Schools in Asia are much more structured and regimented, with stricter rules and regulations, than the public schools in the United States. For example, in Asian countries, students are typically required to wear school uniforms, and they accord high respect to teachers and other school personnel. In the classroom, students in Asia tend to stay quiet and listen to the teacher, and they are not accustomed to the open discussion format often encouraged in American schools. The more flexible, egalitarian, and participatory atmosphere in American schools, especially at the high school level, is often confusing for immigrant Asian American parents and their children. Some teenagers, for example, in their efforts to fit in with their peers, may overzealously respond to this more relaxed atmosphere by setting aside their parents' traditional discipline or motivation for academic achievement. Hence, immigrant parents often complain to teachers that not enough homework is assigned to their children, while the teachers advise them not to put so much academic pressure on their children. This incongruity is a constant point of misunderstanding between immigrant Asian parents and the public schools, as well as a source of tension between these parents and their children (Hong, 1996).

Support Network

When Asian immigrants relocate to the United States, they are typically cut off from the social or emotional support system provided by their network of relatives and friends in their countries of origin (Hong, 1989; Hong & Ham, 1992; Lee, 1996; Shon & Ja, 1982). Some may have immigrated as single individuals. For those with family members in their homeland, U.S. immigration laws allow only a nuclear family with nonadult children to immigrate together as a unit. Hence, it is rare for Asian immigrants to have as extensive a support network of relatives and friends as they used to have in their countries of origin. Rebuilding this social network is a slow process because close friendship takes time to develop. Indeed, as some immigrants put it, they know it would be nice to have a strong social network, but the question is, where can they find one?

For many immigrants, the lack of a support network leads to social isolation and stress, particularly when they encounter difficult situations (Hong, 1989; Hong & Ham, 1992; Lee, 1996; Shon & Ja, 1982). For instance, a couple having conflicts cannot turn to their own families or confidants to ventilate and be consoled. A pregnant wife may not readily get advice on traditional health care, such as what foods to eat and to avoid, from other experienced family members. Parents with a child having physical or emotional problems may have few relatives or friends to consult. At times, such social isolation can be serious enough to lead to dysfunction in the form of marital conflict, feelings of loneliness, depression, or anxiety. In addition to counseling or psychotherapy, clinicians may need to connect these immigrant clients with community resources to serve as a substitute support network. If no community resources are available, a clinician will have to play an active role in locating and, if necessary, adapting mainstream resources to meet the needs of these clients (Hong, 1988, 1989).

New Family Roles

Sometimes relocation may require family members to take on new roles, and this may be a stressful experience (Hong, 1989; Hong & Ham, 1992; Lee, 1996). For example, an immigrant family that is accustomed to having the husband as the wage earner and the wife as the homemaker may find that in the United States both husband and wife have to work to bring in sufficient income. The couple may also have to share household duties and child care responsibilities. These changes in roles and responsibilities may in time create tension and stress for the couple. Conversely, other families in which both husband and wife were working before they immigrated may now find that the wife has to stay home to take care of the children because of the expense and inconvenience of child care or after-school care. In other situations, children of immigrant families may find they have more household responsibilities than in premigration days because both parents are now working. Parents who are limited in English proficiency may find themselves gradually depending more and more on their American-educated and English-proficient children to translate and conduct public transactions for them (Hong, 1989). All these changing roles will affect the functioning of the immigrant family, and dysfunction may occur if the members are too rigid to adapt to these new demands of the situation.

Adaptation to a New Culture

The concerns we have just discussed are more related to the immediate physical or economic needs of immigrants in their relocation process. Another area of concern involves a cognitive, structural, and affective transition to the host U.S. culture (Shon & Ja, 1982). This transition, adapting to the macrosystem, is a slow and gradual process. In this adjustment, immigrants attempt psychologically to incorporate various features of the host culture into their own worldviews, value system, and norms of behavior, as well as all aspects of their cultural knowledge base. In a sense, this is the actual acculturation process. Adaptation to the host culture does not mean complete assimilation or identification with mainstream American culture. Rather, the process of adaptation involves learning, understanding, and internalizing the new culture to the extent that it becomes familiar, controllable, and supportive (Shon & Ja, 1982). This process allows immigrants to function within the new culture with increased confidence and security. By learning about the lifestyle in the United States, Asian immigrants can feel at ease and comfortable with the new culture and with personal interactions and public transactions outside their ethnic community. For some immigrants, this may gradually lead to a complete identification with mainstream American culture. Other immigrants may develop an adaptive bicultural identification that enables them to feel comfortable and function within mainstream American culture as well as their culture of origin. Asian immigrants who fail to make this transition into the host culture may continue to feel uncomfortable with life in the United States unless they are living and working exclusively within the confines of an ethnic enclave.

Unlike the physical relocation, making the cognitive, structural, and affective transition to the host U.S. culture is not an all-or-nothing situation but a continuum. It is typically a lifelong process for the individual immigrant. For immigrant families, adaptation to a new culture is a transgenerational process that takes each successive generation one step further toward acculturation, with the second generation usually being more acculturated than the first, and the third generation being more acculturated than the previous two (Carter & McGoldrick, 1988, 1999; Falicov, 1988). It is not unusual for first-generation Asian immigrants, especially those who came here at a more mature age, to experience greater difficulty in this process. Some immigrants never make sufficient progress in the area of acculturation to feel comfortable with living in the United States. At times, those who can financially afford it may even return to live in their country of origin after their children are grown up and established in the United States.

Migration Stress and the Family Life Cycle

In examining the impact of migration, clinicians must pay attention to a person's developmental life stage (Hong & Ham, 1992; Lee, 1996). Developmental stages represent critical life events in a person's growth and development. Stress or disruption of homeostasis occurs when a person seeks to cope with the new life event and makes the transition from one stage to another. For immigrants, this stress is further intensified by the adjustment issues relating to migration. A person's adjustment to a new ecosystem is often most difficult when he or she is making the transition from one developmental stage to another (Hong & Ham, 1992). The concept of the family life cycle (Carter & McGoldrick, 1988, 1999) provides a useful framework for us to illustrate the impact of migration on the developmental life events of Asian Americans.

The term *family life cycle* refers to a sequence of critical life events, such as "launching of the single young adult," "joining of families through marriage," "families with young children," "families with adolescents," "launching children and going on," and "the family in later life" (Carter & McGoldrick, 1988, 1999). Of course, variations to this pattern occur among families, especially among cultural and socioeconomic groups (Carter & McGoldrick, 1988, 1999). In our examination of immigrant Asian Americans, we are less concerned with the actual number or pattern of family life cycle stages than with the life events that are made particularly stressful by the migration experience.

For immigrant Asian Americans, the developmental stage of having young children is a critical life event that is often made more stressful by the lack of a support network (Hong & Ham, 1992). In Asia, when both husband and wife work, they commonly rely on extended family members to help with child care. Without this support system in the United States, finding help for child care becomes a major stressor. Some couples may have to request one or both of their parents to immigrate to the United States or to live with them temporarily so that they can help take care of the young children. In other situations, a couple, to minimize their own stress, may even send their young children back to their country of origin to be taken care of by the grandparents. Any of these choices will alter family life patterns. Of course, there are couples who can afford to have the wife stay at home to take care of the children or to pay for child care in the United States. However, unless the family is very affluent, the cost of child care is a financial challenge requiring adjustment to their lifestyle.

Often, the stress of child care means that the immigrant couple will have to reprioritize some of their other life goals, such as further education, job training, or career advancement (Hong & Ham, 1992).

For immigrant Asian American families with adolescents and teenagers, an additional stressor is the cultural gap between parents and children (Florsheim, 1997; Hong, 1989, 1996; Hong & Ham, 1992, 1994; Huang, 1976; Lee, 1982, 1996; Sue & Morishima, 1982). The children, being raised and educated in the United States, typically become more identified with mainstream American culture than the parents, who, as immigrants, tend to have stronger memories and emotional ties to their Asian cultural roots. Over time, a cultural gap evolves between children and parents. As depicted by Hong (1996), the family is like a zipper being slowly zipped apart. On one side are parents who are more identified with their culture of origin, and on the other side are children who are more identified with mainstream American culture. This cultural gap is a major stressor for both children and parents and a destabilizing force for the family (Hong, 1989, 1996). For example, in addition to the typical developmental issues faced by adolescents going through the stage of individuation, Asian American adolescents in immigrant families often have to grapple with the different expectations of their parents at home and of people in mainstream settings, such as schools. This confusion may complicate their cultural identity development (Hong, 1989, 1996; Hong & Ham, 1992, 1994; Sue & Sue, 1993, 1999; Triandis, 1995). Conversely, Asian American parents often have difficulties understanding and coping with their children's cultural identity issues, especially when the two cultures hold different views on the roles and behaviors of adolescents. Because Asian cultures prescribe a more hierarchical family structure and more restrictive behavioral norms for adolescents than mainstream American culture, Asian American adolescents frequently accuse their parents of being old-fashioned or controlling. At the same time, immigrant parents often complain that their children are rebellious or corrupted by the host American culture. In some situations, the communication gap widens when the adolescents establish English as their dominant language while their parents remain dominant in their home language. Overall, the cultural gap is a factor that compounds the generation gap in the family, and the friction can be intense enough to lead to family conflicts (Hong, 1989, 1996). From a different perspective, clinicians have to be sensitive to the difficulty faced by many Asian American youths who must negotiate between Asian and mainstream cultures. Even though these youths may be American born and proficient in mainstream culture, they are likely to encounter people who do not perceive them as "full Americans" simply because of their physical features (Chua-Eoan, 1990; Hong, 1996). Such disappointments can be devastating and may lead to the development of a maladaptive bicultural identification (Hong, 1989, 1996; Hong & Ham, 1992, 1994; Sue & Sue, 1993, 1999). These youths may feel that they are in a marginal position, not fully belonging to either culture, or may feel alienated from both cultures.

When immigrant Asian American families are at the developmental stage at which aging and death become a family concern, cultural and migration issues again add to the normal developmental stress (Hong & Ham, 1992). The concept of filial piety in Asian cultures prescribes that children should repay their parent's love and care by providing and caring for them in their old age. It is common for aging parents to live with a married child, preferably a married son, as prescribed by the patriarchal structure of the traditional Asian family. For immigrant couples who have to leave their parents behind in Asia, inability to care for aging parents may create constant guilt feelings, especially when they have no other siblings there to assume this responsibility. Other couples may decide to sponsor their aging parents to immigrate and live with them in the United States. This solution, however, can be stressful for both the couple and their elderly parents (Hong & Ham, 1992; Hong, Lee, & Lorenzo, 1995). At their advanced age, the elderly parents often find it difficult to adjust to the new lifestyle and culture in the United States. For the immigrant couple, the entry of their parents into the nuclear family will change their life patterns. In some cases, the different expectations between the elderly and the younger generation can lead to serious conflicts. Further, Asian American families are not immune to problems between "in-laws." Although the option of placing their parents in senior homes exists, this choice is difficult because it may arouse feelings of rejection and abandonment from the parents. Hence, for immigrant Asian American families, caring for elderly parents is more complicated than it would have been before migration.

Split Households and Reunification

Split households and their subsequent reunification are another area of stress created by the migration experience (Hong & Ham, 1992). The current immigration laws of the United States classify family members into several categories and assign different preferences and quotas for each. For example, a couple can immigrate with their minor children, but their adult children are in a different immigration category and will have to wait longer for their quota. The wait for married children to immigrate is typically even longer. Depending on current immigration regulations, siblings of immigrants may have to wait years, or indefinitely, for their quota. Thus, for many Asian Americans, many years may pass before their whole family, defined from an Asian cultural perspective, can complete the process of migration (Hong & Ham, 1992; Liu & Fernandez, 1987).

This slow process of family reunification greatly affects immigrants' family life in the United States (Hong & Ham, 1992). Because the timing of the migration of other family members is typically determined by immigration regulations and is beyond the control of the applicants, family members may rejoin the family at any life cycle stage. Although the arrival of a family member is a desired event, adding another member may also increase the existing stress level of the established immigrants, who now have to help the newly arrived members cope with the immediate basic issues of migration. This task intensifies the stress of their own migration experience and prolongs their responsibility to the family unit. Such situations may lead to tension and conflicts, especially for families that are already under pressure from other life circumstances. Clinicians should be aware of these themes of separation and reunification in the immigrant Asian American family and should be sensitive to the ambivalence resulting from such exits and entries of family members.

Astronauts and Parachute Kids

For a number of reasons, some Asian immigrant families voluntarily choose to delay the process of settling down together in the United States (Hong & Ham, 1992; Hudson, 1990; Liu & Fernandez, 1987). Most notable are family situations with parents who are known as "astronauts" and children who are known as "parachute kids." Both of these family situations began to be common in the 1980s and typically exist in affluent middle- and upper-class families.

As mentioned earlier in the discussion of employment issues, many Asian professionals find it difficult to secure the equivalent of their premigration jobs or incomes in the United States. Also, individuals who own their businesses may find it too financially risky or unprofitable to start anew here. However, they still want to immigrate to the United States so that their families can enjoy the sociopolitical stability or educational opportunities not available in their countries of origin. So after taking care of the basic migration needs, such as housing for the family and schools for the children, the financial provider, typically the husband, will go back to work in his or her country of origin, while maintaining close contact and visiting the family in the United States frequently (Hong & Ham, 1992; Hudson, 1990). In the Chinese community, such individuals are often nicknamed "astronauts" or "spacemen" because they frequently "fly" back and forth between the United States and their country of origin. Although such split households can be found in all Asian American groups, they seem to be particularly common among more recent Chinese immigrants from Taiwan and Hong Kong (Hudson, 1990; Liu & Fernandez, 1987). There are no data on the number of "astronauts," but their occurrence is common enough for this term to be generally used in the community and to be noted in mainstream American news (Hudson, 1990).

Though members of these split households can afford to visit one another as needed, their separation is still a stressful experience for everyone and will affect the normative development of the family (Hong & Ham, 1992; Hudson, 1990). Often, the decision to have a split household is necessitated by economic considerations and is made reluctantly as the lesser of two evils: temporary family separation versus underemployment or financial downdrift in the United States. Clinicians need to be alert to the effects of such separations on the interrelationships and development of the family members. These separations are highly stressful for the members even though the arrangement is "voluntary" and the family is affluent.

Parachute kids, as they are often called in the mass media (Hamilton, 1993c; Lin, 1998), are Asian children who are sent to the United States to attend grade school while the rest of their families continue to live in their homelands. They are like parachute troopers who are "dropped off from the plane" and left in the United States. Most of these children are from Taiwan, with smaller numbers from Hong Kong and South Korea (Hamilton, 1993c). In the United States, social service agencies typically call these children "unaccompanied minors." Their ages range from 8 to 18, with most being teenagers. Like "astronaut" parents, these children are typically from affluent families that can afford the expenses of sending their children to the United States or other countries for education (Hamilton, 1993b, 1993c; Lin, 1998). There are an estimated 30,000 to 40,000 parachute kids in the United States, with a high concentration in southern California (Hamilton, 1993c; Lin, 1992, 1998). Their living arrangements vary greatly. Some parachute kids may live with their siblings or by themselves in a house or apartment bought or rented by their parents. These living accommodations can be in very nice neighborhoods. Others may live with relatives or family friends who act as their legal guardians (Hamilton, 1993b, 1993c; Lin, 1992, 1998). In some cases, parachute kids may live in dormitories of private schools or in private homes set up like hostels by others in the community who are paid to take care of them (Lin, 1992, 1998).

There are different reasons that these Asian parents send their young children to attend school in the United States. Some parents want their children to benefit from the higher education opportunities in the United States and believe that attending grade school here may provide their children a better transition to college later on. Other parents want to relieve their children from the high-pressure approach to education in Asia. In the case of students from Taiwan, the decision may sometimes be partially related to the parents' desire to help their children avoid the military draft in their homeland (Lin, 1998). Although the decision to go abroad for school is typically made by well-intentioned parents, most children consent to it voluntarily or even see it as an exciting adventure. Also, the children consider attending school in the United States to be a status symbol. However, many parachute kids are not emotionally ready for isolation from their families or close friends, as well as for the different lifestyle in the United States. Loneliness and depression are common problems among them (Hamilton, 1993b; Lin, 1992, 1998). Some parachute kids may get generous financial allowances from their parents but not enough adult supervision and as a result are at high risk of delinquency (Hamilton, 1993a, 1993b, 1993c; Lin, 1992). Though many parachute kids maintain good grades in school and proceed to attend college, a noticeable number of them also develop emotional and behavioral problems that are identified by educators and clinicians working in the Asian American communities (Hamilton, 1993a, 1993b, 1993c; Lin, 1992, 1998). When working with parachute kids, mental health clinicians should be aware of their ambivalence toward living by themselves in the United States. Even though parachute kids may want to be in the United States, they are experiencing the emotional distress of migration and separation from significant others. They need parental care and guidance, but if they returned to their home countries, they would be seen as failures and bring shame to themselves and their families. Clinicians need to explore these issues with parachute kids and, if possible, with the parents or their surrogates in the United States. Use of community resources, including youth programs and after-school activities offered by churches and other agencies, can be considered as an alternative for helping parachute kids to adjust to life in the United States. Advising the parachute kids to return to Asia without considering other options is a clinically simplistic approach. No simple solution exists for the families' dilemma. A clinician must be sensitive to the social and cultural context of the family and help each child and his or her family arrive at their own individual resolution.

Case Illustration of Migration Stress

Mr. and Mrs. K. immigrated from China with their three teenage children. Both of them had the equivalent of postbaccalaureate education and had years of professional experience before coming to the United States. However, they knew they would not be able to find similar professional jobs here because their fluency in English was limited. Also, their credentials from China were not recognized here. Like the immigrants of legendary success stories, they planned to take low-level jobs while they learned English so that they could climb up the socioeconomic ladder. As they put it, they were willing to make some sacrifices so that their children could enjoy the freedom and opportunities available in the United States.

The family's adjustment to their new social cultural environment was difficult. Having limited knowledge of English and being totally unfamiliar with their new surroundings, they had to rely on their relatives to help with everything, from renting an apartment and writing monthly checks for utilities to learning what brands of consumer items to buy and where. Finding their way on public transportation and later learning to drive a car were formidable tasks. Instead of being professional and self-sufficient, they now found themselves constantly in a state of dependency. Overall, the family handled the stress with impressive resilience. Mr. K. worked as a kitchen aide in a Chinese restaurant, and Mrs. K. worked as a custodian in an office building. Both of them attended English classes after work. The children, two sons and a daughter, were good students in a bilingual program in school. Despite the hardships, the family was happy with their choice to immigrate here.

Gradually, however, the stress began to take its toll, especially on Mr. K., who was not used to menial work. His exhausting work schedule made it hard for him to attend English classes. He felt he was trapped in a dead-end situation, with little hope of moving up to a professional career. Mrs. K. also felt exhausted by her job but was determined to keep working. Friction began to develop between them, and this added to the stress level of the family. Meanwhile, the children, being bright and diligent, were doing very well in school. Now being fluent in English, and more acculturated to mainstream America than the parents, they were often called upon to act as interpreters and perform chores for the family. Insidiously, this caused a shift in the power structure of the family. Instead of being respectful and acquiescent, they started to look down on their parents' "ignorance." All their lives, they had looked up to their parents as educated and knowledgeable authorities. Now they saw their parents as vulnerable. Though not openly rebellious, they started to speak scornfully about their parents' lack of assimilation into mainstream American society. Over the next 3 years, the tension within the family grew until Mr. K. decided that he could not take it anymore. He returned to China, where he was able to obtain a professional job similar to his previous one. Mrs. K. stayed in the United States with the children. She wanted to wait for them to complete college before deciding whether she would join her husband in China. She also entertained the possibility that, after graduating from college, the children might be able to support her and her husband to retire comfortably either in the United States or in China.

Initially, this family held together very well under the stress of migration. The family members adapted well to the challenges, although there was a major mismatch between their microsystem—that is, the family's established life patterns—and the new ecosystem of the host U.S. society. They learned new ways of doing things, developed new daily routines, and even accepted menial jobs that totally negated their premigration professional work experience. At the same time, they held onto the patterns of norms and values they had long established in their premigration life in China in order to maintain morphostasis, their sense of balance. The parents continued to be the wage earners and the authorities in the household. The children devoted themselves to school because they were convinced that their scholastic achievement would be an investment for the future of the family. Using our earlier example of the temperature change in a room, like a person bracing for a cold breeze, the family huddled together and braced for this drastic change in environment. However, bracing for a cold breeze for a short period is different from staying in the cold for a long time. The hardship of working at menial jobs was more exhausting than the couple had anticipated. The shift in family power to the children was another unpredicted change. All these changes, as well as other stressors related to migration, created tension within the family. The friction between the parents and the changing attitude of the children were symptoms of developing family dysfunction. From the mainstream American cultural perspective, Mr. K.'s decision to return to China could be interpreted that he was abandoning the family, or that the family was breaking up. However, in the context of Asian immigrant practices, he was simply making the choice of becoming an "astronaut," even though he probably would not be able to visit the family as often as the typical affluent astronaut. Thus, for this family, his departure was a reluctant but acceptable compromise to reduce the tension and stress for himself and for the whole family. In a sense, his departure helped to preserve the family, at least for now.

The next critical point in this family's postmigration adjustment will probably come at the next stage in the family life cycle, when all three children have completed college and are financially established. At that time, Mr. and Mrs. K. will have to decide whether to rejoin each other in the United States or in China. If they choose to live in China, the temporarily separated family will become two permanent units, the parental dyad and the children, on opposite sides of the Pacific Ocean. Also, the couple's decision may be dependent on their children's evolving cultural identification. In the next 4 or 5 years, the children may become more assimilated into mainstream American culture and embrace full individuation as practiced in the United States. They may want to live by themselves and may offer relatively little financial and emotional support to their parents

(Hong, 1989; Hong & Ham, 1992). Even if the children do not drastically change, they may marry individuals who are more Americanized and less inclined to live with parents-in-law. At this postmigration stage, all the previously experienced dilemmas will have to be addressed: Asian versus mainstream American cultural influences, individual lifestyle preferences, and family bonds and loyalties. Thus, to understand this immigrant family, we must continue to examine the interplay of the forces of morphostasis and morphogenesis. On one hand, the family members will seek to maintain the established patterns of the family. On the other hand, they will need to modify these patterns in response to the family's growth and development, as well as to the demands of the host ecosystem of the United States.

Clinical Issues Relating to Migration Experience of Refugee Asian Americans

In addition to the migration stresses that we have previously discussed, refugees typically face even greater hardships at every stage of their migration experience (Carlson & Rosser-Hogan, 1991; Palinkas & Pickwell, 1995; Rumbaut, 1995). In sharp contrast to most recent East Asian immigrants, Southeast Asian refugees did not come from stable or peaceful premigration environments. They lived in countries disrupted by years of war, political upheaval, and social unrest. Thus, in clinical work with this refugee population, clinicians must explore and understand the stress or turmoil that clients may have experienced in their premigration stage.

Most Southeast Asian refugees left their homeland in chaotic and traumatic situations (Hong & Friedman, 1998; Liu, 1979; Rumbaut, 1995; Tayabas & Pok, 1983; Tran, 1988; Uba, 1994). The majority of the early wave of Vietnamese refugees who fled at the end of the Vietnam War had less than 24 hours to evacuate (Liu, 1979; Tayabas & Pok, 1983). Their departure was hasty and chaotic. The second wave of Vietnamese refugees left later by sea in overcrowded small fishing boats (Rumbaut, 1995; Tayabas & Pok, 1983). Many of them drifted about in the sea, suffering starvation and facing possible drowning and death, not sure of their final destination, while being repeatedly turned away by neighboring countries already inundated with refugees. This second wave of refugees also included Cambodians, Hmongs, and Laotians, whose long hazardous trips through the tropical jungle required them to brave the elements, minefields, ambushes, and exhaustion (Tayabas & Pok, 1983). Those Southeast Asian refugees fortunate enough to be granted temporary asylum in nearby countries had to live in overcrowded and sparsely equipped refugee camps while they waited for permanent asylum in other countries such as the United States, France, Canada, and Australia. These countries were among a dozen or so that would eventually accept them for permanent residency (Rumbaut, 1995; Tayabas & Pok, 1983; Tran, 1988). The average wait in the camps was 2 to 3 years (Tayabas & Pok, 1983). During this long wait for asylum, the refugees' lives were literally put on hold. They had little personal control over life events in the camps, and there was no guarantee that they would be accepted by a host country. This uncertainty and the trauma of the actual escape are aspects of the refugee experience that clinicians must appreciate in working with this population.

Southeast Asian refugees who were allowed to enter the United States faced the formidable task of rebuilding their lives from scratch. Most of them had lost all their possessions and had to rely on welfare. Others were separated from their families. All were severed from their familiar communities and established livelihoods. Moreover, the U.S. resettlement policy was to disperse refugees throughout many parts of the country. Many refugees had great difficulty adjusting to the new cultural and social environments and to the unfamiliar cold climate of some locations. After saving up enough money, they gradually undertook a secondary migration to regions such as California in order to be close to their relatives or established Asian communities or to be in a warmer climate (Hong & Friedman, 1998; Min, 1995c; Rumbaut, 1995; Weil, 1983).

The refugees' settlement in the United States was assisted by official government policy and sponsored programs, as well as by charity and religious organizations. However, refugees were not necessarily welcomed by everyone. As early as the first wave arrived in 1975, a Gallup poll showed that 54% of the American public were against accepting them as residents and that only 36% were in favor (Tayabas & Pok, 1983). In addition to long-standing racism against Asians, segments of the general population expressed concerns that the refugees would be competing for jobs or that they would be a burden on welfare and community resources. Later, when Southeast Asian refugees began to relocate in significant numbers to various regions of the United States, many public institutions in those areas, including schools, clinics, and hospitals, felt the strain because they were not prepared to provide culturally responsive services. Although many of these institutions officially tried to accommodate this new constituency, some privately complained that they were a burden on their resources. At times, individual service providers who were set in their ways of practice even felt that this demographic change was making their jobs more difficult or threatening their job security. We have encountered many of these actual situations when we have tried to locate or advocate for services for Southeast Asian refugee clients. In other situations, some community residents feel that the changing ethnic composition of their neighborhood poses a threat to their established way of life or property values. Both blatant and subtle resentment of the arrival of refugees is common. Indeed, the postmigration life of many Southeast Asian refugees is more arduous than one might imagine.

The distress and trauma experienced by Southeast Asian refugees at all stages of the migration experience lead to a high incidence of emotional or psychiatric problems in this population (Carlson & Rosser-Hogan, 1991; Chung & Kagawa-Singer, 1993; Owen, 1985; Palinkas & Pickwell, 1995). Even for those who were able to make the transition to life in the United States successfully, the sense of loss and insecurity caused by the ordeal is likely to take a long time to heal, if indeed it ever heals. As one refugee family told us, after 7 years in the United States, they still felt like new arrivals. Fortunately, they added, they had reestablished contacts with other extended family members now settled in Australia. Both families took comfort in the thought that if either family had to flee again, relatives in the other country would be ready to provide them shelter. For the general U.S. public, such a concern about sociopolitical upheavals in the United States that would force people to flee the country would be totally improbable. However, from the perspective of refugee families, this sense of insecurity is very realistic. These "unimaginable" situations have already happened to them once, and they could happen again. Clinicians must be empathic to such feelings when working with this population.

Case Illustration of Refugee Trauma

Mr. and Mrs. B. and their four children were Vietnamese refugees. They owned a small retail store in Vietnam and fled the country by boat in 1981. Their escape was a traumatic experience. The engine of their crowded fishing boat failed while they were at sea. They drifted about for weeks, starving and not sure whether they could ever reach land. They witnessed fellow refugees falling into the stormy sea and drowning and watched other boats sinking with their passengers. Their boat eventually made it to Malaysia, where they were granted temporary asylum. The B. family considered themselves fortunate because refugees who arrived later were turned away by armed navy boats. These other refugees were not even given the chance to refurbish their food or water supply. The family stayed in a refugee camp in Malaysia for a year and were then transferred to another refugee camp in the Philippines, where they stayed for about 6 months. They were finally permitted to enter the United States in late 1982.

The B. family's resettlement in the United States was aided by a Christian church organization. They literally had to start their lives anew, for they had lost everything they owned. The family moved into a three-bedroom apartment in a low-income inner-city neighborhood where many other Vietnamese refugees had settled. They lived on welfare that was available to Southeast Asian refugees at that time. Mr. and Mrs. B. were in their 50s, and both had little formal education. The oldest child, a son in his 20s, was paraplegic due to a childhood accident. In Vietnam, he did not attend school and stayed at home most of the time. Since settling down in the United States, he had been attending an adult English program for Southeast Asian refugees. His rehabilitation counselor had trouble placing him in a job training program because of his limited English proficiency and lack of formal education. Another son and a daughter were in high school. The youngest girl was in junior high. All three were placed at their grade level based on chronological age, despite the almost 2-year interruption of their formal education when they lived in the refugee camps. Fortunately, because of the relatively large number of Vietnamese refugees in their schools, special bilingual classes with their refugee cohorts were available to help their transition.

In terms of the migration issues discussed in this chapter, this family was fortunate to have church volunteers and other Vietnamese refugees in their neighborhood who could help them deal with their daily physical and economic needs. However, because they had very limited English proficiency, Mr. and Mrs. B. did not dare to venture out of their small ethnic neighborhood unless accompanied by others. Instead of leading the independent and productive life they had in Vietnam, they felt powerless and dependent. This highlighted the mismatch between their premigration and postmigration environments. Like most refugees, the family was relieved to be finally admitted into the United States. They were eager to settle down and hoped not to draw any attention from government or other official sources.

Mr. and Mrs. B. were extremely concerned when the school counselor told them their youngest girl was exhibiting emotional problems in school and was being referred for counseling. The clinician who interviewed both the girl and the couple noticed that Mr. and Mrs. B. themselves were suffering from emotional problems as a result of their refugee ordeal. However, the couple was reluctant to seek mental health services. They had a seemingly resigned attitude of just living day to day, of simply waiting for the children to graduate from school and work to support the family. Mr. and Mrs. B. were also perplexed by the efforts spent by rehabilitation providers working with their oldest son. They could not understand why the rehabilitation counselor and the social worker would not let the son stay at home as he had done during premigration period.

Although settling into an area of the city with a large Vietnamese refugee population helped to ease the family's transition to life in the United States, the family had a difficult time rebuilding the familiar support system of extended family and friends. It took them a long time to develop intimate social and emotional bonds with others in the community. Moreover, unlike voluntary immigrants who could readily contact other people in their homeland by phone or by mail, the family had no available means of communication with anyone in Vietnam because of the postwar relationship between Vietnam and United States at that time. They had no way of even knowing what had happened to relatives or friends who had stayed behind or who fled separately. Thus, the family's support system was thoroughly destroyed. Trying to locate and reconnect with lost extended family members was another stressful task for them.

In the face of such adversity, we again see the force of morphostasis. The family braced itself for survival in the new social cultural environment by holding onto its familiar traditions and culture. The parents maintained their hierarchical position at home and placed their hopes on the academic achievement of the children. They looked forward to the day that the children would graduate from school and could support the family. Like the K. family of the previous case example, the parents had hopes whose fulfillment might be jeopardized by, among other factors, the cultural gap that might develop within the family as the children matured. The parents would have to wait and see whether the children would abandon their cultural roots, especially the cultural values of filial piety and familism, or retain them. Indeed, clinicians working with refugee families need to be aware that in the coming years, there will be a gradual increase in the number of American-born children from this refugee population who, unlike their parents, have no direct experience of the refugee ordeal. Perhaps this widened cultural gap along with the generation gap in the family will provide a breeding ground for misunderstanding, conflicts, and resultant emotional turmoil.

Summary

In this chapter, we have examined the impact of migration on the life patterns of Asian Americans. The process of relocating from a familiar ecosystem to a new social cultural environment is often a stressful task. Asian immigrants need to find a balance between retaining the established patterns of values, roles, and behaviors and accepting the changes initiated by their host U.S. ecosystem. In response to the external stressors relating to the migration process, the morphostatic forces of the family must accommodate both the predictable normative morphogenetic growth of the family and the unpredictable changes brought on by the new social cultural environment. This task is even more difficult for Southeast Asian refugees, who have encountered great trauma in all stages of their migration.

For many refugees, the sense of loss and insecurity caused by their ordeal may take a lifetime to heal. Because the majority of Asian Americans are immigrants or come from families with immigrant parents, mental health clinicians, to work effectively with them, need to have an empathic understanding of these migration and refugee issues.

5

Diagnostic Assessment

Diagnostic assessment is an important part of psychotherapy and counseling. In mental health clinics, a diagnostic assessment typically involves arriving at a formulation as specified in the current (fourth) edition of the *Diagnostic and Statistical Manual of Mental Disorders* (*DSM-IV*) (American Psychiatric Association, 1994). However, other settings, such as family and child service agencies or public schools, may not require formal diagnostic labels as a condition for providing psychotherapy or counseling. Whether or not a diagnostic label is used, a clinician always needs to have a clear understanding of the presenting problems and related issues to formulate a treatment plan for the client. This chapter focuses on the salient cultural and social environmental factors for consideration in diagnostic assessments with Asian American clients. We will start with a review of the major cultural formulations for diagnostic assessment in the literature and then examine specific cultural and social environmental issues that often affect diagnostic assessments of Asian American clients, particularly those who are identified with Asian cultures. Because diagnostic assessment may at times involve psychological testing, we will examine its use with Asian American clients. This chapter also discusses the assessment of cultural identification because the evaluation of a client's degree of identification with Asian cultures or mainstream American culture is critical for providing appropriate services.

Cultural Formulations for Diagnostic Assessment

The *DSM-IV* (American Psychiatric Association, 1994) is the most commonly used diagnostic system in the United States. Although culture was not given much attention in previous editions of this manual, the current edition, published in 1994, gives culture a more prominent position. In addition to including discussions of cultural features of various psychiatric disorders throughout the manual, the *DSM-IV* includes a list of culture-bound syndromes and a set of guidelines on cultural formulation in Appendix I.

According to the *DSM-IV,* a cultural formulation of a psychiatric case includes five aspects: (a) the cultural identity of the client, (b) the cultural explanation of the client's illness, (c) the cultural factors relating to the client's psychosocial environment and levels of functioning, (d) the cultural elements affecting the relationship between the client and the clinician, and (e) the overall cultural assessment for diagnosis and care of the client (pp. 843-844). These guidelines offer a very thorough framework for clinicians to conduct diagnostic assessments for Asian American clients. A very detailed elaboration and explanation of these guidelines is provided by Lu, Lim, and Mezzich (1995). We encourage the reader to consult their work for further information.

Similar cultural frameworks have been proposed by other authors. A very comprehensive and useful system was proposed by Grieger and Ponterotto (1995). These authors introduced the concept of "psychological mindedness," which is defined as a person's familiarity with the Western middle-class conception of counseling. Their assessment framework for multicultural counseling includes six components: (a) the client's level of "psychological mindedness," (b) the client's family's level of "psychological mindedness," (c) the client's and the family's attitudes toward helping and counseling, (d) the client's level of acculturation, (e) the client's family's level of acculturation, and (f) the client's family's attitude toward acculturation.

Both frameworks, the *DSM-IV*'s and Grieger and Ponterotto's (1995), highlight the importance of considering the diverse cultural backgrounds of clients. The *DSM-IV* formulation calls attention to cultural factors affecting a client's psychosocial environment, the client-clinician relationship, a client's cultural identification and perception of a disorder, and treatments for the disorder. Grieger and Ponterotto's (1995) framework emphasizes the worldview and acculturation of a client's family in addition to the individual client's cultural perspective. This focus is particularly salient for mental health treatment of Asian American clients because of the importance of the family in Asian cultures and the possible differences in cultural identification among members of an Asian Ameri-

can family. The two frameworks overlap and can be considered as comple-
mentary to each other. Together, they provide a set of useful guidelines for
clinicians to follow when conducting diagnostic assessments for Asian
American clients. Keeping these frameworks in mind, we will now examine specific cultural and social environmental issues that are crucial elements for consideration in a diagnostic evaluation.

Cultural Factors for Consideration in Diagnostic Assessment

Given the complexity of culture, we will use a simplified framework for
examining fundamental cultural components that are significant in diagnostic assessments for Asian American clients. Our framework includes
the following six major dimensions of culture: (a) kinship and association,
(b) health and nutrition, (c) beliefs and religion, (d) values and norms, (e)
art and folklore, and (f) language. Similar cultural components have been
identified by other authors in their discussion of culture and mental health
services (Axelson, 1993; Lee, 1996; Soriano, Soriano, & Jimenez, 1994).
There are, of course, other dimensions of culture, and the six listed components can be broken down into subcategories or can be reconfigured in
other ways. We are using the current framework for the sake of simplicity
and clarity. The six cultural dimensions identified here are sufficient for
the purpose of our discussion on diagnostic assessment. Because the different cultural elements in our framework may overlap and their effects
may interact with one another, clinicians need to examine their overall implications rather than considering these elements in isolation. We also
want to emphasize that individuals may differ in their adherence to cultural prescriptions. Hence, clinicians need to be cautious about
overgeneralization or stereotyping of Asian American clients.

Kinship and Association

The terms *kinship* and *association* refer to the nuclear and extended
family system, as well as the friendship or social networks in the culture.
This aspect of culture may affect diagnostic assessments of Asian American clients in two major ways. The first pertains to the extent that the relationship or the bonding between a person and his or her family and friends
is considered adaptive or maladaptive. The second pertains to the nature
and the amount of information clients may feel comfortable about disclosing to a clinician.

Asian cultures are collectivistic cultures. They emphasize familism, as
opposed to individualism, which is valued in mainstream American culture (Hong, 1988, 1989; Hong & Friedman, 1998; Hong & Ham, 1992;

Hong & Hong, 1991; Lee, 1997c; Min, 1995a; Shon & Ja, 1982; Sue & Morishima, 1982; Uba, 1994). In Asian cultures, the extended family customarily has strong bonds among its members. Grandparents, uncles, aunts, nephews, and nieces have close relationships with each another. Even family friends, such as intimate or long-time friends of one's parents, are often accorded the respect given to uncles and aunts. These family relationships are often closer than those in mainstream American families. Thus, clinicians can easily misperceive the members of an Asian American family to be overly close, enmeshed, or lacking firm boundaries. They may also be unjustly critical of parents who entrust the daily care of their children to extended family members and may not take into consideration that such a practice is culturally acceptable.

Asian families tend to be more hierarchical than mainstream American families (Hong, 1989; Jung, 1998; Lee, 1996, 1997c; Min, 1995a; Shon & Ja, 1982; Uba, 1994). They place more emphasis on the authority of parents over children and of older siblings over younger siblings. In a sense, the ideal Asian child never individuates from parents in the way mainstream American culture advocates. For example, it is not unusual for adult Asian Americans to live with their parents. It is also a common practice for them to ask parents or older siblings and relatives for their opinion when making important decisions. Sometimes even the younger Asian American generation displays these tendencies. Clinicians can easily misinterpret such living arrangements or deferential attitudes as a dependency trait or even a personality disorder. However, as Lin (1996) has indicated, although dependent personality disorder may be present in some form in Asian countries, its formulation in the *DSM* is culturally inappropriate. For example, in college settings, we often encounter Asian American students who are experiencing emotional conflicts because their parents want them to major in a specific field of study, such as medicine or business, even though they want to major in a different area. Some students may also be confused because their parents do not approve of their girlfriends or boyfriends. A clinician taking a mainstream American perspective may wonder why these college students pay so much attention to the preferences of their parents and why their parents are so controlling. In actuality, these students and their parents are simply demonstrating a cultural trait. Similarly, in work settings, many Asian Americans, in comparison to mainstream Americans, may be more deferential to authority figures. In fact, some analyses of equal-access employment opportunities point out that such deference to superiors and the tendency not to speak up to senior managers may play a role in impeding the advancement of Asian Americans in the corporate world (Lee, 1998). Again, these behavior patterns reflect a cultural trait rather than a personality deficit. Thus, clinicians need to differentiate these Asian cultural traits from behaviors and attitudes that might be considered pathological in the context of Western culture.

Another effect of the hierarchical emphasis of the Asian family is that members of higher rank and members of lower rank may be unwilling to discuss their problems openly in the presence of one another (Hong, 1988, 1989). For example, parents may feel uneasy about disclosing their issues in the presence of their children, and children may feel it is improper to expose their parents' problems in their presence. Clinicians have to be careful about what questions to ask when other family members are present. Often it is advisable to interview the client and family members together and separately. When addressing family members of different rank, Grieger and Ponterotto's (1995) suggestion to consider the family's worldview and level of acculturation is most salient. Because age is one of the major criteria in the social hierarchy, youthful-looking clinicians may be disadvantaged in working with clients who perceive themselves to be older than the clinician. There is no easy solution to this problem except to allow the client more time to develop the therapeutic trust and, at the same time, to try to win their confidence by one's professional demeanor.

The Asian kinship and association system also prescribes what information can be shared with outsiders as compared to insiders (Hong, 1988, 1989). This is explicated in a well-known Chinese proverb, "Family shame should not be spread to the outside" (Hong, 1988; Hong & Hong, 1991). Such a concern has a direct impact on the nature and the amount of information that Asian American clients feel comfortable in disclosing to clinicians in diagnostic interviews. Mental health clinicians are outsiders, or strangers, who are not privy to private information. Unlike other helping professionals such as medical doctors, mental health professionals have no established role in Asian cultures. Consequently, clients who are identified with Asian cultures are often uncomfortable discussing intimate personal or family matters to them. Clinicians need to be patient and ease gradually into these topics (Hong, 1989). In situations where it is pertinent to inquire about these issues expediently, clinicians need to clarify the rationale and the clinical relevance of such inquiries to the client.

Health and Nutrition

Contemporary Western medicine treats the mind and body as separate or dichotomous (Bankart, 1997). In contrast, traditional Chinese medicine, which is the basis of traditional East Asian medicine, views psychological and physiological functions as closely related (Hong & Friedman, 1998; Lin, 1996; Spector, 1996). Health is contingent on the harmony of the *yin* and *yang* forces within the body, and this is associated with a functional balance of the internal organs. Disruption of this balance causes illness (Spector, 1996). External forces, such as weather or emotional aggravation, can upset this harmony and result in physical illness, which, in turn, can be treated through medication, such as herbal soups. Conversely, emotional symptoms may be caused by the imbalance of internal forces. For example, irritability or disposition to anger may be related to an overly strong *yan* force, which is related to the five major viscera of the body, namely the heart, liver, spleen, lung, and kidney. Again, this balance may be restored by medication. Thus, the mind and the body are intertwined. This perspective has significant implications for both diagnosis and treatment. Here we will focus on two diagnostic issues, somatization and hypochondriasis.

Somatization

Asian American clients tend to report physical discomforts when they experience psychological or emotional problems (Gaw, 1993; Hong et al., 1995; Kleinman, 1977, 1982; Lee, 1997c; Lin, 1985, 1996; Sue & Morishima, 1982; Tseng, 1975; Uba, 1994). A major factor contributing to this tendency for somatization is Asian medicine's conceptualization of the close relationship between the mind and body (Hong et al., 1995; Lin, 1985; Tseng, 1975). Because of this factor, mental health professionals must view somatization in the cultural context and not misinterpret the client to be psychologically primitive or alexithymic (Lin, 1996). Also, both medical and mental health clinicians need to consider the possible underlying psychological issues that are being manifested as somatic symptoms and at the same time the possibility that a physical ailment is really present (Hong et al., 1995). They must not indiscriminately dismiss the somatic symptoms presented by Asian American clients as "mere somatization" and proceed with psychotherapy without thoroughly ruling out physical disorders, or vice versa.

Some of the somatic symptoms commonly presented by Asian American clients are insomnia, poor appetite, headaches, diffuse aches all over the body, and general feelings of weakness. These symptoms could be related to mood disorders, especially depression, and to anxiety disorders, as well as adjustment disorders with anxious or depressed mood (Gaw, 1993; Hong et al., 1995; Kleinman, 1977, 1982; Lee, 1997c; Lin, 1985; Lorenzo & Adler, 1984; Sue & Morishima, 1982; Tseng, 1975). However, if a clinician follows the *DSM-IV* mechanically, he or she may arrive at the diagnosis of somatoform disorders. In fact, in the clinical literature, there is a question of whether such a combination of somatic, mood, or anxiety symptoms should be considered as a distinct disorder by itself. In Asian countries such as China, Japan, Korea, and Vietnam, there is general belief in a syndrome that can be translated roughly into "weakness" or "exhaustion" of the nerves (Gonzalez & Griffith, 1996; Kleinman, 1982; Lin,

1989; Ming-Yuan, 1989; Russell, 1989; Suzuki, 1989). Such a syndrome is very similar to what was regarded as neurasthenia in the United States, a disorder that is not included in the *DSM-IV.* However, the possibility also exists that, instead of being a distinct disorder, the somatic symptoms are simply cultural manifestations of mood or anxiety disorders (Gonzalez & Griffith, 1996). At present, there is no definitive answer to this question. It suffices here for us to remind clinicians to approach the issue of somatization in Asian American clients with caution and cultural sensitivity.

Hypochondriasis

According to the Asian medical model, food eaten at daily meals plays an important role in balancing the *yin* and *yang* forces, which regulate one's health. All foods have medicinal values in terms of strengthening the body or nurturing a particular organ or body part. Like the stereotypical mainstream American mother who coaxes her children to eat their portion of vegetables at dinner, many Asian mothers coax their children to eat a hearty bowl of herbal soup at meals. Small talk at banquets often touches upon how the food being served may be good for the body or for a particular organ. Health, nutrition, and food are common everyday topics. In the clinical setting, a clinician using the mainstream American perspective may consider an Asian American client to be excessively preoccupied with health and may raise the question of hypochondriasis. Again, clinicians must be sensitive to this cultural trend and put it in the proper perspective.

Because of the close relationship between mind and body in Asian cultures, in a diagnostic evaluation clinicians will often find it helpful to ask their Asian American clients about their physical health or somatic symptoms, even if they have already been cleared by a physician (Hong, 1993b; Hong et al., 1995). For example, we often include questions such as "How's your appetite?" "Are you sleeping well?" and "How are you feeling physically?" These questions provide information for differential diagnosis and also serve as an "ice-breaker." Asian American clients are more accustomed to answering these sorts of "medical" questions, which are commonly asked by medical providers. The mental health clinician can use these questions to lead into more psychologically oriented questions, such as "How are you feeling emotionally?" "Is there anything bothering your sleep?" This culturally congruent approach meets the expectation of the client regarding somatic concerns. It also provides a smooth transition that eases the client into personal or family topics.

Beliefs and Religion

Here we use the terms *beliefs* and *religion* in a broad sense to include cultural concepts regarding the supernatural and metaphysical forces. In

Asia, there are many folk religions and practices that are often observed along with the major religious practices of Buddhism, Taoism, and Confucianism. Beliefs in metaphysical forces are especially prevalent. Many Asians believe that these forces play a role in determining health and sickness, as well as fortune and misfortune (Chan, 1986; Gaw, 1993; Hong, 1995; Ryan & Smith, 1989). However, these forces are hard to explain because they have no exact counterparts in Western culture.

We use the term *metaphysical beliefs* because these beliefs are not really religious beliefs concerning the supernatural or deities. Rather, the forces that they describe are considered to be an integral part of nature but beyond the scope of Western natural sciences. One example of such Asian metaphysical beliefs is "geomancy" or *feng shui,* which is literally translated as "wind and water." This belief system or practice has been gaining attention in the mainstream United States in recent years. *Feng shui* deals with the harmony of an object with its surroundings and the forces of *yin* and *yang.* For instance, the floor plan of a house, the positions of its doors and windows, the arrangement of furniture, and the landscape around the house can bring fortune or misfortune depending on their harmony. Similar principles of harmony also apply to the location of a business or office and even the grave sites of one's family members and ancestors. All these can have an effect on a person's or a family's material as well as emotional well-being. It should be noted that not all Asians subscribe to a strict belief in such metaphysical forces. However, this belief system is deeply ingrained in the culture. It is a common topic in social conversations and in Asian magazines and newspapers. For many people, it is one of the major considerations in real estate transactions. As such, the concepts will often influence one's thinking either overtly or subtly.

When Asian clients are experiencing psychiatric symptoms, they or their family members sometimes consider the problem to be religiously or metaphysically based and may seek to alleviate the problem by means of religious or quasi-religious practices. For example, a client may consider his or her mood or anxiety symptoms to be related to a disturbance of the balance of metaphysical forces and may seek consultation from a *feng shui* expert instead of a mental health professional. He or she may seek to harmonize these forces by rearranging the furniture in the house, hanging up mirrors in strategic locations, and so on. Clients who are religious may also employ folk religious rituals to dispel evil forces or misfortune. In our clinical practice, we have frequently encountered clients who continue to try these practices even after they have been convinced to come for psychological services. In fact, these clients will bring up these topics for discussion. Some examples of these practices are presented in the case example of C. in Chapter 7. In such situations, clinicians need to put their clients' beliefs in the proper cultural perspective and avoid pathologizing their beliefs as "magical," "schizotypal," or "psychotic" thinking. Conversely, clinicians should also be aware that when a client is really demonstrating pathology, the signs are often readily recognizable. For example, like a mainstream American client who might delusionally profess him- or herself to be "God" or "Christ," an Asian American client may simply profess to be an Asian deity, such as a "Buddha" or "Kun Yin." Also, the client's other symptoms and behaviors are usually bizarre and disturbing enough for even religious people to realize that there is something wrong.

Before leaving the topic of beliefs and religion, we want to emphasize that Asian Americans are not necessarily followers of the traditional Asian religions. They can be nonbelievers and atheists or can be followers of Western religions. As discussed in Chapter 2, a considerable number of Asian Americans are affiliated with Christian churches. The information provided in this section is intended to inform readers about how traditional Asian beliefs may be manifested in clinical data. As with any other piece of cultural information, care should be taken to avoid stereotypes and overgeneralizations.

Values and Norms

The values and norms of a culture shape and guide one's thoughts and behavior. Though recognizing that many values and norms exist in each culture, we will focus on five areas that are particularly significant for diagnostic assessments: (a) interpersonal harmony, (b) educational achievement, (c) work ethic, (d) privacy and stigma, and (e) gender and age issues. It should be noted that although values and norms denote the ideals of a culture, not everyone in that culture will observe them consistently. In fact, some individuals may not follow them at all. For example, honesty is a value in mainstream American culture, as exemplified in the story about George Washington and the cherry tree. However, this does not mean that mainstream Americans will never lie. Similarly, in discussing Asian cultural values and norms, we cannot stereotype and expect every Asian or Asian American to follow these prescriptions precisely.

Interpersonal Harmony

Asian cultures emphasize harmony in interpersonal relationships (Hong, 1989; Hong & Friedman, 1998; Lee, 1997c; Shon & Ja, 1982; Uba, 1994). Disagreements are to be presented indirectly or subtly if possible. Confrontation and open expression of conflict are frowned upon. This cultural norm creates a particularly difficult situation in cross-cultural communication. For example, the mainstream American way of directly voicing one's dissenting opinion in social interactions is often seen by less assimilated Asian Americans as crude or abrasive. In contrast, main-

stream Americans often feel that Asians are evasive or lacking in assertiveness. Culturally uninformed clinicians may easily misperceive their
Asian American clients as deficient in social skills. To make matters
worse, out of respect for the clinician, a client may not express any open
disagreement with the clinician or may veil the disagreement in such polite terms that the clinician does not perceive the client's dissension. This
missed communication can further reinforce errors in a diagnostic assessment. Hence, clinicians need to be sensitive to the social etiquette in Asian
cultures and alert to Asian American clients' subtle indications of dissent.

Certainly, Asians, like others, have disagreements and interpersonal
conflicts. However, social etiquette requires one to be subtle about them in
polite interactions (Hong, 1989; Hong & Friedman, 1998; Jung, 1998;
Lee, 1997c; Shon & Ja, 1982; Uba, 1994). Actually, a seemingly mild or
subtle expression of disagreement can be a very clear and firm statement
of disagreement or even a confrontation, which is clear to others within the
culture. This subtle expression is simply assertiveness expressed in a different way. Of course, there are always situations when heated disagreements or angry outbursts occur between individuals, but these are considered to be in violation of the norm and are frowned upon. Indeed,
avoidance of direct conflict often leads to passive aggressive means of expressing displeasure or dissent. For example, negative feelings can be expressed by tardiness in getting things done for the other person, "forget-
ting" to get something for the other person, or arriving late for a meeting.
These subtle behaviors are more acceptable than direct open aggressiveness. In a sense, passive aggressiveness, when used appropriately, can be
regarded as a culturally syntonic mode of expression rather than a deviant
or pathological trait. Of course, in this context, we are talking of a person
using these subtle expressions in appropriate situations, rather than a person constantly plotting to get even with others by passive aggressive
means. In previous editions of the *DSM,* passive aggressiveness is a pathological personality trait and, if severe enough, can be a personality disorder. In the *DSM-IV,* passive aggressive personality disorder has been
moved from the main text to Appendix B as a set of diagnostic criteria for
further study. We want to caution clinicians to be extremely careful in applying the diagnostic label of passive aggressive trait or personality disorder to Asian American clients without a careful consideration of the cultural context. Also, the passive aggressiveness that is syntonic with Asian
cultures does not involve the negativistic aspect of the personality disorder
defined in the *DSM-IV* diagnostic criteria.

Educational Achievement

Educational achievement is another cultural value that often arises in
a clinical assessment. Traditionally, Asian cultures place a high value on

education (Hong, 1989, 1996; Hong & Friedman, 1998; Lee, 1997c; Lee & Zane, 1998; Min, 1995a; Uba, 1994). Education is seen as the means for achieving moral development and moving up the socioeconomic ladder. In addition to financial rewards, education brings social status. Thus, parents often have high expectations for their children to achieve academically. From an Asian collectivistic perspective, education of children is investment in a family's future. As discussed previously, one of the reasons Asians immigrate to the United States is the opportunities for higher education. It is not unusual to see members of a lower income family pooling their resources together so that the children can go to college. In return, the family hopes that the children, when they graduate, will help the family achieve a more secure financial future. For Asian American children who have academic potential, such positive expectations can be a major motivator for achievement. However, for those whose academic abilities are more limited, this expectation to excel can be a source of undue pressure. This is further complicated by the U.S. mass media, which add to the impression that all Asian American students are whiz kids or superachievers (Brand, 1987; Hong, 1996; Lee, 1998; Lee & Zane, 1998; Williams, McDonald, Howard, Mittlebach, & Kyle, 1984). Consequently, in clinical settings, we have often encountered Asian American children complaining of excessive academic pressure from parents and parents expressing disappointment that their children are not studying hard enough. Some students develop poor self-esteem or other clinical symptoms such as depression and anxiety simply because their work is not as outstanding as that of "other" Asian Americans or because they cannot gain acceptance to top-rated colleges where "most" of their peers go. Whenever clinicians encounter these issues in diagnostic assessments, they need to be sensitive to the value that Asian cultures place on educational achievement rather than to trivialize their clients' concerns. When conflicts arise between parents and children around this issue, clinicians need to be empathic in examining the views of both parties and be aware of how this cultural value affects the interactions within a specific family.

Work Ethics

In addition to education, traditional Asian cultures emphasize the importance of hard work as a means of socioeconomic mobility. Their motto is, diligence and perseverance will lead to success. This Confucian work ethic is seen as the foundation of the great success stories of immigrant Asian Americans (McGrath, 1983; Williams et al., 1984). Along with this orientation of diligence is the tendency to ignore or downplay emotional distress. Unlike a physical illness, which has an undeniable impact on work, emotional distress is often seen as an issue that can be overcome via discipline and resolution. For example, we have often encountered immigrants who said that they were too busy with work to "worry" or to "deal with" emotional distress. They were less willing to spend the time or the money to seek professional help for emotional concerns than for their somatic symptoms. In diagnostic assessments, clinicians should empathize with this cultural orientation rather than dismiss these Asian American clients as resistant or "in denial."

Privacy and Stigma

The cultural values and norms of a society determine whether certain information should be kept private or whether it is shameful if disclosed to others, as well as who is privy to the information. In Asian cultures, as mentioned earlier in our discussion about kinship and association, private personal or family matters and issues considered shameful by the society as a rule are not to be disclosed to non-family members and strangers. Clients who are identified with Asian cultures may find it difficult to overcome this inhibition to disclose private information, even though they understand that mental health clinicians are professionals trying to help them (Hong, 1988, 1989; Lee, 1982; Uba, 1994). This can be a serious obstacle in diagnostic assessments. For example, in one of our clinical cases, two adults accompanied their mother at the initial intake and provided much of the information concerning the presenting problem. However, they never mentioned that their mother had attempted suicide recently by cutting her wrist until the clinician inquired about the bandage around her wrist. Once questioned, they embarrassedly explained that they found it difficult to tell someone outside the family about the incident. In another case, a college student attempted suicide three times, and each time her family told the emergency room staff that the incident was an accident. Eventually, they disclosed the truth to a trusted family friend who happened to know the clinician and requested help on the family's behalf. Besides suicide, many Asian Americans consider major mental disorders, particularly those involving bizarre behaviors or other psychotic symptoms, to be stigmatizing for the individual and the family (Gaw, 1993; Hong, 1988, 1989, 1995; Lee, 1997c; Lorenzo & Adler, 1984; Shon & Ja, 1982; Sue & Morishima, 1982; Uba, 1994). There is a general fear that mental illnesses may "run in the family." Some Asian Americans may also believe that mental illness, like any other major disability or misfortune, may be a retribution or karma for the wrongdoing of one's parents or ancestors (Chan, 1986; Gaw, 1993; Hong, 1995; Ryan & Smith, 1989). Hence, we may encounter clients who are reluctant to disclose any incidence of major mental disorders in their family when they are seeking help for what they consider to be an unrelated matter. In other instances, some individuals may find it embarrassing to discuss the bizarre behaviors of a family member, especially in the member's presence (Hong, 1989). The clinician must address these situations with sensitivity and reassure the client and the family by explaining the clinical importance of the disclosures and confidentiality rules concerning clinical information.

Other common clinical issues considered private or shameful include major family conflicts and sexual issues (Hong, 1989). These topics must be approached with tact. Often, we find it helpful to acknowledge the Asian norm against disclosure to strangers. For example, we may say, "I know, as an outsider, I shouldn't be asking about this, but it is important for me to find out . . ." or "I know it is hard for you to discuss this with an outsider, but in order to help you, I need to know . . ." This acknowledgment, paradoxically, usually makes it easier for the client to disclose more details. In addition to these clinical topics, detailed family or personal history, in contrast to generalities about family composition or social and home environments, is also considered private and personal. Unless it is obviously related to the presenting problem, this detailed background information can best be collected over a number of sessions after a firmer therapeutic relationship is established, rather than at the initial interview (Hong, 1989; Lee, 1982, 1997b). Collecting information too fast will simply inhibit the client from disclosing or will project an impression of impertinence and insensitivity. Clinicians also need to be aware that some immigrants and refugees may feel uncomfortable or may take offense if a clinician pursues the details of their migration history or process, especially when the questions have no obvious relationship to the presenting problems. For some Asian American clients, these questions imply that the clinician is having doubts about the legality of their U.S. citizenship or residence status. For others, these questions may bring back memories of unpleasant dealings with immigration or refugee officials. Some individuals may actually have irregularities or secrets in their migration or refugee process and will not want to be prodded. Hence, when questions concerning these issues have to be asked, a clinician must explain the rationale clearly to the client before proceeding.

Given the inhibition to disclose to outsiders, Asian American clients who are less assimilated into mainstream culture may sometimes ask a trusted friend or family member to accompany them to a diagnostic interview. A clinician needs to be flexible in letting the confidant join the session. In our clinical practice, we will usually interview the client and confidant together and then separately to obtain a clearer clinical picture. At times, an individual may even ask advice from a clinician on a friend's behalf. In this case, we will typically encourage the person to return with the friend. Simply advising the person to tell the friend to make an appointment will probably not be effective because the friend is likely to be too inhibited to call for an appointment or to come alone.

Gender and Age Issues

Traditional Asian cultural norms have very strict guidelines about proper social distance and proper behavior between men and women. Although most Asian Americans have been exposed to mainstream American standards and are less constrained by traditional Asian norms, some may still tend to be more reserved in unfamiliar settings, such as a mental health clinic. A female client may feel uneasy disclosing intimate personal matters to a male clinician, or vice versa—a male client may feel uncomfortable disclosing to a female clinician. Actually, this hesitancy to disclose to the opposite gender is also found among mainstream American clients. However, this behavior is more pronounced in Asian American clients who subscribe to traditional Asian cultural norms. Clinical situations may be further complicated by age issues discussed earlier in the section on family hierarchy. Hence, a young-looking clinician interviewing an older client of the opposite gender has to be particularly alert to the client's possible feelings of discomfort and should approach sensitive topics with caution. In situations relating to marital or sexual issues, clients may prefer to have a clinician of the same gender, at least for the initial assessment. If this is not possible, clinicians will need to be sensitive and patient to allow time for a client to adjust to gender and age differences and to develop trust in them as professionals.

Art and Folklore

In a diagnostic assessment, art and folklore are often manifested in metaphors or symbolism used by clients. These manifestations may be found in a client's conversations with the clinician or, more formally, in a client's responses to projective tests. Interpretation of such materials must be done within the cultural context (Ritzler, 1996) because vast differences exist between Asian and Western cultures. For example, in mainstream American and European cultures, white is the color that symbolizes purity and is worn by the bride in weddings. Yet in China, Korea, and Vietnam, white is the traditional color for mourning, and red is the color for celebrations and weddings. The image of the dragon is another interesting example. In Western cultures, the dragon is typically seen as an evil creature to be slain by the valiant knight. Yet in East Asian cultures, this creature is regarded as a noble and auspicious being and is the symbol of royalty. In fact, even the dragon's physical features, as portrayed in popular art, are completely different in the two cultures. The European dragon is often depicted somewhat like a dinosaur with wings, whereas the East Asian dragon resembles a wingless but flying serpent, with antlers on its head and four short limbs on the torso. Differences in other symbols and folklore between Asian and Western cultures abound. To make accurate interpretations of what a client is expressing, clinicians need to familiarize themselves with common art and folklore in Asian cultures and, when necessary, to consult with others knowledgeable about these issues. A clinician's understanding of symbolism is particularly important in cases where one needs to determine whether a client's ideation is unusual or normal, bizarre or nonbizarre, as in making a differential diagnosis concerning delusional disorders, schizophrenic disorders, and other psychotic disorders.

Language

In this section, we will discuss verbal and nonverbal communication and the use of interpreters.

Verbal Communication

Verbal communication refers to the actual words spoken by individuals in a conversation. A diagnostic assessment will be straightforward if both clinician and client speak the same language, whether English or another language. However, even when an Asian American client is bilingual and fluent in English, clinicians need to be aware that, depending on the context of a conversation, a person's facility in his or her first and second language may differ (Keitel, Kopala, & Adamson, 1996; Yansen & Shulman, 1996). For example, a first-generation Asian American college graduate may have no problems having a discussion in English on matters in his or her professional field. However, this person may find it easier to discuss personal issues or express intimate feelings in his or her home language. This difference is simply a result of the context where a person learned each language and where a person is accustomed to using it. Thus, in assessing clients who speak English as a second language, the clinician needs to be aware that these clients may have difficulty verbalizing feelings or certain symptoms in English. When these difficulties occur, clinicians can often help to clarify the communication by asking a client to give some examples or to elaborate on what he or she is trying to say. Clinicians can also paraphrase, in simple statements, their understanding of what the client may be saying and then ask the client to confirm the accuracy of the paraphrase. However, they need to be careful about putting words in the client's mouth because a client may be agreeing simply out of acquiescence or deference.

Nonverbal Communication

Nonverbal communication involves the tone of voice, facial expression, gestures, posture, and other body language. In a formal setting, individuals who adhere to Asian cultural norms may show a polite smile, speak softly, and gesture less than mainstream Americans. Their demeanor can mask emotional symptoms such as depression or anxiety or may lead clinicians into thinking that the clients are agreeing with them, which may not be true. Children and those in subordinate positions often show their respect to authority figures by avoiding direct eye contact, which is a typical part of clinical data observed by clinicians. This, again, may result in misperceptions. Hence, it is crucial for clinicians to familiarize themselves with nonverbal communication patterns in Asian cultures and interpret them appropriately.

Interpreters

Many clients in the Asian American communities require mental health services in their own Asian language. In major metropolitan areas with large Asian American populations, it may be possible to find clinicians with the appropriate language skills to serve these clients. However, in smaller cities and certain regions of the United States, it is more difficult to find clinicians who speak the home languages or dialects of their Asian American clients. In these situations, clinicians facing the language barrier may have no choice but to enlist the service of interpreters. To avoid miscommunication and loss of clinical data, interpreters must work as a team with the clinician and must be properly trained (Hong, 1989; Lee, 1982, 1997a; Yee, 1997). They need to understand the rationale of the interview questions and have a sense of what clinical information is important to look for. On the basis of our experience in working with interpreters and in acting as interpreters for others, we find that clinicians may sometimes have to rely on the interpreter to make certain judgments. For example, when a client is incoherent, it may be impossible to translate his or her words. The clinician simply has to trust the interpreter's report that the client is incoherent. In other instances, a client may be using peculiar sentence structures or words that have no direct equivalents in English. The clinician will have to rely on the interpreter's input to discern whether the client's statements are signs of speech disturbance reflective of mental disorders. When a client demonstrates a pattern of not providing the information requested, the interpreter's judgment will be important in determining whether this behavior is an indication of the client's tangential thinking, or evasiveness, or simply of the client's inability to understand the questions. In addition to verbal communication, clinicians need to pay attention to nonverbal exchanges between the interpreter and the client. For example, a client may raise his or her voice, or an interpreter may frown when the client is speaking. If these nonverbal expressions do not seem congruent with the translated statements, the clinician may need to ask the interpreter for clarification. This will help to minimize distortion or loss of clinical data. Consistent pairing between the same clinician and interpreter will also help enhance mutual perceptiveness and understanding, which are important in clinical teamwork.

Clinicians should avoid using their clients' family members as interpreters because the family relationship may make it difficult for them to translate in an unbiased manner (Hong, 1989; Lee, 1982). Out of convenience, clinicians may often be tempted to ask English-speaking children to translate for their parents who have limited English proficiency. As mentioned previously in the discussion of family and kinship, the Asian family hierarchy may make this interaction difficult for both children and parents. The children may feel uncomfortable translating a clinician's questions because the inquiry may involve materials for adult-to-adult conversation that the children are not accustomed to. Similarly, the parents may feel uneasy disclosing personal issues to a clinician through their children, who are not privy to such information because of their lower status. Moreover, a clinician has no way of ensuring that the translation is accurate. Thus, clinicians need to use trained interpreters rather than any person or family member who happens to be readily available.

Social Environmental Factors for Consideration in Diagnostic Assessment

Three major areas of Asian American clients' social environmental context may be significant in a diagnostic assessment. The first area involves the impact of migration because most Asian Americans are immigrants. The second area involves racism in U.S. society, particularly the racial incidents that a client may have encountered. The third area relates to specific circumstances such as socioeconomic status, housing, and employment problems, which singly or collectively may compound the presenting problem of a client.

Impact of Migration

We have already examined the impact of migration on Asian Americans in Chapter 4. In this section, we want to focus on the stress related to the migration experience and its possible manifestations in diagnostic assessments. In general, immigrants are happy to relocate from their homeland to the United States. For voluntary immigrants, this move is something they have planned and looked forward to. For refugees, even though their migration is involuntary, arrival at the United States brings a certain sense of relief. However, settling in a new community, starting new jobs, developing a new social and support network, and adapting to a new culture are emotionally and physically demanding tasks. These circumstances may lead many Asian immigrants to think that they have no time to attend to emotional and psychological problems. Their priority is their physical health, which has more obvious effects on their job performance and their basic activities of daily living. Refugees who have experienced major trauma in their homeland and in their flight to asylum may be eager to keep a low profile in order not to attract more governmental attention. Again, many of them tend to perceive mental health problems to be of lower priority than physical ailments. Furthermore, in general, many immigrant Asian Americans are unfamiliar with the various mental health disciplines and service delivery system in the United States and are not likely to initiate requests for psychotherapy or counseling (Chin, 1998; Hong, 1988, 1993a; Lee, 1982, 1997b; Shon & Ja, 1982; Sue & Morishima, 1982; Uba, 1994). Most immigrants are referred to mental health clinicians by medical practitioners, or by teachers if they are children. Even then, many are reluctant to follow through with the referral. In diagnostic assessments, mental health clinicians must avoid overinterpreting the reluctance of their Asian American clients to seek services as "resistance," or their tendency to minimize their level of psychological and emotional distress as "denial." Rather, clinicians need to view the concerns of immigrant Asian American clients in the context of their premigration, migration, and postmigration experiences and try to engage them accordingly.

In some instances, the stress of migration may actually be a precursor to mental disorders. In a cultural analysis of adjustment disorders, Beiser (1996) indicated that migration creates a risk for mental disorders. Berry (1994) raised the issue that acculturative stress may lead to clinical depression and anxiety. Currently, the *DSM-IV* (American Psychiatric Association, 1994) includes "acculturation problem" in the list of "additional conditions that may be a focus of clinical attention" (p. 685). Although this is not a mental disorder per se, its inclusion is an acknowledgment that the distress related to the migration experience may be severe enough to require clinical attention. Tseng (1996) also called attention to migration stress by suggesting that the scope of psychosocial and environmental problems in Axis IV of the *DSM-IV* be expanded to include "conflicts relating to value systems or cultural differences" and "problems relating to socio-ethnic-cultural identity, including culture displacement phenomena as seen in minority populations, refugees, or immigrants" (p. 119). Beiser (1996) went further by proposing a new diagnostic category of "migrant adjustment disorder" that would apply to immigrants who are experiencing distress in adjusting to life in the new host country. Kinzie (1996) operationalized the diagnostic criteria for this disorder by including "the development of emotional or behavioral symptoms in response to a geographic move that results in significant changes in culture, language, or social relations and occurring within 3 months of the onset of the move" (p. 234). At present, the conceptualization of migrant adjustment disorder is simply a proposal, and the description of its symptomatology is likely to undergo refinement and changes as researchers and clinicians further examine the concept. We want to emphasize that the proposed addition of this disorder or the inclusion of acculturation as a psychosocial and environmental problem in the *DSM* does not mean that all immigrants will develop clinical problems. However, these considerations clearly highlight the significance of migration stress that may lead to a mental disorder by itself or may contribute to factors precipitating or complicating another mental disorder. Clinicians must carefully examine this issue in diagnostic evaluations with immigrant Asian American clients. Furthermore, as noted in Chapter 4, the distress experienced by refugee Asian Americans in their premigration environment, their migration process, and their postmigration settlement are also important stressors to evaluate because such calamity and trauma are risk factors for psychiatric problems in this population (Carlson & Rosser-Hogan, 1991; Chung & Kagawa-Singer, 1993; Owen, 1985; Palinkas & Pickwell, 1995).

Racism

Antidiscrimination legislation can change the formal practices of an organization, but it cannot control the attitudes of individuals working in an organization. Despite the progress made in recent decades, racism is still a prevalent issue in the United States. Prejudice against Asian Americans is still common (Uba, 1994; Young & Takeuchi, 1998). It may be manifested blatantly as hate crimes or harassment or subtly as a "glass ceiling"—that is, barriers to promotion in employment—or as slights in social situations. Furthermore, racial tensions exist not only between white and ethnic minority groups but also among ethnic minority groups. In this regard, all clinicians need to examine their own racial/ethnic attitudes when working with clients from different racial and ethnic backgrounds. Conversely, they need to be sensitive to the possible negative racial/ethnic feelings that clients may bring into the clinical setting (Keitel et al., 1996). For example, an Asian American client may have been the target of racism in everyday life or may have had a previous racist encounter with another provider. Possibly, this client will generalize his or her negative feelings to the present non-Asian clinician. These feelings may be demonstrated directly or indirectly in different ways during a diagnostic session. For instance, a client may keep a cordial appearance externally but not trust the clinician enough to disclose intimate personal information. A client may pay lip service to what the clinician is saying but not show up for further sessions. Children and teenagers who have experienced racial incidents in daily life may be openly hostile and may not believe that a non-Asian clinician can understand their issues. Refugees who have had negative racial experiences with officials, such as refugee camp administrators or immigration officers, may perceive a non-Asian clinician as a threatening figure rather than a helper. Thus, in working with Asian American clients, non-Asian American clinicians need to be particularly sensitive to such client attitudes and empathic to their hesitancy in accepting treatment. Clinicians need to understand the social environmental context of their clients to avoid perceiving and interpreting these manifested behaviors as a personal rejection or as pathological traits. Most importantly, clinicians must make a conscientious effort to prevent such client attitudes from biasing their clinical judgment in the diagnostic evaluation and treatment planning.

Besides affecting the clinician-client relationship, racism may be an underlying cause of a client's presenting problem. For example, a middle-age Asian American client in a management position comes for counseling with a complaint of feeling stagnated, especially at work. The clinician may consider these feelings symptomatic of a midlife transition. However, the client's stagnation at work may be related to the barrier for promotion for minorities known as a "glass ceiling," which often exists in major mainstream corporations. Similarly, an Asian American student with academic difficulties may have his motivation for school further lowered by racial taunts from other students or the apathy of some teachers. Sometimes clients may not recognize racism as the source of their problems when, in reality, their problems may be created or compounded by racism. In this regard, clinicians must be alert and evaluate the possible role of racism in contributing to the problems experienced by Asian American clients. Racism operates across socioeconomic class and may affect any Asian American client regardless of his or her cultural identification.

Socioeconomic Status and Related Problems

Asian Americans from low socioeconomic backgrounds, as compared to those with higher socioeconomic status, are more likely to encounter problems in their daily life and in the resettlement process as immigrants. For example, they have to deal with basic life issues such as financial security, housing, employment, and transportation. These social environmental hardships often complicate their migration stress and cultural adaptation. Whether these problems are a part of a client's presenting problem or not, their impact on the person's overall adjustment needs to be assessed in a diagnostic evaluation.

In general, Asian Americans with high educational attainment in the United States, with occupational success, with high income, and with homes in the more affluent mainstream neighborhoods will adapt more readily to mainstream American culture than Asian Americans with limited education, with low-level jobs, with limited income, and with homes in inner-city ethnic neighborhoods. However, there are exceptions to this general observation. For example, a highly educated and financially successful Asian American holding a mainstream professional job may still prefer to discuss personal problems with a clinician who is knowledgeable about his or her cultural heritage. These educated and successful clients are proficient in the mainstream culture, but they may fully embrace Asian cultures in their private lives. In a diagnostic assessment, a clinician needs to keep a client's socioeconomic status in mind while looking beyond it. Conversely, some Asian American teenagers may associate being "Asian" with lower socioeconomic inner-city conditions (Hong, 1996). For them, being "mainstream" is a status symbol. They may resent being referred to a clinician who professes to be knowledgeable about Asian issues because they see this as an insult. Clinicians need to be empathic to such feelings. Focusing on these clients' Asian background too early in the interview is counterproductive because this may aggravate their negative reaction. Their cultural background can be explored at a later time after a clinician has established a firm rapport with the client.

Psychological Testing

Diagnostic assessments may include formal psychological testing. The literature has identified a number of problems in psychological testing for ethnic minorities. The major problems include cultural biases in the content or the norms of a test, improper interpretation or use of test results, and biases in test administration (Keitel et al., 1996; Padilla & Medina, 1996; Suzuki, Meller, & Ponterotto, 1996). In this section, we will examine the implication of these problems in psychological testing with Asian American clients. We will not provide details of specific tests or test batteries because psychological testing is an entire subject area by itself and is beyond the scope of this book. Readers who need information on selecting tests for use with Asian Americans can refer to a very useful overview by Yee (1997). Our intention here is to provide further guidance for clinicians who are already trained in psychological testing and to help other clinicians recognize the limitations of psychological testing and make proper use of the information in test reports.

Cultural Biases in Tests and Test Interpretation

Psychological tests are culturally biased when their content is loaded with items that refer to values, norms, behaviors, or even the history of mainstream Euro-America because these items are unfair for individuals who are less acculturated into mainstream culture (Padilla & Medina, 1996; Ritzler, 1996; Suzuki et al., 1996; Yee, 1997). Though language is one of the most obvious cultural factors in testing, nonverbal tests are not devoid of cultural biases (Harris, Reynolds, & Koegel, 1996; Yee, 1997). For example, picture arrangement is a nonverbal subtest used in the Wechsler Intelligence Scale for Children-Third Edition (WISC-III) (Wechsler, 1991) and the Wechsler Adult Intelligence Scale-Third Edition (WAIS-III) (Wechsler, 1997). This subtest requires a client to arrange pictures into a sequence that tells a story. No verbal response is needed. However, the pictures depict objects, actions, and situations based on mainstream American culture. To what extent can this test be culturally relevant and be a fair indicator of competence for a recently immigrated client from, say, the rural area of an Asian country?

The composition of the standardization sample of a test is another potential source of bias. Newer editions of most of the commonly used psychological tests published in the United States typically use census data to design the ethnic and demographic composition of their standardization samples. Although this procedure is definitely an improvement over samples drawn only from white subjects, it still does not adequately address the issue of cultural fairness for ethnic minorities. This is a particularly salient issue for small minority groups such as Asian and Pacific Islander Americans, who constitute only a small percentage of the U.S. population, 3.7% in 1997 (U.S. Bureau of the Census, 1988). A critical disadvantage for an ethnic minority group is that their presence can become negligible whenever the bigger picture of the general population is examined. For example, the Minnesota Multiphasic Personality Inventory-2 (MMPI-II) (Butcher, Dahlstorm, Graham, Tellegen, & Kaemmer, 1989) included only 19 Asians in its final standardization sample of 2,600 subjects. Both the WISC-III (Wechsler, 1991) and the WAIS-III (Wechsler, 1997) grouped Asian and Pacific Islander Americans, Native Americans, and other small ethnic minority groups into a single "Other" category. Of the 2,200 subjects in the WISC-III standardization sample, only 77 subjects were included in the "Other" category. The WAIS-III had 2,450 subjects in its standardization sample, and only 65 subjects belonged to the "Other" category. The Leiter International Performance Scale-Revised (LEITER-R) (Roid & Miller, 1997), a nonverbal measure of intellectual ability, memory, and attention, included only 55 Asians out of 861 subjects in the standardization sample of its Visualization and Reasoning Battery and 21 Asians out of 391 subjects in the standardization sample of its

Attention and Memory Battery. These examples illustrate the limitations in using census data to ensure cultural fairness in test standardization. Using norms based on the general majority population to score the test performance of an ethnic minority client calls into question whether a clinician is measuring a psychological attribute of the client or simply measuring social cultural differences. Further, when test content is culturally biased, clinicians run the risk of using Eurocentric or mainstream standards to pathologize ethnic minorities (Chin, 1998; Padilla & Medina, 1996; Sue & Morishima, 1982; Suzuki et al., 1996; Valencia & Guadarrama, 1996; Yee, 1997).

To avoid the issue of cultural biases, clinicians can sometimes use psychological tests that have been translated into Asian languages and normed in Asian countries. For example, older editions of the Wechsler Scales and the MMPI have been adapted for use in some Asian countries (Chin, 1998; Yee, 1997). Information about specific tests can be obtained from their respective U.S. publishers who hold the copyrights of the original tests. However, these translated editions are generally hard to obtain in the United States. Moreover, they are appropriate only for use with recent immigrants. Asian Americans who have been in the United States for a period of time, particularly children attending schools in the United States, are usually acculturated to some degree into mainstream America. Their acculturation may make test items that have been modified for individuals living in Asia (e.g., general knowledge of Asian practices or cultures) inappropriate for them or may invalidate norms based on the population of their country of origin. At the same time, these Asian Americans may not be acculturated enough into mainstream American culture to be assessed accurately by test items and norms based on the general U.S. population. Because there is no easy solution to this dilemma, it is imperative for clinicians to apply clinical judgment in using test norms. Test scores cannot and should not be used in isolation from other clinical data (Matarazzo, 1990; Roid & Miller, 1997; Suzuki et al., 1996). Clinicians must always interpret an Asian American client's test responses in the context of the client's culture, migration experience, and other social environmental issues.

In test reports, clinicians need to comment on the validity of the results or on the limitations of norms used in scoring the test. For example, in our practice, sometimes we may emphasize that the scores are based on comparisons with the general U.S. population. In reporting intelligence tests, clinicians must be aware that readers of these reports, including school personnel, clients, and their family members, tend to focus on the actual numeric scores. Hence, in some situations, we may want to emphasize that these scores reflect the client's achievements in the context of mainstream culture rather than the client's intellectual ability. In other situations where misunderstanding of the results by the reader is likely to occur or have serious consequences, we may choose to give a clinical or qualitative description of the client's performance rather than reporting the numeric scores. As Harris et al. (1996) cautioned, clinicians need to emphasize what is considered to be the accurate interpretation of a test rather than to report a biased score and then qualify it with subsequent caveats.

Cautions in Test Administration

The validity of a psychological test may be affected by its administration. Poor rapport between clinician and client, or negative attitudes of either party, may also affect test performance (Keitel et al., 1996; Padilla & Medina, 1996). Hence, in addition to a comfortable physical setting, tests must be administered in a congenial and nonthreatening psychological atmosphere. In working with Asian Americans with limited acculturation into mainstream America, clinicians need to be aware that many of these clients are not familiar with psychological testing. For example, in our clinical practice, we have encountered clients who erroneously thought that psychological testing would involve the use of electrodes and equipment similar to polygraph or EEG machines. Other clients, especially students who are recent immigrants, may feel apprehensive about test taking because tests and examinations in Asian schools are often taken very seriously and may have dire consequences such as retention or expulsion from school. Refugees who had experienced oppression and maltreatment from authorities may also view the testing situation with suspicion (Yee, 1997). Hence, it is imperative for referral sources and clinicians to explain to their clients the purpose and the nature of the psychological tests well before the actual administration of the tests. In settings such as hospitals, where providers may be wearing institutional attire that makes them look official and solemn, clinicians need to pay particular attention to putting their clients at ease. While interpreting test results, clinicians need to consider extenuating factors present during the test administration and describe them accurately in the test report.

Language Issues in Test Administration

To be valid, a psychological test should be administered in a client's most proficient language (Keitel et al., 1996; Padilla & Medina, 1996). For an Asian American client with limited English proficiency, the preference, of course, is to have the test administered by a clinician who speaks the client's first language. If an interpreter is necessary, he or she must be properly trained and be familiar with the tests and their purposes (Lee, 1997a; Yee, 1997). Clinicians should be aware that the difficulty level of test items may be changed when test items are translated from English into an Asian language. For example, the months of the year in Chinese, Korean, Japanese, and Vietnamese are named numerically: January is "One" Month, February is "Two" Month, March is "Three" Month, and so on. This sequence is much easier to figure out than the unrelated names in English. Consequently, a clinician must use utmost caution in interpreting test scores based on items translated informally by him or her or by an interpreter. Results from such translated items need to be evaluated clinically rather than statistically and must be examined in light of other information.

In working with bilingual Asian Americans, clinicians need to determine whether a client is truly proficient in English. Even though clients appear to be fluent in English, their second language, at times they may be constructing their responses according to the organizational pattern of their primary language (Keitel et al., 1996; Yansen & Shulman, 1996). This can lead to misinterpretation by the clinician. Also, as mentioned earlier in this chapter, there are bilingual clients whose proficiencies in English and their first language are specific to particular subject areas. They may also speak with a mixture of both languages in a casual conversation. Often, these clients may have to be tested bilingually (Yansen & Shulman, 1996). In our practice, for example, we may let a bilingual Chinese American child switch between English and Chinese in responding to a test. Often, unless this child is clearly dominant in Chinese, we will begin by administering a test in English and then readminister the failed items in Chinese. This method is particularly useful for school-related psychological testing because it provides information on how the client could perform in a mainstream English medium, as well as how the client could perform if his or her first language were taken into consideration. This approach is more efficient, and less tedious or time consuming, than administering complete versions of the tests in both English and the client's first language.

Summing up this discussion on psychological testing, we want to emphasize that, as Suzuki et al. (1996) observed after a comprehensive review of test instruments in the *Handbook of Multicultural Assessment,* "There is currently no such thing as a 'culture free' or 'culture fair' instrument or assessment method" (p. 677). Hence, clinicians must be vigilant about the proper use of psychological testing for Asian Americans.

Assessment of Cultural Identification

For ethnic minority clients, their level of acculturation into mainstream American culture and their culture of origin are factors that play crucial roles in diagnostic formulations, psychological testing, and other areas of clinical services (American Psychiatric Association, 1994; Grieger & Ponterotto, 1995; Keitel et al., 1996; Padilla & Medina, 1996; Suzuki et al., 1996). Thus, exploration of an Asian American client's cultural identification is an integral part of the diagnostic assessment.

Most of the instruments or questionnaires designed for assessing cultural, racial, and ethnic identity are based on Nigrescence and Afrocentric models, which focus on an individual's stage of racial/ethnic development (Kohatsu & Richardson, 1996). Some of these instruments, such as the Multigroup Ethnic Identity Measure (MEIM) (Phinney, 1992), are designed for use with any ethnic group. Instruments developed specifically for use with Asian Americans are scarce. Review of the literature (Leong, 1998; Leong & Chou, 1998; Suinn, 1998) indicate that the Suinn-Lew Asian Self-Identity Acculturation Scale (SL-ASIA) (Suinn, Richardson-Figueroa, Lew, & Vigil, 1987) is the most frequently used acculturation measure in research on Asian Americans. The original version of this scale (Suinn et al., 1987) is composed of 21 multiple-choice items that cover the areas of language, identity, friendship choice, behaviors, generation/geographic history, and attitudes. The Revised-SL-ASIA (Suinn, 1998) has five additional items and takes into account that acculturation may not be a unidimensional or linear process. Two brief forms of the SL-ASIA, each containing five items, have been developed by Leong and Chou (1998). These acculturation scales are very helpful for obtaining quantitative measures of Asian American cultural identification, especially for use in research. However, given the complexity of cultural identification, quantitative measures need to be complemented by qualitative approaches, such as interviews, observations, and life and oral histories, to produce a more accurate picture (Kohatsu & Richardson, 1996; Sabnani & Ponterotto, 1992). In the context of clinical work, a clinician can include one of the quantitative scales as part of the intake questionnaire to obtain a preliminary idea of the client's cultural identification. However, a clinician's quick impression based on the quantitative scale needs to be explored further in the diagnostic evaluation. In our experience, we have found that qualitative data on cultural identification obtained in a diagnostic interview are often sufficient without the use of quantitative instruments.

In a diagnostic interview, a client's cultural identification can be assessed by inquiring about certain issues that are similar to the typical contents of ethnic/racial identity scales. These issues include (a) country of birth and years or generations in the United States; (b) languages spoken at work, at home, and in social settings; (c) upbringing experiences; (d) education in the United States; (e) residence, community, and social network; and (f) occupation and location of job (mainstream setting or ethnic community). These issues can be discussed in any order and can flow with the interview. Some of them tap into common background questions that are already included at intakes. However, they also yield information about a client's cultural identification. Take for example, this 25-year-old Korean American man: (a) born in Korea and came to the United States 6 years ago; (b) fluent in English and Korean but prefers to speak in Korean at home and in social settings; (c) brought up by parents who adhere to Korean culture; (d) received precollege education in Korea and attended college in the United States; (e) resides in an Asian American neighborhood and socializes mostly with Korean Americans; and (f) works as an accountant in a workplace where coworkers and clientele are mainly Korean Americans. This information suggests that this person is likely to have a strong identification with Korean culture. However, considering his education, years in the United States, and profession, he may also have adopted some values and behaviors of mainstream American culture. The degree of his biculturalism will need to be explored further in the rest of the diagnostic interview or later in the treatment sessions. In our clinical practice, we generally find such interview data to be more helpful than asking clients directly about their cultural identification. Individuals may not necessarily be aware of their cultural identification. For instance, some individuals may overtly claim to be very identified with Asian cultures without realizing that they have become very Westernized. There are many amusing anecdotes in Asian American communities about immigrants who returned to their country of origin for a visit after an absence of a few years and were shocked to have friends there remark about how Americanized they had become. Conversely, there are other individuals who overtly claim to be very Westernized without being conscious that their ideas and actions are still strongly influenced by Asian cultures. Thus, clients' own statements about their cultural identification should always be considered in conjunction with other information.

Actually, assessment of cultural identification needs to be an ongoing and interactive process. Throughout a diagnostic interview, as well as throughout the course of treatment, clinicians can obtain information about their clients' cultural identification by noticing how they conceptualize their problems or symptoms, as well as how they express their positions about specific cultural values and issues. Similarly, throughout this process, clients often gain insights about their emotions, thoughts, and behaviors and thereby develop a better understanding of their cultural identification. Information gathered during the initial interview provides a preliminary guideline rather than a definitive designation of a client's cultural identification. Clinicians need to be flexible in using such preliminary data and ready to modify their assumptions about a client's cultural identification as more information emerges.

In addressing a specific cultural issue, clinicians cannot assume that their clients are definitely approaching this issue from, say, a Korean orientation simply because they are generally identified with Korean American culture. As discussed in Chapter 3, individuals may consciously or unconsciously choose the cultural elements of mainstream American society that they want to attain in the process of accommodation, assimilation, or acculturation. For example, an Asian American client may have a strong identification with Asian cultures but may take a mainstream American position on a particular issue. The opposite can also be true of Asian Americans who are strongly identified with mainstream culture. Consider the case of a Vietnamese American college student who sought counseling because he had strong disagreements with his father over the choice of his major field of study. He came to the United States as a young child and considered himself very Americanized. In addition, he was very articulate in English. He felt that as an adult he should have autonomy in his academic choices and that his career was "none of his father's business." Yet in the course of counseling, it became clear to the clinician that he also held onto the traditional Asian views on parental authority, which gave his parents a more significant role in this matter than mainstream American parents had. He was deferential to his father and was unable to defy him. In fact, to the extent that he was experiencing an emotional conflict over this issue, he was already expressing to the clinician, without being aware of it, that he still adhered to traditional Asian cultural views on parental authority. If he had been as strongly identified with mainstream culture as he claimed, he could have simply declared his autonomy as an adult and brushed aside his father's wishes. Instead, he was very relieved later when he was able to convince his father to let him have his way. This case is a good illustration of the complexity of cultural identification. When a cultural issue is unclear, rather than making an assumption, clinicians need to explore the cultural underpinnings of their clients' perceptions, attitudes, emotions, and behaviors with them.

Summary

In this chapter, we have examined the major cultural and social environmental factors that often affect diagnostic assessments of Asian American clients. These cultural and social environmental issues may be manifested in the interview content: that is, the information provided by the client. These issues may also affect the interview process, which includes the interaction and the relationship between the clinician and the client. In using psychological tests, clinicians need to be aware of the possible cultural biases in the content or the norms of a test, in test interpretation, and in test administration. Other clinical data must always be integrated with test results to ensure accurate findings. Finally, in applying the issues discussed in this chapter, clinicians need to remember that Asian Americans may differ in their cultural identification and that a client's cultural position should be assessed in an ongoing and interactive process throughout the course of psychotherapy and counseling. As with any other piece of cultural information, we need to avoid stereotypes and overgeneralizations.

6

Engaging the Client in Psychotherapy and Counseling

Psychotherapy and counseling are often referred to as a journey, a unique process that begins when strangers meet for the first time (Bruch, 1974). The first step of the therapeutic process is for a clinician to engage a client in treatment by establishing a therapeutic relationship or working alliance (Egan, 1997). This clinician-client partnership begins with the initial meeting (Brammer, 1973; Haley, 1976). Whatever the client experiences at this initial encounter may determine the course of therapy. Furthermore, to work effectively with a client, the clinician needs to continue developing the therapeutic relationship throughout the treatment process. Regardless of a clinician's theoretical orientation, therapeutic work cannot take place if the client does not return for further sessions because of a poor working alliance.

This chapter discusses the cultural and social environmental factors that clinicians need to consider in engaging Asian American clients in psychotherapy and counseling. Though highlighting the pitfalls in the development of the therapeutic relationship, we also want to emphasize that Asian American clients do stay and benefit from mental health services when clinicians engage them appropriately. Once again, we remind readers that Asian Americans differ in their cultural identification and in their social environmental experiences. The information presented in this chapter is focused on Asian Americans who are identified with Asian cultures. Clinicians must judiciously apply this information to their Asian American clients and avoid stereotyping them.

Cultural Factors for Consideration
in Engaging Asian American Clients

Many of the cultural issues examined in Chapter 5 are also relevant to the development of the therapeutic relationship and the engagement of Asian American clients in psychotherapy and counseling. In this chapter, we will identify additional cultural factors that are particularly salient in the initial stage of the therapeutic encounter with Asian American clients.

Expectations Regarding Psychotherapy and Counseling

Many Asian Americans are unfamiliar with the concept or the process of psychotherapy and counseling. Their expectations and objectives of these clinical services may be very different from what Western or mainstream-oriented clinicians are accustomed to providing. The following discussion addresses three aspects of this issue.

Unfamiliarity With Mental Health Services

Historically, the theories and the practice of psychotherapy and counseling are based on European cultures. They are foreign concepts, not ingrained in Asian cultures. Many Asian American clients are not familiar with the concept of "talk therapy" (Bankart, 1997; Hong, 1993a; Hong et al., 1995; Lee, 1980, 1997c; Shon & Ja, 1982; Sue & Morishima, 1982; Uba, 1994). In Asia, the general public typically associates mental health services with the use of medication or psychiatric care, a practice catering to individuals with severe mental disorders. Psychotherapy and counseling are not widely perceived as modes of addressing mental health or psychoemotional problems. The idea of "talking" with someone as a way to address a mental health problem and not giving him or her a medical prescription is quite perplexing for many individuals. A client's unfamiliarity with mental health services is further compounded by the cultural prescription about privacy regarding personal and family matters. Consequently, when personal or family problems arise, many Asian Americans may seek advice from respected relatives or confidants rather than mental health providers. Hence, in general, Asian Americans are often reluctant to seek psychotherapy and counseling. When they do so, it is often as a last resort or at the insistence of another culturally familiar professional, such as a medical doctor or a teacher (Gaw, 1993; Hong, 1988, 1993b, 1996; Hong et al., 1995; Lee, 1997c; Shon & Ja, 1982; Sue & Morishima, 1982; Wong, 1985).

In the initial stage of treatment, clinicians need to be aware of and sensitive to the importance of maintaining privacy and the stigma attached to mental health services. During a session, when a client appears to be hesitant in a conversation, the clinician must be cautious in attributing this behavior to the client's resistance. Rather, the clinician should consider whether this hesitancy is related to the client's discomfort or apprehension about psychotherapy or counseling itself. Brief expressions of reassurance and encouragement from the clinician throughout the first few sessions are often useful in helping the client overcome the inhibition of seeking psychotherapy and counseling.

Quick and Direct Relief

When Asian American clients consult a mental health clinician, many of them expect quick relief from their symptoms (Gaw, 1993; Hong, 1988, 1993a, 1993b; Hong et al., 1995; Lee, 1980, 1982, 1997c; Shon & Ja, 1982; Sue & Morishima, 1982; Uba, 1994). For example, they may expect medication to help them sleep better, to "calm" them down, or to eliminate psychotic symptoms. Many clients simply want to take medication without concurrent psychotherapy or counseling. When presenting problems are life issues rather than physically and medically related, clients may expect the clinician to provide advice or to answer their questions directly. For example, when seeking services relating to marital conflicts or parent-child issues, they often see the clinician as a mediator or an advisor who will instruct them on ways of resolving the problems. In other words, whether the help sought is medication or advice, Asian American clients most often expect the clinician to be an expert who will intervene swiftly and directly to resolve their problems or symptoms. They assume that mental health services are treatments using problem-solving or symptom relief strategies rather than insight. Once the initial problems or conflicts are resolved, their tendency is to terminate psychotherapy and counseling.

To engage Asian American clients in treatment, clinicians need to be seen as "actively" involved with the presenting problems during the initial sessions (Hong, 1989, 1993b; Hong et al., 1995; Lee, 1997b; Uba, 1994). One effective way is to focus the discussion on the presenting problems (Haley, 1976; Hong, 1989, 1993b; Hong et al., 1995) and refrain from too much inquiry about family, occupational, developmental, or other background information unless these are obviously related to the problems. We are aware that giving a client advice for solving the presenting problems during the first session is often premature. So, after discussing the presenting problems, clinicians need to explain to their clients how they plan to help them. This explanation reassures the clients that they have been heard and that the clinician is actively working with them to address their problems. For many clients, this approach will sufficiently engage them and motivate them to return for treatment, at least for a few more sessions.

Some clients, however, may continue to press for advice on what to do between sessions. At this point, clinicians have to use their judgment and examine the following issues: Will the client return to treatment if he or she is not given some advice? Does the clinician have enough information about an issue to give advice? A rule of thumb is to restrain from giving advice until there is enough information. If clinicians give inappropriate advice based on insufficient information, clients will lose confidence in their competency and will not return. Even though Asian American clients want their clinicians to be "actively" addressing their problems, clinicians will have a better chance of engaging them by clearly explaining the rationale for not giving advice at this time and the necessity for more sessions to explore the issues. Also, clinicians need to use part of the first few sessions to inform the clients about the nature and process of psychotherapy and counseling.

Expert Advice

Many Asian American clients expect the clinician to be an expert or teacher who has the knowledge to solve their problems (Hong, 1988, 1989; 1993b; Lee, 1982, 1997b; Shon & Ja, 1982; Uba, 1994). A misguided egalitarian approach or "pseudo-modesty" will undermine a client's confidence in the clinician. For example, some clinicians routinely use statements such as "We will find out together how to deal with this problem" or "You are the only one who can solve your problem—I cannot tell you what to do." These statements may be misinterpreted by clients as a clinician's admission to incompetence. Conversely, being an expert or being authoritative does not mean that a clinician has to be authoritarian or arrogant (Hong, 1989, 1993b). Being an expert simply means conveying an image of confidence and professional competence, a quality that the client expects. Needless to say, the clinician must also demonstrate a courteous and respectful attitude, as well as sensitivity to the client's feelings and level of functioning. In giving expert advice, clinicians can identify a number of alternatives and help the client examine them instead of dictating a particular resolution. In the initial sessions, clinicians can also emphasize the tentative nature of their suggestions and encourage a mutual exploration of them. We have found this approach to be very helpful in engaging our Asian American clients to continue treatment.

Treatment Planning

Depending on a clinician's theoretical orientation, a treatment plan may be general or specific. A crucial consideration in treatment planning is determining whether the plan is acceptable to the client. A treatment plan, no matter how theoretically sound, is useless if the client rejects it and does not return for further sessions. The goals and directions of treatment are more likely to be accepted by an Asian American client if they are defined from the individual's cultural perspective and level of functioning.

Length of Treatment

Because many Asian American clients are skeptical about the effectiveness of psychotherapy and counseling (Gaw, 1993; Hong, 1993a; Hong et al., 1995; Lee, 1980, 1997b; Lorenzo & Adler, 1984; Shon & Ja, 1982; Sue & Morishima, 1982; Uba, 1994), we find it helpful to identify goals that can be achieved in about 8 to 12 sessions, or a reasonable number within the limitations of insurance and other third-party payment policies. This strategy gives clients some realistic objectives rather than allowing them to expect an immediate cure in one or two sessions. When long-term treatment is anticipated, our usual practice is to engage a client with short-term goals and, at the same time, to discuss with the client the necessity of longer treatment to address the problem fully. The purpose is to give clients a chance to experience the effects of psychotherapy and counseling, which, hopefully, will convince them to continue services. Telling clients bluntly in the initial treatment plan that their problems will require long-term therapy of months or years will simply turn most of them away. Asking a client to consent to long-term treatment at the initial stage of psychotherapy and counseling is akin to asking someone to sign a long-term lease for a car or a piece of property when the person is not sure whether he or she wants the item to start with.

Identifying Treatment Goals

The formulation of culturally appropriate treatment goals requires clinicians to consider their clients' perceptions and cultural explanations of their problems or symptoms (American Psychiatric Association, 1994; Grieger & Ponterotto, 1995; Lee, 1997b; Lu et al., 1995). These issues are discussed in Chapter 5 in the context of diagnostic assessments. In this chapter, we want to emphasize the importance of infusing cultural issues into treatment planning to make the plan credible and acceptable to clients (Hong, 1989; 1993b; Hong et al., 1995; Lee, 1997b). For example, a client may be suffering from depression but during the initial sessions may focus only on somatic symptoms such as insomnia and poor appetite. In this situation, the treatment goals need to highlight the alleviation of these somatic symptoms along with addressing the cognitive and affective aspects of depression. This treatment plan allows a clinician to engage the client by focusing on the somatic concerns at the beginning stage of treatment and, as therapy progresses, gradually addressing the cognitive and affective issues that are the source of the somatic complaints.

Treatment Procedures

Culture may significantly affect a client's perception of the appropriate way to resolve a problem (American Psychiatric Association, 1994; Gaw, 1993; Grieger & Ponterotto, 1995; Hong, 1993b; Hong et al., 1995; Lee, 1982, 1997c; Lu et al., 1995; Shon & Ja, 1982; Sue & Morishima, 1982). For example, Asian American clients who believe that their somatic symptoms are related to the imbalance of forces within their bodies are likely to try traditional Asian medicine or folk remedies rather than psychotherapy. Parents who believe their children's poor academic achievement to be the lack of effort or discipline instead of psychoemotional difficulties are more likely to seek help from after-school tutors than from mental health professionals. Throughout the initial treatment sessions, clinicians need to be willing to accept the cultural perspective of their clients and not to dispute or dismiss their beliefs or practices as wrong or irrelevant (Hong, 1988, 1989, 1993b; Hong et al., 1995; Lee, 1997b). To engage Asian American clients in treatment, clinicians can incorporate the clients' cultural perspectives into the treatment plans. For example, instead of instructing clients with somatic concerns to stop using folk remedies, clinicians can tell their clients to continue the folk remedies but to come for psychotherapy and counseling at the same time. Similarly, clinicians can advise parents concerned with their children's poor academic performance to continue after-school tutoring in addition to seeking psychotherapy and counseling.

Throughout the course of treatment, and particularly during the initial sessions, we often find it helpful to begin each session with a discussion of a client's presenting problems and then to ease gradually into content that concerns the clinician (Hong, 1993b; Hong et al., 1995; Lee, 1997b). Take for example, a depressed client with somatic symptoms. A clinician can begin a session inquiring about the client's appetite and sleep patterns during the past week, or the time period between the present and previous sessions. Then he or she can proceed to discuss how these somatic symptoms are affecting the client's daily activities. The clinician can gradually ease into an exploration of the client's work or family functioning, other life events, or emotional problems. Eventually, when there is sufficient information, the clinician can, depending on his or her theoretical orientation and the client's actual clinical situation, explore ways for the client to, say, address a particular life situation, which in turn will alleviate the feelings of depression and associated somatic symptoms. Likewise, for treating children with school-related problems, clinicians can spend some time at the beginning of each session checking with parents about their children's recent school performance, quiz results, or reports. If a child is seen for individual session, this can be done alone with the parents or conjointly with parent and child, prior to the individual session. Clinicians need to assure parents that they are actively addressing the child's school performance rather than "abstract" psychoemotional issues "overly emphasized" in American culture. We have found that systematic checking up on the presenting problems at the initial phase of treatment can be very useful in engaging reluctant Asian American clients. These discussions serve as an "ice-breaker" at the beginning of sessions and create a comfortable environment for clients to discuss personal issues.

Traditional Healing Practices

Some Asian American clients may follow both Western and traditional Asian healing practices (Gaw, 1993; Hong, 1993b; Hong et al., 1995; Lee, 1997b). We find this practice more common among the immigrant population, who are more knowledgeable about traditional Asian healing methods than the American-born generation. For example, they may use herbal medicine or acupuncture to alleviate somatic symptoms associated with mental health problems. Some individuals, like the client C. whose case will be discussed in the next chapter, may also use folk religious or metaphysical practices to restore the "balance of nature" in their environments. Occasionally, recent immigrants faced with a major disorder or disability that Western medicine has failed to cure may even take the drastic step of returning to their country of origin to seek traditional Asian remedies, which are less available in the United States (Hong, 1995).

Clinicians often find it futile to discourage Asian American clients from using traditional Asian medical or folk practices as a way to cure their mental health symptoms. These practices are deeply ingrained in Asian cultures. If clinicians tell their clients to stop using these practices, the clients are likely to ignore the advice and simply avoid bringing up the topic again. The clients may also perceive the clinicians as typical Western professionals who are not knowledgeable about Asian cultures and the effectiveness of Asian healing practices. This perception will make it more difficult for clinicians to engage the clients in treatment. Instead of advising against the traditional Asian remedies, clinicians can discuss these practices in the psychotherapy and counseling session (Hong, 1993b; Hong et al., 1995). For example, when a client brings up the topic of herbal soups, a clinician can inquire whether he or she feels that the particular soup is helpful. A clinician can even initiate a discussion about traditional Asian healing practices by asking a client whether he or she has tried any of these remedies. These discussions are helpful for engaging a client and can easily lead to an extensive exploration of a client's presenting symptoms and daily activities.

Clinicians do not need to be concerned that use of traditional Asian health practices will divert their clients' attention away from mental health services. Basically, the clients are seeking counseling or psychotherapy because these traditional practices are not alleviating their presenting symptoms (Hong et al., 1995). Because many traditional soups and folk practices are aimed at strengthening the body, the clients may simply be using them as an adjunct or backup. In fact, some herbal soups can be taken as a beverage or part of a regular meal that even nonafflicted family members can share. Clinicians need to respect the decisions of their clients to use these healing methods as long as they do not have adverse effects on treatment. If clinicians are knowledgeable about these cultural practices or seek consultation with others who are familiar with the culture, they may find that many of these practices can be an adjunct to "Western" therapy rather than an interference (Hong, 1993b; Hong et al., 1995; Lee, 1997b). At the very least, we usually find that discussing the efficacy of these practices with a respectful and accepting attitude is a good way to engage a client.

Of course, there are situations where a traditional healing practice is contraindicative: For example, a particular herbal soup is a stimulant and the client is drinking it before relaxation exercises. Whenever clinicians are unsure about the effects of a healing method, they should consult with other knowledgeable providers. A clinician can also explain the rationale of his or her treatment method to a client and ask the client to check with the person who recommended or prescribed the particular herb or practice. This inquiry is especially important if the client is taking psychotropic medication because there is the possibility of drug interactions. Psychiatrists will find it important to check about the traditional Asian medicine that their clients may be taking. In case of doubt, they can advise their clients to stop taking the Asian medicine "for a while" and see how the Western medication works. Clients are likely to comply with this advice if the rationale is clearly explained to them because the concept of drug interactions also exists in Asian medicine. The basic issue is for clinicians to engage their clients by demonstrating respect for and acceptance of clients' cultural perceptions and practices. Clinicians need to be particularly cautious about dismissing traditional Asian practices as "unscientific," "old-fashioned," or "superstitious." This attitude can be conveyed, blatantly or unintentionally, by clinicians who are not familiar with traditional Asian healing practices, and it will simply alienate their Asian American clients from treatment (Hong, 1993b; Hong et al., 1995). Conversely, nonmedically trained clinicians need to be cautious about taking the extreme opposite position and recommending or promoting traditional

Asian medicine to their clients. Alternative medicines are currently gaining a lot of attention and popularity in the mainstream American mass media. However, recommending or promoting them without the proper training or licensure would be unprofessional and unethical.

Liaison Work

Many Asian American clients seeking psychotherapy and counseling are referred by other professionals, such as medical doctors or teachers (Gaw, 1993; Hong, 1988, 1989; Hong et al., 1995; Lee, 1997b). Initially, mental health clinicians often have to rely on the authority of these referral sources to engage the client in treatment. For example, clinicians may need to emphasize that they will be exchanging information with the referring doctor or teacher. Of course, this is done with the client's consent. At times, clinicians may need the referring professional to reinforce the necessity or efficacy of mental health services to a client. Thus, creating a collaborative relationship and maintaining a clear line of communication with the referring professional is important for engaging clients. Typically, it will take a number of sessions for clinicians to gain the confidence of their clients and familiarize the clients with the nature and process of counseling or psychotherapy. Only then will the clients feel comfortable to share more details of their life and family issues.

In our experience, word of mouth is a very effective referral source in the Asian American communities. Because clients often prefer to consult a clinician recommended by their friends or relatives who know the clinician, mental health professionals need to network actively with community organizations, including churches, temples, civic groups, and professional organizations, as well as service agencies (Hong, 1988, 1996; Hong et al., 1995). Clinicians can use community activities as a way to promote their services and make themselves visible in the potential client population. This connection with the community helps to demystify a clinician, making him or her an actual person rather than a stereotype. Also, we find that acknowledging a particular referral source in small talk at the beginning of the initial session can be an effective ice-breaker that helps to establish therapeutic rapport.

Social Etiquette

In Chapter 5, our discussion of diagnostic assessment has examined some of the nuances concerning language and communication styles and the values and norms concerning social interactions, including gender and age issues. In this section, we will elaborate upon three areas that are critical in developing therapeutic rapport with Asian American clients who are less assimilated into mainstream American culture.

Physical Contact

In contrast to Western cultures, Asian cultures generally sanction less physical contact between individuals in social settings. This is particularly the case for interactions between males and females. In general, most Asian Americans are familiar with the handshake as a greeting. Recent immigrants from less Westernized localities, such as certain rural areas of Asia, may be more accustomed to a simple bow or nod. However, even these new immigrants will accommodate quickly and accept a handshake as a gesture for greeting another person in mainstream settings. Beyond this simple initial greeting, clinicians need to exercise caution in physical contacts with their clients. For example, hugging or embracing a client can be problematic because these gestures may be perceived as having sexual connotations and may cause misunderstanding and embarrassment. Even though clients may know that a hug or an embrace may simply be a friendly gesture, they may still feel uneasy if they have limited exposure to mainstream American culture and are not accustomed to these gestures. Other common gestures like patting a person on the shoulder or a child on the head are regarded by some people, particularly some Southeast Asians, as a curse or an act that can bring bad luck. Considering the cultural issues and nuances relating to physical contact in social interactions, we advise clinicians to refrain from any behavior beyond a gentle handshake or a simple nod with a smile, particularly when they are unsure of their Asian American clients' cultural identification. It is prudent for clinicians to be cautious rather than to behave in ways that make clients feel uncomfortable or that may even be perceived by clients as inappropriate.

Communication Style

Differences between the communication styles of a client and a clinician may lead to misperceptions and misunderstandings and hinder the development of therapeutic rapport. Unlike the open expression of thoughts and feelings favored by mainstream American culture, indirect statement and nonverbal expression are common styles of communication in Asian cultures (Hong, 1989; Lee, 1997c; Shon & Ja, 1982; Uba, 1994). The Asian cultural value of interpersonal harmony and the concept of "saving face" discourage open confrontations in social settings. Thus, Asian American clients are less likely to show direct disagreements with a clinician. They may verbalize disagreements in a mild or roundabout manner (Hong, 1989). Indeed, even if clients disagree with their clinicians, they may not show any indication of disagreements. Instead, they may sit politely through a session and perhaps smilingly accept a second appointment while having no intention of returning. In the context of Asian cultures, this behavior is considered acceptable and polite, while directly turning down the next appointment may be considered rude or confrontational. Often, clients express their disagreements with clinicians in a polite and indirect manner (Hong, 1989). For example, a client may say, "Some people say I should try . . ." instead of directly saying that he or she disagrees with the clinician's advice. This indirect statement helps to distance clients personally from a disagreement and is considered to be more socially refined or polite. We often find it helpful to follow the same subtlety in communicating with Asian American clients. For example, a culturally appropriate way to respond to the above comment is to continue to refer to the third party: "Those people are wrong . . ." or "But there are others who say. . . ." This response helps to distance the disagreement and is face-saving for both the clinician and client. Other times, to convey disapproval of a course of action that a client is taking, we may say, "Some people have problems similar to yours. . . . I often tell them that it is useless to. . . ." This indirect statement distances the disapproval and again is considered more socially refined than a direct disapproval. The message, however, is still very clear for the client.

At times, taking a step backwards can actually allow a clinician to go forward. For instance, as suggested in Chapter 5, in approaching topics concerning sensitive personal or family information, clinicians can use apologetic phrases such as "I know, as an outsider, I shouldn't be asking about this . . . but in order to help you, it is important for me to know. . . ." This apology is a culturally polite way to approach a sensitive issue and helps to put a client at ease in discussing the information. By observing Asian social etiquette, clinicians may have more success in engaging Asian American clients in treatment.

The indirect approach may be very uncomfortable for clinicians who are accustomed to the direct communication style in mainstream American culture, especially clinicians who mechanically emphasize the use of "I" statements. Clinicians need to remember that an indirect communication style is based on cultural values and norms and is not a clinical protocol. Clinicians should always speak directly if a therapeutic intervention requires it. For example, there are times when a clinician may need to emphasize an issue by directly saying, "I suggest you try this" or "Don't do this." However, such remarks have to be made judiciously, tactfully, and with cultural sensitivity. Otherwise, a clinician may be perceived by the client as arrogant or socially crude.

Sensitive and Intimate Issues

The issues of privacy and stigma have been discussed in Chapter 5, along with suggestions for clinicians to approach sensitive and intimate topics with Asian American clients. In this section, we want to emphasize that clinicians need to be alert to these issues throughout the course of psychotherapy and counseling, rather than just at the diagnostic interview. Topics such as intimate details of family interactions or the marital relationship, particularly sexual behavior, are typically assigned a higher degree of privacy in Asian cultures than in mainstream American culture. Thus, clinicians need to understand the discomfort and embarrassment that Asian American clients may be feeling when they have to discuss these intimate details of their lives. This uneasiness may be particularly strong when clients have to discuss sexual or marital issues with clinicians of the opposite gender or when they have to confide intimate personal or family matters with clinicians whom they perceive as "too young" in the context of the Asian age hierarchy. If these topics are initiated by a clinician, he or she needs to provide a clear rationale for inquiring about such matters. Acknowledging the client's discomfort is also helpful. For example, we often begin inquiring about and discussing sensitive issues by saying, "I know it may be difficult for you to talk about this, but it is really important for me to know . . ." This type of remark conveys to clients our awareness of the culturally sensitive contents and our understanding of their feelings. This remark also provides an opportunity for clients to express their concerns in discussing these intrusive topics. Whenever therapeutically possible, clinicians are in a better position to engage their clients if they gradually approach sensitive and intimate subjects over a number of sessions. Otherwise, their clients may perceive them to be socially abrasive, intrusive, or insensitive and will not return for further sessions.

Acknowledge and Discuss Cultural Issues

Learning the nuances of culture is a difficult and infinite task. Clinicians, whether they are Asian American or not, may discover that they are unfamiliar with certain Asian cultural issues or practices. In many instances, basic clinical skills, empathy, genuineness, and an attitude of respect for the client can compensate for this unfamiliarity. Whenever clinicians are unsure of a cultural issue, they can definitely ask their clients about it. Most clients do not mind giving a clinician some help in understanding their own culture, especially when the clinician is from a different ethnic group. Of course, clinicians need to limit their inquiry, for the purpose of a session is to help clients resolve their problems rather than to give clinicians lessons on Asian cultures. Clinicians also need to express an attitude of respect for a client's culture, rather than treating the client's explanations as amusing anecdotes of "exotic" cultural views or practices. If clinicians ask for clarification about cultural views and practices genuinely and respectfully, they will demonstrate their cultural sensitivity to their clients and will be more likely to succeed in engaging their clients in treatment.

Social Environmental Factors for Consideration in Engaging Asian American Clients

The process of engaging Asian American clients in psychotherapy and counseling entails creating social environmental conditions that help them feel comfortable, or at least less reluctant, to seek services. Clinicians need to examine these conditions in the context of the referral network, the intake process, the social and physical environment where treatment is provided, and the availability of adjunct services. Moreover, clinicians must be empathic to the social environmental stressors experienced by their clients, including migration or refugee issues, and must help their clients address them. The following discussion examines the major social environmental factors that may affect a clinician's effectiveness in developing a therapeutic relationship with Asian American clients who are identified with Asian cultures and in engaging them in treatment.

The Referral Network

Many Asian Americans are unfamiliar with the medical and mental health system in the United States, particularly the diversity of clinicians and specialists (Gaw, 1993; Hong, 1988, 1993a; Hong et al., 1995; Shon & Ja, 1982; Sue & Morishima, 1982; Takeuchi, Mokuau, & Chun, 1992; Uba, 1994). They are often unsure about how to seek help and where to go for services. This uncertainty is particularly common among immigrants, especially those who are from lower socioeconomic backgrounds and those with limited English proficiency. Quite often, we have seen clients who are referred back and forth by various institutions, including mental health clinics, medical clinics, rehabilitation centers, schools, social service agencies, or even the legal system and protective service agencies. Being transferred from one provider to another and from one agency to another and being asked to wait for appointments for each referral is often a confusing and frustrating experience for a client. Many clients may simply give up and not follow through with a referral. Mental health clinicians will be in a better position to engage a client in treatment if the referral process is streamlined so that the client will not get lost among the various institutions. For example, the current practice in many clinics is for the medical professional to give the phone number of a mental health clinic to a client and expect the client to contact the clinic directly. However, Asian American clients who are already skeptical of psychotherapy and counseling may simply procrastinate on calling for an appointment and may eventually decide not to follow through with the referral. In our experience, a mental health clinician's direct contact with a client at the time of referral, either by phone or in person, is very helpful in engaging the client to go for treatment. For example, a medical professional can phone a mental health clinic while a client is still waiting in his or her office and then put the client on the phone so that the client can make an appointment directly with the intake worker. In other institutions such as schools, mental health clinicians may find it easier to engage their clients if they are regularly available on site, such as a few hours each week (Soriano & Hong, 1997). This regular presence allows school personnel to introduce parents and children directly to the clinician who will be seeing them at a mental health clinic or at the school. We will discuss such collaborations in greater detail in Chapter 9. No doubt, a great deal of effort is required for mental health professionals to establish and maintain close relationships with different referral sources. However, clinicians must be willing to take this effort so that they can enhance the likelihood that their Asian American clients will follow through with referrals for treatment (Hong, 1988; Takeuchi et al., 1992).

The Intake Process

A crucial step in engaging Asian American clients is to act quickly and offer them appointments as soon as possible to capitalize on their willingness to accept the referral and try psychotherapy and counseling (Hong, 1988; Hong et al., 1995; Takeuchi et al., 1992). Many mental health programs, including health maintenance organizations, have long waiting periods between the referral and the initial appointment or between intake and actual therapy sessions. Such practices often dampen clients' willingness to seek services because they are reluctant and skeptical to start with. The long wait for appointments simply offers clients a rationalization to back away from a referral. As mentioned in the previous section, direct phone contacts and face-to-face meetings are very helpful in engaging Asian American clients. Even though a full evaluation session is not always immediately possible, clinicians can have a brief meeting or a phone discussion with a client to review the referral and to make an appointment for a full session at the nearest date. Such introductory contacts help to lower the barrier between the clinician and the client and increase the likelihood that the client will actually show up for the appointment. If it is impossible to offer an appointment soon enough to meet the urgency of the problem or the amenability of the client, a clinician can at least use this brief contact to explain to the client the reason for the delay and discuss alternatives, such as making a referral to another clinician who is more readily available.

Currently, a common practice of many mental health programs is to have different clinicians conduct the intake interview and provide the actual treatment. These institutional procedures are not helpful for engaging Asian American clients (Hong, 1988, 1993b; Hong et al., 1995). Instead, we recommend that the clinician who conducts the intake screening and the initial evaluation also be the person who provides the actual treatment. This continuity helps a client become familiar with the clinician and overcome the cultural inhibition of disclosing personal matters to a "stranger." Also, it minimizes the repetition of questions typically asked by providers, such as "What brings you here?" "How do you feel about this incident/situation?" and "How is it affecting your relationship with your family or others?" Such repetitive questioning by different providers is often very frustrating and annoying for a client who is already skeptical about the effectiveness of psychotherapy and counseling.

We can anticipate some resistance from mental health professionals in adopting the suggestions discussed in this section. Some professionals may even argue that it is impossible for the same clinician to follow a client all the way because of different specializations. We agree that a referral to another clinician should be made whenever it is necessitated by the nature of a client's problem or a clinician's expertise. However, in many cases, the same clinician is competent enough to provide the intake, evaluation, and treatment. In such cases, this clinician can be the sole provider. Mental health professionals need only look at the private practice sector to witness the feasibility of this approach (Hong, 1988; Vane, 1986). In private practice, the typical procedure is for the same clinician to do the intake, evaluation, and treatment for each client. There is no reason to insist on the "assembly line" approach in the public sector. Having the same clinician working with a client from intake to termination will help to foster the therapeutic relationship and to engage the client.

The Social Milieu

A clinician's attitude, behavior, and overall demeanor contribute to the process of engaging the client. Likewise, these characteristics apply to the entire staff of a clinic or treatment program. Staff members include anyone who has contact with clients, such as telephone operators, receptionists, cashiers, billing clerks, secretaries, and clinicians. Misunderstanding and misperception may occur at any stage of a client's contact with a clinic or program. For example, an Asian American client who is uncomfortable about contacting a mental health clinician and who does not know exactly what is entailed in an initial appointment may ask a lot of questions over the phone. He or she may feel intimidated or offended by the curt responses of a phone operator who is under time pressure to answer other incoming calls. A refugee client, already apprehensive about governmental screening or investigation, may be intimidated by a stern-faced receptionist who, without proper explanation, asks him or her to fill out a form concerning personal history or to produce tax returns for a sliding-scale payment request. As these examples indicate, cultural sensitivity and courtesy of the entire staff are critical for engaging Asian American clients in treatment.

The Physical Setting

The physical setting where psychotherapy and counseling take place can often affect the therapeutic alliance and process. To facilitate therapeutic rapport, mental health services need to be provided in a setting where clients feel at ease. In addition to the usual amenities expected of a clinic, such as private counseling areas to ensure confidentiality and to minimize distractions, additional steps can be taken to help Asian American clients feel welcome and comfortable. Culturally syntonic decor in a clinic or office is one way to create an inviting atmosphere for Asian American clients. For example, a room can be decorated with Asian artwork or photos to help clients who are less assimilated into mainstream culture feel as if they are in a familiar environment, or at least in an environment that acknowledges their cultural background. These decorations do not have to be expensive or elaborate. Even simple posters of Asian scenery or landmarks may serve the purpose. In particular, we have found clients to enjoy seasonal decorations observing major Asian holidays and celebrations. Depending on the particular clinic, these seasonal decorations can even be made by clients, such as children, day treatment clients, or clients in acculturation and other preventive programs. Of course, decorations should be tasteful, appropriate, and not stereotypical. For example, though lanterns and dragons are common cultural motifs, if used ineptly, they might make the place look more like a restaurant than a professional facility.

We also find it helpful to provide magazines in Asian languages in the waiting area of a clinic. Newspapers in Asian languages can be provided, but they may be costly because they have to be changed daily. Other written materials suitable for display include Asian language informational brochures about the clinic or about clinical topics relevant to Asian Americans. Our intention for providing these reading materials is simply to make the client feel at home rather than to provide library service. This literature, together with other informational items in Asian languages, such as directional signs and door plaques, will help the clinic to convey a congenial atmosphere to the Asian American client and engage them in services. We want to emphasize that popular mainstream magazines and other informational items in English also need to be visibly displayed along with materials written in Asian languages. As discussed in previous chapters, Asian Americans, even those within the same family, may have different attitudes and feelings about their cultural affiliation. Clinicians need to ensure that clients who are less proficient in Asian languages will not feel alienated if they need to come to the clinic for services along with other family members who are proficient in Asian languages.

Location of Services

In comparison to clinics in mainstream settings, community clinics or programs that are located directly in Asian American neighborhoods are considered less intimidating by Asian American clients who are less assimilated into mainstream culture (Lee, 1980, 1982; Sue, 1977; Takeuchi et al., 1992). These community-based services can be provided by independent clinics or satellite offices of a mainstream mental health program. Another way to engage Asian American clients is to provide mental health services in institutions familiar to them, such as schools or social services agencies. Clinical services provided in these settings have the additional advantage of helping to destigmatize psychotherapy and counseling. In turn, this helps to overcome client reluctance to seek services. This approach calls for a more flexible model of service delivery that involves collaboration between mental health agencies, schools, and other community organizations. This collaborative model is viable despite issues such as funding, limited resources, and interagency politics (Adelman & Taylor, 1993; Dryfoos, 1994; Fine & Carlson, 1992; Soriano & Hong, 1997). We will discuss this approach in greater detail when we examine innovative service delivery models in Chapter 9.

An important factor for consideration in this discussion regarding location of services is the issues of funding and resources. Providing mental health services in culturally appropriate locations requires clinicians to address the more general and systemic social environmental issue of racism, particularly institutional racism. Mainstream institutions are often resistant to change because they are insensitive to the needs of Asian Americans and other ethnic minorities. Policy makers and providers in mainstream institutions frequently refuse to diverge from their established models, practices, or regulations. Hence, clinicians who are dedicated to serving Asian American clients will need to advocate and address community issues and client concerns on a systemic level.

Availability of Adjunct Resources

Clinicians can engage in treatment many Asian American clients who expect immediate and direct resolution of their problems by connecting

them with support services that are adjuncts to psychotherapy and counseling (Hong, 1988; Lee, 1980, 1982, 1997b; Takeuchi et al., 1992; Uba,
1994). For example, a delinquent child may benefit from an after-school
program, or a parent experiencing stressful life events may need help with
child care. Job training, job placement, and adult English programs are
also commonly needed adjunct services in the communities. For some clients, the absence of support services is actually a major source of their presenting problems. This is particularly true for lower socioeconomic status
Asian Americans living in impoverished ethnic communities. Helping
these clients locate appropriate support services, including financial aid,
can be an effective way to establish the therapeutic relationship as well as
to resolve their presenting problems. It is an excellent way of demonstrating to clients that the clinician truly understands their situation and cares
about them.

Take, for example, a divorced Chinese American woman referred by her
children's school to seek therapy for her two boys, aged 12 and 14 years,
who were having conduct problems. At the initial session, the woman related that her family had limited financial resources and lived in a small
apartment in a poor inner-city neighborhood. The two boys were sharing
an old bed and were constantly bickering about the crowded sleeping conditions. The woman requested the clinician to help her find resources to
purchase separate beds for the sons. She had tried many community agencies but had been told repeatedly that being without a bed was not a "serious hardship" that would qualify for assistance. Having ascertained that
her request was authentic, the clinician agreed to help but also explained
that this would take time. In the next 2 months, while providing psychotherapy to the family, the clinician checked with various agencies and advocated for the family. Eventually, the clinician was able to find two community organizations to share the cost of the beds. Although the process
took a long time, the boys were delighted to have their own beds. By helping this family locate resources and advocating for them, the clinician
showed them that he understood their predicament and cared about them.
This action was very helpful in establishing the therapeutic relationship
with the mother, and especially with her two sons. The beds were a concrete expression of care they could easily see and appreciate. Despite their
defiance toward authority figures in school and their resistance to the referral for therapy, the boys always maintained a respectful attitude toward
the clinician.

To locate appropriate adjunct services for clients, clinicians must be
knowledgeable about both mainstream and community resources. Besides government agencies, these resources often include public and private community organizations, such as merchant associations, family associations, churches, and temples, which may have greater flexibility in

providing services and allocating funds than publicly funded agencies. When advocating for their clients, clinicians often need to help these organizations understand the importance of the clients' needs. Moreover, Asian American clients who are not proficient in English will need adjunct services provided in their first language, and this may not be readily available in mainstream agencies. The availability of services varies from locality to locality. Funding for resources is often a political issue that is closely related to institutional racism. Once again, clinicians may need to advocate and address the availability of adjunct services on the systemic level.

Immigration and Refugee Issues

We have repeatedly emphasized how important it is for clinicians to be sensitive to the stress associated with the immigration or refugee experiences of foreign-born Asian American clients. In addition to being unfamiliar with mental health services, recent immigrants have to cope with the adjustment stress of relocation. The specific stressors include settling down in a new community and new culture, starting new jobs or new schools, and developing a new social and support system (Hong, 1989; Hong & Ham, 1992; Lee, 1982, 1997c; Shon & Ja, 1982). Clients often convey that they simply do not have time to "talk" about psychoemotional issues with a clinician. Rather, they feel that a better use of time is to be helped with managing daily life tasks. Refugees who have had traumatic experiences and have encountered obstacles in gaining asylum in the United States may want to conceal the details of their background or avoid further governmental attention. In therapy sessions, they may be very guarded about personal details. Clinicians need to be empathic about the feelings of these clients and proceed with patience to gain their trust, rather than callously dismissing their reluctance to seek services or their cautious attitude as resistance. Often, outreach programs are needed to engage these clients. These programs will be discussed in detail in Chapter 9.

To engage immigrant and refugee Asian American clients, clinicians must be prepared to discuss and provide information to them regarding life and customs in the United States. Sometimes the information can be as simple as telling a client how to take public transportation or drive to certain places or explaining the observance of certain holidays that are not celebrated in Asia, such as Thanksgiving Day. There are also occasions when a clinician needs to inform clients where to obtain certain services or where to buy certain items. Take, for example, a Vietnamese American teenager with a physical disability referred by his school for counseling. At the first appointment, he asked the clinician to help him get replacements for the padding on his crutches. The teenager could have solved this simple problem by telephoning his disability caseworker or checking the phone directory yellow pages for a supply store. However, being a refugee who was too intimidated to ask for help, he did not want to "bother" his non-Asian American caseworker with this "minor" problem. Also, being new to the United States, he had no idea where to find a supply store to buy the replacement. For months, he had been using the worn-out padding, which was very uncomfortable. Finally, when he was referred to the present Asian American clinician for counseling, he found the courage to disclose this "nonclinical" problem. In our clinical practice, we routinely have immigrant and refugee clients who request information relating to issues such as housing, child care, after-school programs, adult English classes, social services, and legal services. These questions may be raised at any point during psychotherapy and counseling. Clinicians need to respond to these inquiries rather than to dismiss them as irrelevant, as demonstrating a lack of boundaries, or as a distraction from the "real clinical" issue. By answering these questions, clinicians can convey their empathic understanding of the relocation stress experienced by their clients and thus help to develop therapeutic rapport. At times, we may even contact a particular resource with a phone call during the session because of a client's limited English-speaking ability or other inhibiting factors. Again, this action demonstrates a clinician's genuine concern and willingness to help the client. A mental health clinician who takes a rigid traditional approach and refuses to address these "nonclinical" issues is likely to be perceived by Asian American clients as bureaucratic, aloof, or uncaring. To help immigrant and refugee clients address their life issues, clinicians need to familiarize themselves with the common problems faced by Asian Americans in adapting to life in the United States. In this way, clinicians will be prepared to answer their clients' inquiries and engage them in treatment.

Actually, adjunct activities to help immigrant and refugee clients adjust to the U.S. way of life can be an integral component of a treatment plan. This, for example, is the model implemented at the Community Living Program provided at Coastal Asian Pacific Mental Health Services (Coastal), a program of Los Angeles County Department of Mental Health. The Community Living Program is designed specifically for Vietnamese American trauma victims, many of whom have diagnoses of post-traumatic stress disorder. According to Richard Kim, a clinical psychologist formerly at Coastal who designed their Community Living Program, the program includes an educational component that teaches clients about the American way of living. In addition to medication, psychotherapy, and other activities, clients in this program receive weekly adult education classes that address a variety of issues, including daily living skills such as how to pay bills, get bus passes, and use services at the post office and banks. They make field visits to various institutions, such as post offices and banks, to learn directly how to access their services. These adjunct services have been found to be very effective in helping the recovery of these clients.

Finally, when working with foreign-born Asian American clients, we often find that "small talk" about immigration issues is helpful for establishing therapeutic rapport and for serving as an ice-breaker in the initial sessions. For example, clinicians can ask their recent immigrant clients (in a casual and chatty tone of voice), "You have been here 10 months already—are you getting used to living in the United States?" With clients who have been here longer, clinicians can ask a similar question: "You have been here 10 years—have you been back to . . . [country of origin]?" In the Asian American communities, questions like these are commonly asked as part of a light conversation. These questions provide a socially pleasant way for a clinician to convey understanding of a client's background and to help engage the client in treatment.

Case Illustration

We have examined the major cultural and social environmental factors to be considered in engaging Asian American clients in psychotherapy and counseling. The following case by Yoshi Matsushima, LCSW, is a good illustration of many of the issues discussed in this chapter.

The client M. was a 48-year-old, third-generation Japanese American man. He was married to a white American woman. The presenting problem was major depression. He had previously been seen at a non-Asian clinic for about 6 months. He had been referred to the present clinician because he wanted to have an Asian American therapist. He felt that "white people don't understand my problems." He was on psychotropic medication in addition to being seen for psychotherapy.

The clinician, a first-generation Japanese American man, noted that M. was strongly influenced by Japanese culture in a number of ways. For example, M. had a tendency to avoid masculine authority figures. This was not unusual within the cultural context. Indeed, in Japan, there is a saying that there are four things to be afraid of in life: earthquake, thunder, fire, and father. M. also had a xenophobic attitude and tended to avoid associating with strangers—that is, non-Japanese. In such situations, he would be polite but not trusting. His usual communication style was nonconfrontative and indirect. This mode of interaction was in accordance with the traditional cultural principles of saving face for self and others and maintaining interpersonal harmony. However, this manner of communication, when compounded with his idiosyncratic style of speaking in

short, abrupt sentences, was causing problems and misunderstanding between him and his wife, as well as other people. The clinician had to address this issue as part of therapy.

The clinician, being a male and an authority figure (therapist/expert),
was particularly concerned that M.'s intense negative feelings toward his
father and Japanese supervisor would interfere with the formation of the
therapeutic alliance. Thus, he made an active effort to build a positive relationship with the client. When M. came for his appointments, the clinician
would try to make the situation informal and relaxing. He made a point of
speaking to M. with a relaxed facial expression before M. started talking.
If the clinician had a necktie on that day, he would remove it before the session. He also avoided wearing black pants and white shirts, as this attire
was stereotypic of Japanese men. These visible signs made it less likely
for M. to perceive him as similar to his father or work supervisor.

The clinician was also aware that some American-born Japanese have a
strong identification with Japanese culture and a deep longing to be accepted by the people of Japan. In contrast, some immigrant Japanese
Americans, especially recent arrivals, have a disparaging attitude toward
Japanese Americans who have been in the United States longer. This situation is also found in other Asian American groups. Being aware and sensitive to this issue, the clinician, a first-generation Japanese American, tried
to avoid any signs that could be misinterpreted as a disparaging attitude toward American-born Japanese. He made an effort to point out to M. that
the two of them shared many characteristics, such as physical resemblance
and liking for certain foods, Japanese movies, Japanese songs, and hob-
bies. He also made a special effort to avoid communication styles that
were more typically Japanese than Japanese American. In a way, this accentuated their common identity as Japanese Americans rather than creating a division between Japanese and Japanese Americans.

Like many Asians, M. viewed mental illness as a strong stigma. He had
difficulty accepting the fact that he had a major mental illness. He explained his problem as a disability, not as mental illness. He expressed
doubts about the wisdom of taking medication for his depression. He had
difficulty complying with medication instructions because to take medication was to admit to himself and others that he was mentally ill. He was
very ashamed of having a mental illness. This feeling of shame was one
reason he did not go out of his home. He was concerned that he would meet
someone he knew and would be asked how he was doing or would be asked
about his job or his "disability." To deal with M.'s feeling of shame, the clinician repeatedly offered him encouragement and support through statements like "So, you are disabled, but you are making your best effort to
live each day with your disability. That's important." The clinician also
tried to instill the idea that the client had a right to protect his privacy and

did not have to answer all the questions that others asked him. The clinician coached him in using the communication techniques of "many politicians," such as responding to questions without answering anything. Along with this strategy, the clinician also called M.'s attention to his problematic communication style and discussed its effects and possible consequences. In sessions, he would reframe what M. said into language more congruent with mainstream American society. At other times, he would ask M. to reframe his own speech into ways that would be more easily understood correctly by others.

Discussion

This client presented a situation that would have been difficult for any clinician, whether Japanese American or not. He could not trust a white therapist because he felt that white people would not understand him. He could have had difficulty with a male Japanese American therapist because this could have accentuated his apprehension of and negative attitudes toward male authority figures. A female Japanese American therapist would also be problematic for this client because in traditional Japanese culture women have lower social status than men. In this case, the clinician skillfully addressed these issues of hierarchy and gender by deliberately presenting a relaxed demeanor. He even took the extra but subtle step of making sure not to wear a necktie or any other stereotypic Japanese male attire.

The provision of culturally sensitive services requires a clinician to be constantly alert to his or her own beliefs, attitudes, and behaviors as well as those of the client. In this case, the clinician was sensitive to the issues and possible interpersonal dynamics concerning himself, an immigrant Japanese American, and the client, an American-born Japanese. He subtly addressed this issue by emphasizing the commonalities between himself and the client and made sure that the client would not feel rejected in the cultural sense. It was through all these delicate and skillful maneuvers that the clinician was able to engage the client in therapy.

This case demonstrates the importance of discerning when to accept a client's cultural perspective and when to realize that a culturally based behavior may have become maladaptive. When the client sought to escape the stigma of mental illness by defining it as a disability, the clinician did not dispute the client's interpretation or pathologize his thinking as denial or resistance. Instead, he discussed the problem as if it were a disability. When the client disclosed that he was embarrassed to talk to others about his "disability," the clinician empathized with his need for privacy and coached him in answering people's inquiries. In these instances, he was working from the client's perspective. However, the clinician also realized that the client's communication style was a source of problems in his marital and social relationships. Instead of blindly accepting everything as cultural, the clinician realized that the client's communication problem was created by a combination of cultural and idiosyncratic factors. He discussed and clarified this problem with the client and sought to teach him to communicate more effectively.

Finally, this case highlighted the importance of not making assumptions about the cultural identification of a client. The client was third-generation Japanese American and was married to a white woman. A clinician could easily have made the erroneous assumption that the client was primarily identified with mainstream American culture. Instead, the client was strongly identified with Japanese culture, which strongly influenced his worldview. This cultural identification was reflected in his attitude toward male authority figures, his ideas about mental illness, and his communication style. Again, the clinician was alert to the issues and correctly identified their cultural underpinnings.

Summary

In this chapter, we have examined the cultural and social environmental issues to be considered in engaging Asian American clients in treatment. These issues may be manifested in the content of psychotherapy and counseling: that is, the information discussed by clinician and client. The issues may also affect the process of psychotherapy and counseling, such as the verbal and nonverbal interactions and the relationship between clinician and client. To engage Asian American clients, treatment procedures and treatment planning must meet clients' cultural expectations. In addition to relational compatibility between clinician and client, issues on the institutional and systemic level may affect the therapeutic relationship. The institutional setting and its procedures, as well as the cultural sensitivity of the entire staff of an agency, are important factors affecting a client's willingness to seek treatment. Another crucial factor is the availability of culturally appropriate adjunct services. Because differences exist in Asian American clients' cultural identification and in their social environmental experiences, once again, we want to caution clinicians that the clinical strategies discussed in this chapter need to be applied judiciously. Clinicians must avoid overgeneralization and stereotypes and approach each client on the basis of the individual's cultural orientation, social environmental experiences, and clinical needs.

7

Application of Major Therapeutic Orientations

Psychoanalytic Therapy, Person-Centered Therapy, and Cognitive Behavioral Therapy

This chapter discusses the cultural application of three major therapeutic orientations commonly practiced by mental health professionals in the United States, namely psychoanalytic therapy, person-centered therapy, and cognitive behavioral therapy. Specifically, we will examine the practical application of these three approaches in clinical work with Asian American clients who are identified with Asian cultures. We are assuming that the reader has already been trained to use these theories and therapeutic strategies, and we will focus our discussion on selected aspects of these approaches that need special attention when applied to Asian American clients. As mentioned in Chapter 1, *therapy* is used as a generic term encompassing both psychotherapy and counseling.

All three approaches discussed in this chapter have their proponents among Asian American clinicians (Chin, Liem, Ham, & Hong, 1993; Mokuau & Matsuoka, 1992) and are considered relevant for use with Asian American clients. The critical issue for clinicians is to be constantly mindful that the concepts and techniques of these therapeutic orientations are developed in the context of Western worldviews and cultural values. Our challenge as clinicians is to relate these concepts and strategies to the cultural and social environmental contexts of Asian American clients. In this chapter, we will focus on selected concepts and strategies of these three therapeutic approaches rather than on comprehensive descriptions, which are beyond the purpose and scope of this book. Our selection of the specific treatment concepts and strategies for inclusion in the following discussion is based on our experience of applying these approaches to Asian American clients who are identified with Asian cultures. Our intent is to heighten the awareness of clinicians to a cultural application of these approaches. Because engaging clients in treatment and developing clinician-client rapport are important for any therapeutic orientation, the suggestions discussed in Chapter 6 must be kept in mind in the present discussion. At the end of this chapter, we will briefly review some culturally specific therapeutic approaches based on Asian cultural foundations.

Psychoanalytic Therapy With Asian American Clients

In psychoanalytic therapy, a clinician's major task is to uncover and interpret the meanings of conscious and unconscious thoughts, feelings, and motivations, as well as the projections, and other ego defenses, that a client brings to a therapy session (Freud, 1912/1958a, 1911-1915/1958b; Friedman, 1985; Gray, 1994; Kohut, 1984; Meissner, 1974; Langs, 1974, 1988; Stark, 1999). With this therapeutic approach, clients are encouraged to use free association: that is, to speak freely about whatever comes to their mind. Clients need to be willing to freely verbalize their thoughts and feelings to the clinician. As explained in our discussions in previous chapters on traditional Asian cultures, Asian American clients who are identified with Asian cultures are often uncomfortable about disclosing intimate personal information and feelings to outsiders, including mental health clinicians (Hong, 1988, 1989). Traditional Asian cultural values also emphasize that a person should exert control over his or her feelings to ensure relational and social harmony and not to disrupt harmony among others (Hsu, 1985; Tang, 1997). Such an orientation may further contribute to the reluctance of Asian American clients to talk freely about their negative feelings. This is a challenge for clinicians seeking to apply the psychoanalytic approach. On the positive side, psychoanalytic therapy's emphasis on achieving insight through uncovering one's unconscious thoughts, feelings, and motivations is congruent with traditional Asian cultural concepts of seeking self-understanding and developing self-control. As such, the insight-oriented nature of the psychoanalytic approach can be appealing to Asian American clients. But although the search for insight is compatible with Asian cultural tradition, self-examination in traditional Asian cultures is primarily a private process and is not to be revealed completely to others (King & Bond, 1985). Hence, a psychoanalytically oriented clinician must still be attuned to the possible discomfort experienced by Asian American clients when they examine their intimate thoughts and feelings within their interior world with the help of an unfamiliar person, such as a clinician.

To maximize the effectiveness of psychoanalytic therapy with Asian American clients, clinicians must attend to their clients' expectations for treatment. As discussed in Chapter 6, many Asian American clients expect quick symptom relief when they seek mental health services (Gaw, 1993; Hong, 1989, 1993a, 1993b; Hong et al., 1995; Lee, 1980, 1982, 1997c; Shon & Ja, 1982; Sue & Morishima, 1982; Uba, 1994). They expect structure, such as questions and directions from the clinician, rather than free association. In addition, they want therapeutic discussions focused on their symptoms and problems, rather than on childhood events and distant memories. Indeed, one of the most frequent complaints we hear from Asian American clients concerning psychoanalytic therapy involves their impatience with a clinician's pace in addressing their symptoms or problems, or a clinician's apparent focus on the past rather than on the present, which they consider to be more relevant. To engage these Asian American clients, clinicians using the psychoanalytic approach need to adapt the pace of intervention to their expectations. In the initial sessions, clinicians can provide greater structure and attend more to the presenting problems and symptoms than they would in work with clients who were identified with mainstream American culture. Actually, discussions with clients about life events that they consider to be significant, such as migration experience, may lead to associated descriptions of other life events, such as memories of childhood or parental influences. These client descriptions provide valuable clinical data for the psychoanalytically oriented clinician (Tang, 1997; Yi, 1995). During this initial exploratory stage, a clinician can gradually inform a client of the nature and rationale of psychoanalytic therapeutic strategies while easing the client into this process.

Asian and Western Worldviews: Ajase Complex and Oedipus Complex

Although the core concepts and techniques of psychoanalytic therapy are applicable to clinical work with Asian American clients, clinicians need to be aware of the similarities and differences between Asian and Western cultures' worldviews and values. These cultural beliefs are subjective realities, often expressed in the stories, folktales, and myths in a culture (Jung, 1971; Tien, 1989). Perhaps the most cogent example is the contrast between two cultural stories, the Asian Ajase story and the Western Oedipus myth, that have the same theme: the parent-child relationship. Each story is used to symbolize a complex in its culture, a fixation about the parent-child relationship. The saga of Ajase, the cultural story signifying the Ajase complex, has been proposed as an Asian alternative to the Western myth of Oedipus, the tale illustrating the Oedipus complex (Hedstrom, 1994; Okonogi, 1978; Roland, 1988; Yamamoto & Chang, 1987). The Oedipus complex, a prominent concept in psychoanalytic therapy, is named after the well-known myth about Oedipus, a Greek king from antiquity, whose primal conflict with his father dominated his life events. In contrast to this Western myth, the Ajase complex is named after the story of Ajase (the Japanese translation of the Sanskrit name Ajatashatru), a historical Indian prince described in Buddhist scriptures. Like the Oedipus myth, the Ajase story is concerned with the father-son conflict. However, the central theme of the Ajase story is the magnificence of maternal love in the mother-son dyad, a theme that is considered to be more syntonic with Asian cultures than the Oedipus myth (Hedstrom, 1994; Okonogi, 1978; Roland, 1988; Yamamoto & Chang, 1987).

The Ajase complex was originally conceptualized by Heisaku Kosawa, a pioneering Japanese psychoanalyst who studied in Vienna and presented his ideas on this subject directly to Freud (Okonogi, 1978, 1979). There are different versions of the Ajase story, but their central themes and essential elements are the same (Hedstrom, 1994; Okonogi, 1978, 1979; Roland, 1988; Yamamoto & Chang, 1987). Ajase (Ajatashatru) was the crown prince of the Magadha kingdom in India who lived during the time of Buddha (Encyclopedia Britannica Online, 1999). The story begins with events surrounding his birth. During this time, Ajase's father, King Binbashara (Bimbisara in Sanskrit), caused Ajase's mother, Queen Idaike (Vaidehi in Sanskrit), much emotional pain and distress. When Ajase grew up and learned about his mother's emotional sufferings, he imprisoned his father out of sympathy for his mother. Later, Ajase learned that his mother, out of loyalty to her husband, was secretly saving him from being starved to death in prison. He also found out that his mother was involved in certain dark secrets concerning his birth. He became outraged and tried to kill her. A court minister counseled him against this action. Ajase, overcome by remorse, developed a severe skin disease with an odor so horrible that it repelled everybody except his mother. She forgave his transgressions and cared for him. Ajase eventually recovered, and mother and son were reunited in mutual forgiveness.

The Ajase saga is a tale of compassion, forgiveness, and reunion, in contrast to the Oedipus tragedy, which evokes the fear of eternal guilt and permanent punishment. The differences in the focuses of the two stories are reflective of the differences between Asian and Western cultural values and worldviews. When Kosawa personally presented his thesis on the Ajase complex to Freud in 1932, his ideas gained no particular recognition (Okonogi, 1978). As Okonogi (1978, 1979), a protege of Kosawa, later speculated, the worlds and cultures of Freud and Kosawa were too far apart for Freud to comprehend the value of Kosawa's thesis and, likewise, for Kosawa to recognize how a cultural chasm prevented Freud from understanding his concepts.

In a similar vein, clinicians applying Freudian concepts to Asian American clients must be on the alert for cultural blind spots and follow Kosawa's exemplary effort in adapting these Western concepts to the Asian cultural context.

Transference and Countertransference

Transference and countertransference are important concepts of the psychoanalytic approach. In working with Asian American clients, clinicians, whether they are Asian American or non-Asian American, will find that the transference process is highly affected by the differences in cultural and social assimilation between themselves and their Asian American clients. Because the transference process is based on trust and idealization, Asian American clients may have difficulty establishing transference, an unconscious identification, toward a clinician whom they perceive as different in race, social class, culture, and life events such as migratory experiences. Hence, clinicians must take race and culture into consideration in analyzing the transference relationship (Chin, 1993; Comas-Diaz & Minrath, 1985; Yi, 1995). Several transference themes are common among Asian American clients. These include authority in hierarchical transference, power in racial transference, ethnic/self identity in self-object transference, and ethnic gender roles in preoedipal transference (Chin, 1993).

Hierarchical Transference

The concept of hierarchical transference refers to clients' assumptions about authority figures that dominate the client-clinician relationship. Many Asian American clients bring to their relationship with clinicians the Asian value of filial piety and respect for authority. For these clients, this Asian perspective of authority may contribute to their understanding of the clinician's role as well as influencing their expectations for the therapy. Because authority figures are idealized in Asian culture as benevolent, these Asian American clients frequently experience hierarchical transference as a positive relationship with the clinician that is similar to the relationship between a parent and child, in which a child expresses compliance and respect to a parent (Chin, 1993). By offering a positive interpretation of this culturally based hierarchical transference, clinicians can be more effective in assisting their Asian American clients to work through their transference, as well as to validate their cultural values.

Racial Transference

Racial transference may occur when Asian American clients have experienced blatant racial discrimination or indirect exclusion in their life situations. These experiences are based upon the power differential in their social environmental situation and often lead to negative attributions and assumptions about a clinician who is a member of the oppressing race. The attitude of these Asian American clients toward the clinician may have been elicited not by the therapy itself but rather by some reality-based situations that sustain their lack of trust in a clinician or in the therapeutic process (Chin, 1993). Often Asian American clients who are sensitive to their clinician's racial difference will experience feelings of powerlessness and helplessness, or at times resentment, that prompt them to withdraw from the clinician or to leave therapy. To resolve racial transference, clinicians need to support their clients in developing a positive racial identity while working through the transference relationship (Chin, 1993). Empowerment, or self-control over one's racial identity, is often one of the therapeutic goals in these situations.

Self-Object Transference

This concept is related to the cohesion or organizing capacity of the self (Chin, 1993). A positive self-object transference relationship is crucial because it can influence and create the interactional patterns that form the basis of self and object representations and, in turn, a healthy self-concept (Yi, 1995). For Asian American clients, as for most ethnic minority clients, this will often include a prominent ethnic dimension (Chin, 1993). Hence, in working through the self-object transference, a clinician must validate, maintain, or restore an Asian American client's positive ethnic identity in the therapeutic relationship (Chin, 1993). Clinicians need to be especially sensitive to Asian American clients who are struggling with the issue of biculturalism and split loyalties. On one hand, these individuals want to maintain traditions from their Asian cultural heritage, such as the traditional values emphasizing hierarchy, roles, and social etiquette, as well as interdependence and mutual obligations in familial and all interpersonal relationships (Tang, 1997; Yi, 1995). On the other hand, they feel compelled to adopt the cultural values and practices of mainstream United States. Indeed, this is a major challenge in the normal developmental process of Asian Americans. At times, Asian American clients may resort to sophisticated splitting mechanisms and may view their experiences in discontinuous terms (Chin, 1993). For instance, given the incompatibility of certain cultural values and practices, an individual may resolve to follow Asian cultural practices in some situations or areas, such as moral education for his or her children, and follow mainstream cultural practices in other situations or areas, such as business transactions. The clinician must acknowledge the realistic necessity of this splitting, rather than simplistically branding it as a primitive defense mechanism, as it is generally regarded in traditional psychoanalytic theory (Chin, 1993).

Preoedipal Transference

A client's unconscious recapitulation of the very early childhood relationship with a significant caretaker, typically the mother, leads to preoedipal transference. Its focus is on the mother-son dyad, and it is generally considered, in traditional psychoanalytic thought, a more primitive process than the Oedipal or erotic transference, which is focused on the father-son dyad (Chin, 1993). However, as indicated in our discussion of the Ajase complex, the magnificence of maternal love in the mother-son dyad is more congruent with Asian cultural values and worldviews than the Oedipus complex, which is Eurocentric and focused on the fear of retaliation from the father. In applying the Ajase story to Asian American clients, psychoanalytically oriented clinicians will need to consider the themes of guilt, somatization, and unconditional maternal love in understanding and working through the preoedipal transference (Chin, 1993). For example, a female clinician may trigger an Asian American client's primitive wishes for reunion with the preoedipal mother, as well as fears of either engulfment or abandonment by the mother. Without appreciation of Asian cultural values and norms, such as those illustrated by the Ajase story, clinicians may misinterpret the nature of the client's preoedipal transference. However, clinicians also need to be aware that ethnic gender roles are shifting for many Asian Americans. The traditional Asian worldviews that emphasize male dominance are being challenged as Asian countries become exposed to contemporary Western influences and, in particular, as Asians immigrate to the United States and enter into a Western society in which women have made significant gains in the direction of gender equality. Clinicians need to be aware that this evolving shift in dominance may create gender role ambivalence for Asian American clients in both their conscious and unconscious states of mind and in the manifestation of transference in therapy.

Countertransference

The concept of countertransference refers to a clinician's unconscious distortion of the client during the therapeutic process. Although Asian American clinicians may believe that they can more fully understand their Asian American clients because of perceived similarities between themselves and their clients, countertransference can develop whether a clinician is Asian American or non-Asian American (Aponte, Rivers, & Wohl, 1995; Atkinson et al., 1998; Sue, Ivey, & Pedersen, 1996; Sue & Sue, 1993, 1999). Even though Asian Americans throughout the world may share similar cultural beliefs and values, their life experiences are unique. Hence, the responsibility of all clinicians is to recognize and mediate their own internal states and tensions throughout the therapeutic process. To be skillful in self-mediation when working with Asian American clients, clinicians will need to explore their own perceptions, attitudes, and feelings about Asian Americans and Asian cultures. Such self-awareness and self-exploration are particularly crucial for clinicians using the psychoanalytic approach in therapy for Asian American clients.

The Technique of Interpretation

A major technique in psychoanalytic therapy is interpretation: That is, the clinician interprets and points out alternative ways clients can understand their own behaviors, emotions, and thoughts (Freud, 1912/1958a, 1911-1915/1958b; Friedman, 1985; Langs, 1974, 1988; Stark, 1999). In doing so, clinicians, whose interpretations can be effective only when they are relevant to their clients' experiences, must be knowledgeable about the cultural and social environmental contexts of their Asian American clients.

The decision of what to interpret is contingent on the cultural meaning given to the behaviors and experiences of Asian American clients. For example, when a client shows discomfort or hesitates to answer questions or to engage in conversation, culturally informed clinicians will reflect upon whether their inquiry is infringing on the client's sense of privacy from an Asian cultural perspective rather than interpreting the client's behavior as resistance. If the client's behaviors or feelings are normative or expected within the Asian cultural context, then they are not particularly significant for interpretation. In working with immigrant Asian American clients, clinicians need to be particularly cautious in attributing their clients' current functioning or problems to the effects of previous life events, specifically childhood events. Because of the cultural differences between Asian and Western child-rearing practices, normal Asian parenting may easily be misperceived as abusive or neglectful (Hong & Hong, 1991). Clinicians having a Western or mainstream American perspective on child rearing may misinterpret or even pathologize their clients' premigration childhood experiences that occurred in the Asian cultural and social environmental contexts.

In presenting an interpretation to a client, a clinician needs to attend to appropriate communication styles within the context of Asian cultures. In making interpretations about the internal emotional state of an Asian

American client, a clinician should be particularly sensitive to the client's feelings of shame or embarrassment. For example, issues concerning sex, an important content of the unconscious in psychoanalytic theory (Ford & Urban, 1963), are often embarrassing for many Asian American clients to discuss with a clinician because these issues are considered culturally to be very private matters (Hong, 1989). If clinicians draw attention to their clients' manifestation of these underlying emotions with an interpretation, they may only amplify already unbearable feelings that their clients are experiencing (Tang, 1997). This discomfort may lead to their clients' premature withdrawal from the therapeutic process. In these situations, indirect methods of attending to clients' internal states may be a more effective approach. For example, a clinician may refer to a client's internal state indirectly by using general comparisons, such as "Some/many people in this situation may feel . . . ." Sometimes, for a client who is more identified with and knowledgeable about Asian cultures, a clinician may offer an interpretation by using a culturally based saying, proverb, or metaphor to help the client achieve insights (Hong, 1993b). Regardless of the actual contents of interpretations, they must be communicated to the client in a socially and culturally appropriate manner that is congruent with the client's communication style and educational background. Otherwise, a clinician runs the risk of driving the client away from therapy.

In sum, when working with Asian American clients, clinicians using the psychoanalytic approach must be careful to engage their clients by relating to them in socially and culturally appropriate ways and proceeding in a manner that meets their clients' expectations. Culturally and social environmentally informed interpretations about transference and other aspects of the clinician-client relationship, and about clients' life experiences, particularly premigration childhood events, are key considerations in the effective application of psychoanalytic therapy with Asian American clients.

Case Illustration

P., a female college student from the Philippines, was referred for therapy by one of her professors. P. had been an outstanding student for the first half of the semester, but recently she had begun missing classes and assignments. At the same time, she had also started having severe stomach pains, headaches, insomnia, and crying spells. She had seen a physician for her ailments but had been told that no physical problem was evident.

P. was very reluctant to see a mental health clinician. She finally came because she felt so unhappy and was so concerned about her studies and inability to attend classes. In the initial session, she was willing to describe only her behaviors related to school and to her study habits. The clinician

encouraged P. to continue with her studies and refrained from making interpretations about her inability to attend classes or to complete assignments. In this initial session, the clinician reassured P. that in time she
would be able to return to class. She also suggested some methods for relaxation prior to bedtime so that P. could sleep through the night.

As the sessions continued, the clinician encouraged P. to talk about her
decision to come to the United States for her education. P. was very willing
to discuss this issue, which led to discussions about her immediate and extended family in the Philippines. As she talked about her family members
she would often cry, speak longingly of them, and express her wish to return home. However, whenever the clinician offered support of her expressed thoughts of returning to the Philippines, P. would stop talking and
remain silent for a long time. Then she would resume talking in a soft hesitating voice. The clinician simply encouraged P. to continue talking about
her family and to reexperience her feelings through tearful retelling of
family events, rather than offering interpretations on the manifestations of
her unconscious need for her family. This pattern for the sessions continued for almost 6 months. Toward the end of this period, P. was able to return to class. By this time, both the clinician and client had formed a firm
working alliance with each other.

For the following 4 months, P. discussed issues related to her class participation. Throughout this period of treatment, the clinician connected
the family vignettes P. had described in earlier sessions with descriptions
of her thoughts about her professors and classes. These interpretations
helped P. gain insights about the associations between her family and her
academic experiences. At the end of the first year, a breakthrough occurred. P. confided to the clinician that she had been raped by her uncle a
few months after she came to the United States. This uncle was her
mother's brother, who had agreed to let P. live with him and his family
while she was attending college in the United States. P. had always liked
this uncle and his family, so she initially felt very happy and secure living
with them. However, soon after her arrival, P. was aware that her uncle was
sexually interested in her and that he often touched her breasts "acciden-
tally." Several months later, he came into her room one night and raped her.
P. was terrified but felt she could not tell her parents or anyone else what
had happened.

For the 6 months of treatment following this disclosure, the clinician explored with P. the reasons for her inability to discuss the rape with her
mother, whom she loved dearly as her closest confidant. With the clinician's encouragement, P. was able to discuss the shame she felt for having
"provoked" her uncle to rape her. "It was my fault," she said, "How could I
ever bring shame to him by telling my mother what her brother did?" Even
though P. was able to talk about the rape in therapy, she was not able to tell

her mother or any other member of the family what had happened to her. After the second year of therapy, she decided to return to the Philippines. In her last session, P. told the clinician that her "secret" would remain with memories of the therapy and the clinician but would never be told to anyone else.

Discussion

In working with this client, the clinician was culturally sensitive to her desire to seek immediate relief for her somatic complaints and resolution of her school-related problems. In the initial stage of therapy, the clinician engaged the client by focusing on these issues and offered suggestions to help her sleep and handle school, rather than challenging her with interpretive analyses of the underlying causes of her symptoms. Throughout the first part of therapy, the clinician respected the client's perspective and was careful not to jump to conclusions and make direct interpretations or confrontations about the client's behaviors or emotions. For example, the clinician could have reacted to the client's hesitating soft voice and frequent periods of silence by interpreting her manner of communication as apparent resistance to approaching the issues of returning to the Philippines. If the clinician had followed through with this interpretation, she would have heightened the client's awareness that she had breached a cultural norm in disclosing family issues to an outsider. Also, the clinician would have intensified the client's shame and embarrassment about losing her emotional composure and about failing to meet her parents' expectation to succeed in college. Instead, the clinician simply encouraged the client to continue discussing situations concerning her studies and her family. When the client disclosed the rape incident, the clinician attended to both the cultural and social environmental aspects of the client's predicament. The clinician knew that, from the client's cultural perspective, if the incident were disclosed to other family members, the client would experience feelings of shame, as well potential disruption to her family relationships. The clinician appreciated and respected the client's eventual decision not to inform her family of the incident. From an Asian cultural perspective, this was a noble act of self-restraint and sacrifice. The clinician was also aware that, as a newcomer to the United States, the client's social environmental situation provided her with no close friends or confidants for emotional support except her uncle's family, from which she was alienated. Because the clinician understood the effects of social isolation on the client, she respected and supported the client's decision to return to the Philippines. She understood the client's decision as a reasonable choice that, at this stage of therapy, was a conscious and deliberate decision made with a sense of resolution rather than distress. The client demonstrated her trust in the clinician by confiding a secret to her and by respectfully terminating from therapy. By adapting the psychoanalytic approach to the client's Asian cultural perspective, the clinician was able to gain her client's trust and to help her client arrive at a resolution that was congruent with her cultural and social environmental contexts.

Person-Centered Therapy With Asian American Clients

Person-centered therapy is practiced by many clinicians with a humanistic orientation. The theoretical concepts and therapeutic methods of the humanistic orientation are based on the client's subjective and phenomenological point of view, and they emphasize the client's potential for self-direction and self-actualization (Corey, 1996; Ford & Urban, 1963; Lietaer, Rombauts, & VanBalen, 1990; Mokuau & Matsuoka, 1992; Raskin & Rogers, 1995; Rogers, 1957). Many key concepts of person-centered therapy are syntonic with traditional Asian cultural worldviews and values. The most remarkable parallels are this therapeutic approach's premise of the innate goodness of human nature and its concepts of empathy, insight, self-knowledge, and self-actualization, which are similar, in substance, to the fundamental concepts of Asian philosophies concerning human benevolence, compassion, and the quest for self-understanding, virtue, enlightenment, and perfection (Ham, 1993; Tu, 1991; Yamamoto & Chang, 1987). Thus, the key concepts of person-centered therapy are appropriate for application to Asian American clients who are identified with Asian cultures. The challenge for clinicians is to ensure that the therapeutic strategies and techniques are likewise applied with cultural sensitivity (Ishiyama & Westwood, 1992; Westwood & Ishiyama, 1990).

Person-centered therapy does not emphasize the use of therapeutic techniques. Its focus is on the therapeutic process and on the personal qualities, attitudes, and beliefs of a clinician. The clinician-client relationship is the basis of therapeutic interventions and is the critical variable responsible for therapeutic change. This relationship is characterized by three core conditions: (a) congruence—a clinician's genuineness and authenticity; (b) unconditional positive regard—a clinician's acceptance, respect, and deep and genuine caring for a client; and (c) empathy—a clinician's sensitivity and understanding of a client's subjective experiences and feelings, as if the clinician were in the "shoes" of the client (Corey, 1996; Rogers, 1957, 1975; Truax & Carkhuff, 1967). These three core therapeutic conditions are expressed through clinical skills such as active listening, attending, clarifying, reflecting, summarizing, and appropriate self-disclosure. The therapeutic process of healing begins immediately, at the first encounter between a clinician and a client. A clinician begins to establish a therapeutic environment by showing respect for a client and by initiating the therapeutic process in whatever way makes a client comfortable. Throughout the therapeutic process, a clinician relies on a client's capability of making decisions about the process of therapy: for example, introducing content for discussion, disclosing problems, and determining the frequency of the therapy. Clinicians, using person-centered therapy, maintain a nonjudgmental stance, listen empathically, and then demonstrate empathic understanding to their clients. In the following discussion, we will adhere to the theoretical focus of this therapeutic approach by emphasizing the clinician-client relationship rather than elaborating on clinical techniques. We will also focus on particular aspects of the therapeutic process that need special attention when applied to the cultural and social environmental contexts of Asian American clients.

Nondirective Focus

The person-centered approach minimizes the importance of diagnostic assessment and advice giving by a clinician. In the initial stage of therapy, a clinician does not emphasize taking a detailed history or background information of a client. Rather, he or she prefers to let the client take the lead in bringing up issues in the therapy sessions and refrains from giving instructions and advice. However, as discussed in Chapter 6, many Asian American clients expect a clinician to take an active and visible role in assessing their presenting problems, as well as giving instructions for symptom relief or guidance for problem resolution (Gaw, 1993; Hong, 1998, 1993a, 1993b; Hong et al., 1995; Lee, 1980, 1982, 1997c; Shon & Ja, 1982; Sue & Morishima, 1982; Uba, 1994). Thus, a nondirective focus, if used mechanically, may create a very uncomfortable situation for Asian American clients and may even create enough tension for them to discontinue therapy. To engage these clients, clinicians need to remember that one of the basic tenets of person-centered therapy is to provide a therapeutic environment where clients can feel psychologically safe enough to explore their problems, to flourish, and to progress toward self-actualization. In this regard, clinicians can help their Asian American clients feel more comfortable by providing structure and therapeutically appropriate instructions or advice. Instead of mechanically applying a nondirective format, clinicians need to practice the spirit of person-centered therapy by being sensitive to their Asian American clients' cultural orientation and offering them guidelines, particularly in the initial stage of therapy. Clinicians can gradually inform their clients of the rationale and process of person-centered therapy and then ease them into a nondirective process. Moving too fast into a nondirective mode, especially in the first few sessions, may simply discourage Asian American clients from continuing therapy.

Empathy

Empathy is a fundamental skill and a process in person-centered therapy. To be empathic, a clinician needs to possess an attitude of profound interest in a client's world of meanings and feelings and to offer a client a sense of appreciation and respect (Raskin & Rogers, 1995). In an empathic therapeutic process, clinicians feel along with their clients, intellectually understand their clients' experiences, and, most importantly, communicate to their clients that they are being accurately understood. This is essentially a multistep process: (a) perceiving verbal and nonverbal behaviors of the client; (b) accurately understanding the meanings of the client's behaviors; (c) experiencing affective responses to the client's messages while remaining as free as possible from cognitive distortions such as stereotyping and value judgments; (d) separating feelings shared with the client from those held alone by the clinician; and (e) accurately communicating feelings back to client so that he or she feels understood (Ham, 1993; Keefe, 1976; Rogers, 1957, 1975; Truax & Carkhuff, 1967). When working with Asian American clients who are identified with Asian cultures, empathy can become a bridge connecting the worlds and cultures of clinicians and their clients (Ham, 1993). However, to be truly empathic with these clients, clinicians need to be aware of the broad conceptualization of empathy. Empathy is a complex construct that includes at least five dimensions: affective empathy, cognitive empathy, predictive empathy, cultural empathy, and active empathy (Buie, 1981; Ham, 1993; Jenkins, 1997; O'Hara, 1997; Wu, 1987; Yamamoto, 1982; Yamamoto & Chang, 1987). These five dimensions are interrelated as trait (affective empathy), skills (cognitive and predictive empathy), and process (cultural and active empathy) (Ham, 1993).

Affective Empathy

Because of our human nature, we often find ourselves responding spontaneously to strong emotions exhibited by other individuals. This aspect of emotional response is an example of the affective dimension of empathy. In a therapeutic relationship, clinicians may experience feelings similar to the feelings of their clients, at the levels of intensity expressed by their clients (Buie, 1981). This sharing of feelings does not necessarily lead to an accurate understanding of clients' feelings. However, even when clinicians misinterpret the meanings that clients give for their own feelings, they still have a sense that their clients are experiencing certain emotions. This shared emotional experience, an empathic resonance, enables clinicians to have an intuitive awareness of their clients' feelings. When clinicians use their trait of affective empathy, they become aware of their internal state of emotional resonance with their Asian American clients, regardless of how unfamiliar their clients' experiences are to them. For example, a clinician may not know much about the stress and tension of life in Vietnam during the Vietnam War. Yet the clinician can still sense a Vietnamese American client's intense emotions as the client describes her premigration experiences in the war-torn country. This sensitivity or emotional resonance serves as a connection between clinician and client. In working with Asian American clients, clinicians need to make use of this intuitive awareness to get attuned to their clients' emotions.

Cognitive Empathy

This dimension of empathy refers to clinicians' cognitive awareness of their clients' unique social and cultural experiences and to their understanding of their Asian American clients' cultural traditions, values, and worldviews. In particular, clinicians trained in the United States and Asian American clients identified with Asian cultures may have very different cultural and social schemas: that is, cognitive structures for taking in, processing, and communicating information (Ham, 1993; Yamamoto & Chang, 1987). Clinicians who are knowledgeable about cultural and social schemas recognize that Asian American clients identified with Asian cultures may cognitively structure their social experiences and express their emotions in ways that are different from mainstream American culture. Take, for example, a client who has suffered a misfortune. He is feeling sad and distressed. However, from a traditional Asian point of view, he also accepts the misfortune as fate and is resigned to it. A clinician with affective empathy may be able to sense this client's sadness, yet, lacking cognitive empathy, may not be able to comprehend his belief in fate. Without cognitive empathy, a clinician may misperceive this client's acceptance of fate as a manifestation of despair and hopelessness. A culturally informed clinician would be more likely to understand this client's idea of fate as a sense of resolution and consolation—that is, a positive cognitive expression that he could rebound from grief and move on with his life. Such perceptual errors are hard to detect because, in this case, the clinician would be partially correct in sensing the client's sadness. Hence, to work effectively with Asian American clients, clinicians must develop their cognitive empathic skills by learning, from the literature and from direct interpersonal experiences, about Asian cognitive structures embedded in cultural and social schemas (Ham, 1993).

Predictive Empathy

In interpersonal interactions, we often rely on inferences to anticipate what others may feel and how others may behave. Clinicians, using their personal and training experiences, often predict or make inferences about their clients before they engage in a therapeutic relationship with them. This predictive empathy, which is closely related to cognitive empathy, is a double-edged sword, particularly when applied to Asian American clients (Ham, 1993; Wu, 1987). If clinicians have accurate knowledge of their clients' cultures and worldviews, this process can help to engage their clients in therapy. However, if clinicians rely on faulty preconceived notions and stereotypes about Asian American characteristics and values, they will create a contaminated therapeutic environment based on inaccurate data and a distorted version of reality. This situation will certainly not be conducive to their clients' therapeutic progress. For example, a client who is strongly identified with Asian cultures is looking for instructions and advice in the initial sessions. A clinician with accurate predictive empathy will understand this client's expectation and will address his or her needs by offering directions or by explaining the rationale for not doing so. The clinician will do this in the early stage of therapy and thus preempt the need for the client to express concerns about the lack of directions. A clinician who does not have sufficient knowledge or experience about Asian Americans will be unable to anticipate this client's needs and will instead have to wait for the client to voice a complaint about the lack of instructions and advice. By that time, the client may already be disappointed at the clinician or doubtful of the clinician's sensitivity and competence. Clinicians with accurate predictive empathy are like gracious hosts or hostesses who can anticipate what their guests will like and dislike, or what their guests will need from time to time, and who can accordingly provide for the comfort of their guests. In contrast, less responsive hosts or hostesses will wait for their guests to point out to them that something is missing or unsatisfactory.

Given the differences between Asian and mainstream American cultures, clinicians need to examine carefully their own interpersonal experiences to ensure that they are making accurate inferences about their Asian American clients. Besides didactic training and literature review, participation in field experience and immersion in community activities are ways for clinicians to develop predictive empathy skills.

Cultural Empathy

This dimension expands Rogers' (1975) concept of empathy by adding to other dimensions of a person's empathic skill the ability to step into the culture of another person (Wu, 1987). Clinicians' ability to do this allows them to appreciate fully the cultural underpinnings of their clients' experiences and emotions. One common assumption is that culture is learned behavior that can be acquired or understood through experience. However, many behavioral norms and symbolic representations in a particular culture are invisible to individuals within the culture (Wu, 1987). Clinicians' unconscious acceptance of their own cultural norms and values may limit their appreciation of the cultural context of clients from other cultures. Hence, clinicians who are fully identified with their own culture may have difficulty feeling affection and devotion toward the culture of their Asian American clients. These clinicians, to work effectively with clients who are identified with Asian cultures, will need to develop their intercultural empathy (Ham 1993).

Cultural empathy is experienced and communicated as both intracultural empathy and intercultural empathy. Intracultural empathy, the emotions or intrapsychic feelings commonly experienced by individuals within the same culture, is developed from shared experiences, as when a child feels joy along with others over a festival or feels awed along with others by a religious ritual. When individuals within a culture have experienced similar feelings in response to shared cultural events, they are better able to engage in an intracultural empathic process (Ham, 1993; Wu, 1987). To develop intercultural empathy, clinicians need to experience the feelings associated with the cultural events of clients from other cultures. Much like anthropologists learning about cultures, clinicians can enhance their cultural empathy by consulting the literature, analyzing and contrasting cultural themes in Asian versus Western myths and folktales, and observing individuals in their social interactions and social groupings (Ham, 1993; Wu, 1987; Yamamoto & Chang, 1987). Because cultural empathy requires clinicians to experience subjectively their Asian American clients' cultures, immersion and direct participation in the social cultural environment of their Asian American clients through internships and other community work can be a helpful way to develop cultural empathic skills.

Active Empathy

In the final step of the empathic process, clinicians must communicate to their clients that they understand and intuitively feel their emotions and experiences. For empathy to be effective in a therapeutic relationship, clinicians must respect and acknowledge their clients' perceptions about the empathic interaction. Only clients themselves know whether they feel understood and whether their clinicians' empathic communication is accurate. Consequently, if a client does not perceive a clinician as empathic, then the clinician has not accurately communicated empathic understanding to the client (Ham, 1993; Keefe, 1976; Rogers, 1957, 1975; Truax & Carkhuff, 1967). Clients need to realize that the clinician truly understands, cares, and respects them. Thus, empathy is more likely to be understood by Asian American clients if it is communicated in a culturally syntonic manner.

In Asian cultures, care and respect for others are expressed not solely by words but often by actions, such as doing something or giving something to the other person (Hong, 1989; Shon & Ja, 1982). This practical manner of expressing care and concern to another person is known as *active empathy,* a term coined by Yamamoto (1982). It conveys the Asian cultural emphasis on actively demonstrating, in the empathic process, appreciation and understanding of another person. As applied to therapy with Asian American clients, active empathy involves a clinician's demonstrating care and respect to a client by trying to do something helpful to solve a client's problems (Ham, 1993; Hong, 1993b; Yamamoto & Chang, 1987). This may involve, or even warrant, giving the client instructions, advice, feedback, or other information, depending on the particular situation. Active empathy goes beyond a clinician's verbal expressions of understanding a client's feelings and situation and actually demonstrates to clients that a clinician cares enough to do something about their problems (Hong, 1993b).

Enhancing Client Involvement and Self-Expression

In person-centered therapy, a clinician encourages clients to express themselves more fully as a way to gain insight and self-awareness and move toward self-actualization (Mokuau & Matsuoka, 1992; Rogers, 1957, 1975). However, conventional therapeutic procedures emphasizing a client's verbal expressions may not always be effective, particularly for those Asian American clients who feel inhibited about freely expressing themselves to strangers and outsiders—in this case, a clinician. If the therapy is conducted in English, verbal expression may be problematic for clients who speak English as a second language (Keitel et al., 1996; Yansen & Shulman, 1996), as discussed in previous chapters. Compounded with the nuances of cross-cultural communication, mutual misunderstanding can easily occur between these Asian American clients and a non-Asian American clinician. All of these problems create serious challenges for clinicians using the person-centered approach. One solution for these obstacles is to use alternative ways to facilitate the clients' involvement and self-expression (Ishiyama, 1995; Westwood & Ishiyama, 1990). Westwood and Ishiyama (1990) have suggested a number of alternative strategies that can be used in cross-cultural counseling to enhance the active involvement of clients in the process of communicating with clinicians. These strategies are syntonic with the person-centered approach and can be considered for application when a client's verbal expression is impeded. In the following discussion, we will describe some of these strategies that may be particularly helpful in working with Asian American clients identified with Asian cultures.

Express Feelings in the Client's First Language

One way to enhance client involvement and self-expression is for clinicians to encourage clients to speak in their first language when they are describing feelings (Westwood & Ishiyama, 1990). This provides an opportunity for ventilation of feelings and free expression of thoughts. Even if a clinician does not understand a client's verbal language, the paralanguage, such as voice tone, intonation, and pitch, can reveal information about the client's emotional state.

Use Alternative Modes of Communication

Clinicians may find that metaphorical ways of communication, such as acting, storytelling, music, drawing, and other activities can help increase a client's comfort and involvement with therapy (Westwood & Ishiyama, 1990). In using any of these methods, clinicians often discover that not all clients may benefit from the same activity or respond with the same levels of comfort to a particular activity. For example, some clients may find acting or role playing helpful in expressing themselves, whereas others may find they are embarrassed to participate in such activities. Because of clients' varying reactions to these therapeutic activities, clinicians need to be mindful of arbitrarily imposing any of them on clients and, in all circumstances, must respect a client's decision not to perform them.

Checking the Clinician's Perceptions and Interpretations

Because nonverbal expressions such as gestures, mannerisms, body posture, and personal space are often culturally based, clinicians need to check with their clients about the accuracy of their perceptions and interpretations (Westwood & Ishiyama, 1990). However, clinicians need to be aware that clients may feel overly self-conscious or embarrassed when too much attention is given to their appearances, mannerisms, or other behaviors. Attention to cultural sensitivity and social etiquette is essential in checking perceptions and interpretations.

Learn Culturally Meaningful Phrases

Clinicians can gain a better empathic understanding of their clients' emotions and perceptions by learning culturally meaningful phrases used by their clients to express their inner processes (Westwood & Ishiyama, 1990). Clinicians may even ask their clients to teach them these expressions or phrases. However, the focus of this "teaching" activity must remain on the therapeutic process, such as reinforcing the clinician-client alliance, enhancing a client's sense of competence, and involving a client in the communication process. This activity should not be done for the purpose of simply satisfying a clinician's own curiosity or need for knowledge.

In sum, even though the core theoretical concepts of person-centered therapy, such as insight development and self-actualization, are consonant with Asian cultures, clinicians still need to adapt their therapeutic strategies to meet the expectations and needs of Asian American clients. This often requires a clinician to focus more on an active demonstration of empathy rather than on a nondirective empathic approach. Furthermore, the central role of empathy and the clinician-client relationship in person-centered therapy provides a compelling reason for clinicians using this approach to be knowledgeable about the cultural and social environmental issues concerning Asian Americans. In addition to reading the literature and attending workshops, clinicians may find it helpful to experience the cultural and the social environmental contexts of their Asian American clients by direct participation in their cultural events and community activities.

Case Illustration

H., a 40-year-old woman who immigrated from Hong Kong to the United States 12 years ago, was mandated to seek therapy by a state social service agency because of her violent behavior toward her middle child, a boy age 9. Initially, H. herself called the police to report that her son had threatened to harm her with a knife. Later, the police informed the social service agency of possible family violence and child abuse, and H. was mandated to seek therapy.

H. was first assigned to see a white social service clinician who described having a difficult relationship with her. Even though H. openly discussed the factual aspects of her family history, which were filled with violence and abuse, the clinician felt that H. was unwilling to express her attitudes and deeper feelings. She often sensed that H. was overly compliant and accepting of her suggestions and might just be pretending to cooperate. She felt that H. was withholding information about her feelings and relationships about other people in her current life, such as her husband or her son's teacher. Not only was the clinician sensing that H. lacked trust in her, but the clinician herself was beginning to recognize her own feelings of mistrust for H. After three sessions, the clinician recommended that H. be seen by a clinician with a better understanding of her Asian cultural perspective, and she transferred H. to an Asian American clinician.

In the first session with the Asian American clinician, H. expressed relief to be reassigned to someone who would understand her cultural background. She then focused on the rage she felt toward the state system for betraying her: "They told me to ask for help, and then they made me feel as if I had done something wrong." In using the person-centered approach, the clinician conveyed empathy for H.'s situation by accepting H.'s feelings and attitudes. In subsequent sessions, the clinician continued to provide a nonjudgmental and supportive therapeutic environment that helped H. to ventilate and to explore her intense rage toward the police and the social service agency. Throughout these sessions, the clinician demonstrated a caring, attentive, and respectful attitude that reassured H. that the clinician could tolerate her anger. This attitude also conveyed to H. that the therapy sessions were a safe context for her to openly express her feelings and thoughts. H. gradually became less angry in the therapy sessions and started to seek advice and guidance from the clinician about ways of addressing her family situation. Once the clinician was confident that H.'s expectations for therapy were culturally appropriate, she began to focus more on the use of active empathy in the sessions, such as offering advice on ways for H. to contact and speak with her son's teacher and with the social service agency.

After 4 months of therapy, H. expressed gratitude to the clinician and commented that she felt respected and heard. In subsequent sessions, H. talked about her problematic relationship with her mother, whom she perceived as critical and controlling. In these discussions, she often expressed feelings of worthlessness. She shamefully related to the clinician that she had become a mother similar to her own. Her fervent hope was for the new country, the United States, to transform her into a new person. After 6 months of therapy, many of H.'s issues had been resolved. H. had established a positive relationship with her son's teacher, and the social service department terminated their supervision of H. and her son.

Even though H. was no longer mandated to seek therapy, she voluntarily continued treatment with the Asian American clinician. In the therapy sessions, she continued to discuss her self-esteem issues. She also enrolled in a college as a fulfillment of an adolescent dream of getting a college degree in the United States. However, in the eighth month of therapy, the clinician sensed tension in the therapeutic relationship. During one session, H. seemed particularly uninvolved with and distant from the clinician. The clinician shared her observation with H. H. agreed and then admitted that she no longer wanted an Asian American clinician as a role model and confidant. Her comment was, "How can you understand me when I am trying to be an American and not so Chinese?" Although the clinician disclosed her own experiences of acculturation as an effort to demonstrate empathic understanding for H.'s feelings, H. seemed to see the disclosure as a directive on how to be an "American" and responded that she considered the clinician's disclosure as unhelpful. After this session, she telephoned the clinician to terminate therapy.

Discussion

The clinician's appreciation and empathic understanding of the cultural and social environmental contexts of this client were particularly germane for understanding the dramatic shifts in her therapeutic progress. As an immigrant who was unfamiliar with mainstream American institutions and cultural attitudes toward family violence, the client called the police for help, thinking they would help her. Instead, she found herself being investigated and placed under the social service agency's supervision. Because she did not understand the nature of therapy, she reacted to it as if it were a punishment and an interrogation. Possibly, the client's mistrust of the white clinician was created by their racial differences. Also, being assigned a white clinician may have heightened the client's perception that she was being misunderstood and unfairly treated by the "foreign" white institutions. Taken together, these issues could have contributed to the client's problematic relationship with this white clinician. Furthermore, as the clinician admitted, she might have been overly suspicious of the client simply because of her own cultural misperceptions and lack of cultural knowledge. This, in turn, could have fueled the client's mistrust further. Transferring the client to an Asian American clinician made it easier for the client to feel that she would be heard and understood accurately. Using the person-centered approach, the Asian American clinician presented a therapeutic environment that was understanding, accepting, nonjudgmental, and respectful. This safe environment helped the client feel that she was not being investigated or punished. Hence, she opened up to this clinician and later chose to continue therapy when she was no longer mandated to do so.

At the beginning of therapy, the client had very low self-esteem and was burdened with her intense negative and conflicting feelings about her mother and herself as a mother. These were feelings that she had never dealt with directly or disclosed to anybody. In the supportive and nonevaluative therapeutic environment of the person-centered approach, the client felt psychologically secure enough to examine her feelings about her role as a mother, as well as her desire to start a new life as a "new person" in the United States. Once free from her fear of negative criticism, the client was able to move toward trusting her own self-evaluations and ideas. Her decision to seek out experiences that she perceived as different from her Asian heritage and to terminate from a therapeutic relationship that she perceived would prevent her growth was, paradoxically, a sign of therapeutic success. Instead of doubting herself, she was confident enough to recognize that she could pursue her development outside the context of therapy. At termination, she had gained significant insights and clarified issues concerning herself and her life goals.

Cognitive Behavioral Therapy With Asian American Clients

The cognitive behavioral orientation emphasizes assessing the behaviors, thoughts, and perceptions associated with clients' problems and emotions and offers advice and instructions for resolving these issues. Clinicians using this therapeutic approach seek to help clients replace maladaptive behaviors, thoughts, and perceptions with adaptive ones and learn new behaviors, new ways of thinking and of making inferences about the events that are affecting them emotionally (Beck, 1976, 1995; Corey, 1996; Ellis & Dryden, 1997; Masters, Burish, Hollon, & Rimm, 1987). In addition to instructions, advice, and practice during the therapy sessions, clinicians may also give homework assignments to clients, such as having clients practice or try out certain skills and behaviors, implement a contingency management plan, or engage in specific activities between sessions. Clinicians using the cognitive behavioral approach assume a role analogous to that of advisers or teachers who actively provide instructions to clients, or to that of medical doctors who give "prescriptions" to alleviate clients' symptoms and problems. The action-oriented format and problem-focused nature of this therapeutic orientation are culturally congruent with the expectations of many Asian American clients. These clients expect a mental health clinician to be an authority or expert who will focus actively on their problems and will provide instructions for symptom relief or problem resolution (Hong, 1988, 1989, 1993b; Lee, 1982, 1997b; Shon & Ja, 1982; Uba, 1994). With such congruence, the cognitive behavioral approach can be very appealing to Asian American clients who are identified with Asian cultures.

Although Asian American clients often expect their clinicians to assume the role of an authority figure or expert, clinicians need to be aware of the distinction between being authoritative and being authoritarian (Hong, 1989, 1993b). Clinicians should be authoritative in the sense of being professionals with expert knowledge about treating or relieving their clients' problems, as opposed to being authoritarian, arrogant, and arbitrary. They need to be courteous, respectful, and empathic to their clients' ideas and feelings and particularly to their clients' culture. Most importantly, clinicians using the cognitive behavioral approach need to avoid the pitfall of being too task oriented and neglecting the significance of establishing and maintaining rapport with clients. Small talk and other social culturally appropriate ice-breakers in the therapy sessions are often helpful for easing clients into discussions of their intimate thoughts, perceptions, and behaviors.

A key factor for successful application of cognitive behavioral therapy with Asian American clients is a clinician's ability to accurately assess a client's behaviors, thoughts, and perceptions in the context of Asian cultural values, norms, and worldviews and in the context of a client's social environmental condition. This assessment includes determining treatment goals that are syntonic with a client's cultural and social environmental contexts. A related factor is a clinician's skill in communicating and clarifying to clients the therapeutic methods, objectives, and concepts in a culturally syntonic manner. We will focus on these issues in the following discussion.

Assessing Problems and Determining Treatment Goals

Problem identification and assessment play an important role in cognitive behavioral therapy. A clinician typically begins therapy by acquiring specific information about the various dimensions of a client's problems, such as frequency, duration, intensity, and other related circumstances. The process of therapy continues as a clinician identifies the contingencies, the rewards and punishments, related to a client's problem behaviors or examines the maladaptive thoughts, irrational beliefs, perceptions, autonomic thoughts, and cognitive errors or distortions that contribute to a client's emotional distress. A clinician then makes plans for instructing a client on ways to modify the maladaptive behaviors, thoughts, and perceptions into adaptive ones and to learn and practice new behaviors, new thoughts, and new ways of perceiving problematic life events (Beck, 1976, 1995; Corey, 1996; Ellis & Dryden, 1997; Masters et al., 1987).

In working with Asian American clients, clinicians need to define and identify adaptive and maladaptive behaviors and cognitions within their clients' cultural and environmental contexts. One example is the definition of assertiveness. As discussed in Chapter 5, Asian and mainstream American cultures have different conceptualizations of what constitutes assertive behavior (Hong, 1989; Hong & Friedman, 1998; Lee, 1997c; Shon & Ja, 1982; Uba, 1994). A misinformed clinician can easily misperceive an Asian American client to be lacking in assertiveness and then offer assertiveness training as an intervention strategy. Even for clients who can benefit from assertiveness training, a clinician must be alert to the cultural differences in the expression of assertiveness. We have frequently encountered Asian American children who learned "assertiveness" from school counseling programs that followed the mainstream model and ignored the Asian cultural context. As a result of this training, these children were criticized by their parents or community as being socially abrasive, curt, or simply rude when they "expressed" themselves "directly" at home or in community settings. Hence, a culturally responsive assertiveness training program needs to include discussions of social cultural contexts to direct clients to learn different ways of behaving assertively in different settings. At times, some immigrant Asian American clients do not lack assertiveness, but they can benefit from learning about the norms of behavior for expressing their ideas and needs in mainstream settings. A clinician may use the technique of assertiveness training to help these clients to learn and practice new ways of behaving and expressing themselves. However, if a clinician uses the phrase *assertiveness training* to describe treatment goals, the clients may question the clinician's diagnostic accuracy, treatment competency, and cultural sensitivity. Instead of using this phrase, our own practice is to discuss with these clients that we are teaching them the norms of mainstream behavior that are essential for clear communication and success in their new host society. This explanation defines the treatment goal as learning a "survival skill" for daily living in the United States, rather than remediating a personality or social "deficit."

In a similar way, when clinicians assess their clients' problems and formulate treatment goals and strategies, they need to apply other cognitive behavioral constructs and techniques, such as contingency management, reinforcers, irrational beliefs, autonomic thoughts, and cognitive errors or distortions, to Asian American cultural and social environmental contexts. A culturally syntonic approach to conceptualizing problems will increase the likelihood of clinicians' designing an appropriate intervention program (Hong, 1993b; Hong et al., 1995; Mokuau & Matsuoka, 1992).

Application of Asian Cultural Concepts and Practices

Many cognitive behavioral therapeutic concepts and techniques commonly used by clinicians are actually very similar to ideas and practices found within Asian cultures. For instance, the cognitive behavioral concepts about modifying a person's expectations, irrational beliefs, or cognitive distortions are syntonic with traditional Asian philosophical concepts about achieving internal peace or character development through self-restraint, seeking harmony, being content, eliminating greed, lowering one's desires, and avoiding extreme emotions and attitudes. When working with clients identified with Asian cultures, we often find it helpful to relate cognitive behavioral therapy concepts and strategies to Asian cultural concepts (Ham, 1989; Hong, 1993b; Hong et al., 1995). This "bridging" (Ham, 1989) may help clinicians gain their clients' trust and cooperation. Usually, just a brief discussion of the similarities between the cognitive behavioral strategies and the Asian cultural concepts will be sufficient. Sometimes clinicians can also use a simple example from Asian folk traditions or philosophical principles to illustrate an issue (Hong, 1993b). In most situations, a clinician does not need to give a lengthy discourse on these concepts. The point we want to emphasize here is that we find it more effective to teach Asian American clients new cognitive behavioral skills by using terms and concepts that are familiar to them than by using Western-based professional jargon that is foreign to them.

Relaxation Exercises

Among the various cognitive behavioral techniques, relaxation exercises are probably the ones that have generated the greatest number of questions from the Asian American clients in our clinical practices. These clients often want to know the relationship between relaxation exercises and certain traditional Asian health exercises that they have heard about or are already practicing.

There are different forms of relaxation techniques in cognitive behavioral therapy. The commonly used forms include meditative-breathing exercises, use of peaceful or relaxing imagery, and muscle relaxation. These exercises are very similar to Asian health or spiritual practices discussed in Chapter 2, such as *Qi Qong* (*Chi Kung*), a form of meditative exercise with a focus on breathing; *Tai Ji Quan* (*Tai Chi Chuan*), a form of martial arts roughly analogous to aerobics in slow motion, combining calisthenics, dance, meditation, and controlled breathing; and Zen meditation, a meditative exercise with focused thinking, as well as other practices (Bankart, 1997; Smith, 1991; Wallace & Benson, 1972). Among these Asian practices, *Qi Qong* (*Chi Kung*) and *Tai Ji Quan* (*Tai Chi Chuan*) are particularly popular and are commonly practiced as health-enhancing exercises, especially in China. When we teach relaxation exercises to clients identified with Asian cultures, we often point out the similarities between these techniques and the traditional Asian practices. This explanation makes the relaxation exercises more culturally palatable to the clients and is very helpful for engaging them in therapy. However, we are also careful to inform clients that relaxation exercises are not identical to the traditional Asian practices, even though their basic principles are similar. For example, there is a cultural belief that practicing *Qi Qong* (*Chi Kung*) improperly may lead to psychoticlike symptoms. This condition is actually identified in the *DSM-IV* (American Psychiatric Association, 1994) as a culture-bound syndrome called *Qi Qong* psychotic reaction. If clients believe that practicing relaxation exercises is identical to practicing *Qi Qong* (*Chi Kung*), some psychologically vulnerable clients may worry excessively about practicing the exercises incorrectly and also may be at risk of developing the psychotic reaction. In addition, some forms or schools of *Qi Qong* (*Chi Kung*) and Zen meditation have strong spiritual and religious connotations that, if equated with relaxation exercises, may create internal conflicts for clients who hold other religious beliefs. Hence, clinicians must also draw the fine line between relaxation exercises and these practices.

As discussed in Chapter 5, Asian American clients have a tendency to report physical discomforts when they experience psychological or emotional problems (Gaw, 1993; Hong et al., 1995; Kleinman, 1977, 1982; Lee, 1997c; Lin, 1985, 1996; Sue & Morishima, 1982; Tseng, 1975; Uba, 1994). We have often found relaxation exercises to be very effective for Asian American clients who are manifesting anxiety through somatic symptoms (Hong, 1993b; Hong et al., 1995). Inclusion of relaxation exercises in therapy sessions also addresses the clients' desire for immediate symptom relief. Instead of "talk therapy," which clients often perceive as ineffective, relaxation techniques can be presented to clients as a set of actions or procedures that they can use to induce both physical and psychological relaxation. This active approach is syntonic with the Asian cultural perspective on the interrelationship of the mind and body affecting health and sickness.

In sum, the cognitive behavioral orientation has the advantage of being direct and symptom focused. This is appealing to many Asian American clients who seek immediate relief of their problems. Many of the key constructs and techniques of this therapeutic approach are congruent with Asian cultural concepts and practices. However, clinicians need to avoid the pitfall of mechanically applying the methods and techniques without giving sufficient consideration to the cultural and social environmental contexts of their clients. Also, clinicians must restrain from overfocusing on techniques and neglecting clinician-client rapport.

Case Illustration

C. was a 48-year-old Chinese American man who had been in the United States for 30 years. He had been working as a cook in Chinese restaurants for most of this time. He and his wife spoke very little English, and their social network was exclusively within the local Chinese American community. They had two children who were in college. C. described his family life as satisfactory and the family's financial status as modest but secure.

C.'s presenting problem was an intense fear of crowded places and enclosed places. He related that the symptoms had started about a year ago. One day, he was walking on a crowded street with his family, and suddenly he felt he was suffocating. He was so frightened that he went home immediately. Since then, he had been extremely fearful of crowded or enclosed places, such as public transportation, noisy restaurants, cinemas, shopping malls, and even driving on congested highways. Whenever he was in any of these situations, he would experience suffocating feelings, heart palpitations, and dizziness. He would associate these feelings with symptoms of a stroke or heart attack. However, he would feel better once he left these places. Despite reassurance from his family physician who had known him for years, C. was convinced that he had a physical illness. He had consulted a number of other physicians, including practitioners of traditional Chinese medicine. Finally, an acupuncturist persuaded him to accept his family physician's original recommendation for psychotherapy.

C. was able to perform his job as a cook and carry out all activities of daily living. However, to avoid public transportation or driving on highways, he had changed his job the year before so that he could work closer to home. He also tried to avoid all places that could become crowded, such as department stores, restaurants, and certain streets. His fear of enclosed places was also evident during the therapy sessions. He always requested to turn on the fan in the therapy room because he felt the room small and suffocating.

C. was seen weekly for psychotherapy by a clinician using the cognitive behavioral approach. At the beginning of therapy, C. clearly stated that he was still not convinced that his problem was psychological. To engage him, the clinician spent a considerable amount of time in each session listening repeatedly to his descriptions of his "physical" symptoms. With C.'s permission, medical records were obtained from his family physician, and phone consultations were conducted to exchange case information. The clinician also set up a joint session with a psychiatrist to clarify C.'s lingering somatic concerns. Meanwhile, the clinician started using part of each session to teach C. relaxation exercises. After 2 months, the clinician introduced systematic desensitization through the use of imagery and continued the process in subsequent sessions.

Throughout this period, the clinician continued to discuss C.'s "physical" symptoms with him. In fact, the clinician purposely invited such discussions by frequently inquiring about his physical health, appetite, and sleep patterns. He also discussed the various ways C. had tried to deal with his symptoms. C. related that besides prescriptions from herbalists, he had tried fortune-tellers and *feng shui,* or geomancy, which aims at addressing the balance of metaphysical forces in the environment and the individual. For example, at one time, he was told that his father's burial site in China was probably in an unfavorable location. He remitted money to his relatives in China, and asked them to rearrange the landscaping and perform certain folk religious rituals to balance or reset his "feng shui." This course of action did not relieve his symptoms. At another time, he was instructed by a Chinese fortune-teller to use a particular red dye (a common ingredient in folk rituals) to paint certain symbols on the doorposts of his house. Again, this ritual did not work. The clinician listened empathically and discussed the details of all these remedies with him but never challenged him about the wisdom of trying these practices. By showing respect and acceptance of C.'s cultural beliefs, the clinician slowly gained C's trust and was able to get him to disclose and explore other background information. C. gradually opened up and confided that although he was a stocky and robust-looking man, he was really a very timid person. He related that when he first came to the United States as a teenager, he was trapped in an elevator and that since then he had avoided going into elevators by himself. He also related that about the time of his symptoms' onset, he had a friend who died suddenly of a stroke. Through these discussions, C. gradually gained insights about his own symptoms and understood the possible psychological basis for his problems. The clinician was also able to help C. redefine his physical symptoms, such as heart palpitations and feelings of suffocation, as signs of anxiety rather than signs of a stroke or heart attack.

After 4 months of therapy, C. felt reassured and confident enough to try in vivo systematic desensitization with the clinician accompanying him to various places. The first step of this procedure began with C. and the clinician taking public transportation together. Later, the clinician accompanied him into a department store, then to a shopping mall, and eventually into an elevator. C. made steady progress and subsequently was able to go to these places on his own as homework assignments. After 10 months of therapy, C. was able to go to all the places he had once feared, including shops and cinemas. His progress was sufficient enough for him to terminate therapy.

Discussion

The Asian cultural context of the client permeated this case. Like many Asian Americans, this client saw his symptoms as somatic rather than psychological. Initially, he rejected the advice of his family physician to seek psychotherapy. For a whole year, he looked for any medical provider, whether a practitioner of Western medicine or of traditional Asian healing practices, who would confirm his somatic suspicions. He came for psychotherapy only after exhausting all these medical resources as well as nonmedical folk practices. Even then, he was skeptical about the effectiveness of psychotherapy. The clinician had to work within this cultural context in approaching the client's problems. Instead of rejecting his notions about phobias or giving him a lesson on somatic symptoms, the clinician accepted the client's doubts about the helpfulness of psychotherapy and spent a considerable amount of time discussing the client's physical health. He further reassured the client that he understood and respected the client's views and culture by empathically exploring the client's experience with folk remedies. In turn, the client confided in the clinician other personal information, such as his timidity, fear of elevators, and fear of strokes and heart attacks after his friend's sudden death.

In this case, the clinician balanced between the client's initial skepticism of psychotherapy and the client's eagerness for expert advice and symptom relief by introducing relaxation exercises early on. However, the clinician held back from cognitive reframing and desensitization until the therapeutic alliance was established. Moving too fast into these intervention strategies without engaging the client through a respectful discussion of his views and conceptualization of his problems would very likely alienate him. Patience, flexibility, empathy, respect, and sensitivity to the client's cultural and social environmental contexts are the keys to successful cognitive behavioral therapy with Asian American clients, as they were with this client.

Culturally Specific Approaches

In the above discussion, we have focused on psychoanalytic therapy, person-centered therapy, and cognitive behavioral therapy. All of these therapies are among the major therapeutic orientations currently taught and practiced in the United States. Although these therapies were developed in the context of Western cultures, they are considered to be universal or etic models that can be adapted for use with different client populations. However, there are actually therapeutic approaches that have been developed in Asia and based on Asian cultural perspectives. The most prominent of these are Morita therapy and Naikan therapy, both developed in Japan. These two treatment approaches are based on the Japanese worldview and cultural values (Bankart, 1997; Hedstrom, 1994; Ishiyama, 1986, 1991a, 1991b; LeVine, 1993a, 1993b; Reynolds, 1976, 1983, 1989a, 1989b). Likewise, in recent years, mental health professionals in mainland China have been developing a therapeutic approach based on the principles of Taoist philosophy ("China Develops," 1998). Because these culture-specific or emic approaches are usually not included in the curricula of the training programs at universities in the United States, we will not elaborate upon them in this chapter. Clinicians who are interested in learning more about them are encouraged to refer to the publications cited, especially the books by Reynolds (1976, 1983, 1989a). Interestingly, although Morita therapy and Naikan therapy were developed specifically for use in Japan, some mental health professionals have considered their use in other cultural settings (Hedstrom, 1994; LeVine, 1993b; Reynolds, 1989a). For example, Reynolds (1989a) reported that he had applied Morita and Naikan therapies in Los Angeles with Chicanos, Puerto Ricans, blacks, Arabs, Jews, and other groups. In this regard, the distinction between the etic and emic models is not necessarily dichotomous (Hong & Ham, 1994; Hong et al., 2000). In the coming years, the introduction and adaptation of Asian therapeutic concepts to Western cultures may lead to a new frontier for mental health practitioners and researchers.

Summary

In this chapter, we have examined selected therapeutic concepts and techniques of psychoanalytic therapy, person-centered therapy, and cognitive behavioral therapy that require modification and special attention when applied to psychotherapy and counseling with Asian American clients. Because all three therapeutic orientations were developed in the context of Western culture, clinicians need to be judicious in applying their concepts as a template to analyze, interpret, or understand an Asian American client's conscious or unconscious thoughts, behaviors, perceptions, or emotions. The cultural and social environmental contexts of a specific Asian American client must always be taken into consideration when applying concepts and techniques from these therapies. If these Western-based approaches cannot fully meet the therapeutic needs of an Asian American client, modifications will be warranted. Furthermore, clinicians need to be sensitive to their Asian American clients' desire for quick symptom relief or problem resolution, an expectation that is common among Asian Americans identified with Asian cultures. To engage these clients, clinicians using the psychoanalytic and the person-centered approaches need to be more problem focused in the early stage of therapy. During this period, clinicians can gradually inform clients of the rationale of their particular approach and ease clients into a particular therapeutic orientation and process. Conversely, clinicians using the more action-oriented cognitive behavioral approach need to attend to the therapeutic relationship and to avoid overfocusing on techniques and symptoms. For all three approaches, clinicians must make every effort to meet their clients' expectations by acting as professionals with expert knowledge who are actively addressing their clients' problems. At the same time, clinicians must always be professionals who are courteous, respectful, caring, and empathic to their clients' preferences, needs, and cultural and social environmental contexts.

8

Application of Relational Treatment Modalities

Family Therapy and Group Therapy

This chapter discusses the cultural application of two relational treatment modalities: family therapy and group therapy. We are assuming that the reader already has a working knowledge of these treatment modalities, and we will focus our discussion on selected aspects of these approaches that need special attention when applied to Asian American clients who are identified with Asian cultures. As in our observations in the previous chapter, clinicians using family therapy and group therapy must be responsive to their clients' cultural and social environmental contexts and must work at their clients' level of functioning. In this chapter, we will offer practical suggestions for applying these two treatment modalities to Asian American clients and will illustrate our clinical strategies with case examples. Because engaging clients in therapy is essential for all treatment approaches, clinicians must be mindful of the suggestions for developing clinician-client rapport discussed in Chapter 6. Also, as mentioned in Chapter 1, *therapy* and *treatment* are used as generic terms denoting both psychotherapy and counseling.

Family Therapy With Asian American Clients

Our discussion about family therapy is intended to identify techniques and interventions that can be applied to Asian American families. We are specifically interested in providing a bridge between Asian cultural characteristics and Western practices of family therapy (Ho, 1987; Kim, 1985). Our examination is focused on the core interventions that most family therapists use in therapy sessions. These core interventions can be grouped in three broad categories (Seaburn, Landau-Stanton, & Horwitz, 1995): here-and-now interventions, transgenerational interventions, and ecosystemic interventions.

Here-and-now interventions emphasize the process of change as it is demonstrated in the present, even during the therapy session itself (Seaburn et al., 1995). The interventions address a family's organization (Minuchin, 1974), its communication, or both (Madanes & Haley, 1977) or specific problems or solutions that are goal oriented and problem or solution focused (De Shazer, 1985; Haley, 1976). These interventions lead to brief family therapy that accentuates behavioral changes rather than insights (Berg & Miller, 1992; Ho, 1990). Interventions can be enacted during a therapy session, or directives may be prescribed for the family to accomplish between sessions. Regardless of the specific intervention method, a family is continually encouraged by a clinician to work on tasks that are designed to facilitate change. With here-and-now interventions, a family therapist accepts the responsibility for facilitating change and is active and sometimes directive. In this regard, the here-and-now interventions are congruent with the expectations of many Asian American clients who anticipate a clinician to provide advice and instructions. These interventions are useful for engaging Asian American clients in the early stage of therapy but are particularly helpful in identifying methods for problem resolution and for goal setting (Berg & Jaya, 1993; Berg & Miller, 1992; Sue & Zane, 1987). However, family therapists must also be careful that these directive interventions are congruent with the particular cultural and social environmental contexts of an Asian American family, for a broad continuum of variation exists between Asian and mainstream American perspectives, particularly in the area of values, norms, and behaviors concerning family hierarchy and child-rearing practices (Hong, 1989; Hong & Hong, 1991; Lee, 1996, 1997b; Sue & Zane, 1987).

The emphasis of transgenerational interventions is on tracking the evolution of both problems and solutions across many generations of the family (Seaburn et al., 1995). The implementation of a transgenerational approach to intervention relies on the family's willingness to explore patterns or problems in the past. Although transgenerational patterns are linked to present concerns, clinicians address family-of-origin issues that are impinging on the present. Several basic assumptions underlie the transgenerational interventions: (a) Current problems often involve resolving relationship issues emanating from past experiences with family members; (b) families are held together through time by invisible strands of loyalty (Boszormenyi-Nagy & Spark, 1973), and (c) family difficulties are most likely to emerge during transitional periods from one life cycle phase to another. A family therapist tends to be less directive when using transgenerational interventions. The responsibility for change in the family is shared. A family therapist may coach a family throughout the process of their exploration history but does not intervene with a direct action. A family has a greater responsibility for taking charge of its therapy. In applying these interventions to Asian American families, a clinician must be sensitive to the Asian cultural prescriptions on privacy in family matters and nondisclosure to outsiders (Hong, 1988, 1989). When working with families with a strong Asian cultural identification, family therapists need to be highly attuned to the cultural meanings that their clients give to questions about the family. For example, in keeping with an Asian perspective, Asian American clients may consider questions about transgenerational family members and themes as too intrusive, or too historically based, to be relevant to their identified problem. Asian American clients may, in fact, interpret these clinician-generated questions as a sign of a clinician's insensitivity to their culture and social etiquette. Because the content of a family's history can only be generated by family members as clients (McGoldrick & Gerson, 1985), family therapists must respect their clients' decision to determine their degree of disclosure about their family and family process (Berg & Miller, 1992). In keeping with this respect, collaboration between family members and the family therapist becomes a therapeutic process (Anderson, 1995, 1997) that enables both the family therapist and the Asian American family to explore generational issues and to connect these issues to current life concerns. Family therapists may find that Asian American families are more willing to participate in this therapeutic process when they are given explicit explanations about the purpose and goals of the interventions and are given time to ease into the family exploration (Hong, 1989, 1993b; Jung, 1998; Lee, 1996, 1997b; Soo-Hoo, 1999; Uba, 1994).

An ecosystemic approach has been characterized by Auerswald (1968) as a balanced interaction of family and larger social systems and by Imber-Black (1988) as an interaction of multiple factors both within the family and beyond the relational bonds of the family (Seaburn et al., 1995). Proponents of ecosystemic methods of intervention include in their therapeutic framework aspects of larger social systems and institutions that shape an ecosystem. These influential determinants often include factors such as political and economic issues; ethnicity, race, and culture; religion; gender; language and social construction; and geographical and historic events (Seaburn et al., 1995). This biopsychosocial approach to intervention (Engel, 1980) defines a problem as the manifestation of multiple factors inside and outside the family (Epstein, Bishop, & Levin,

1978). The family is only one system among many larger systems that influence family functioning. The larger multisystem or contextual perspective focuses on the "problem-determined system" (Anderson & Goolishian, 1988) and includes everyone who is involved in conversation about the presenting problem. Meaningful solutions are coconstructed in the dialogue that occurs among the participants (Anderson & Goolishian, 1988; Goolishian & Anderson, 1987; Hoffman, 1990; White & Epston, 1990) and are inherently collaborative. To implement an ecosystemic approach, clear, specific interventions cannot be identified. Rather, this approach includes many interventions of the "here-and-now" and "transgenerational" approaches. The ecosystemic family therapist uses therapeutic interventions as resources for engaging the family in a partnership. Together, the family therapist and the family members, perhaps with other social resources, will define the family's problems and develop solutions for them. As discussed in Chapter 4, the ecosystemic approach to family therapy can be a useful tool for integrating the migration experience of Asian American families (Ho, 1987; Lee, 1982, 1997b) because of its emphasis on interactions between a family and larger social systems and political institutions. The "ecological fit" of individuals is a measure of the consonance and dissonance between their ecosystems before and after migration. In addition, a family's "ecological fit" is a collective measure of their ability to consolidate the multiple migration experiences of all the family members (Falicov, 1988). In applying ecosystemic approaches to Asian American families, clinicians must be knowledgeable about the social environmental barriers and stressors experienced in general by Asian American families and particularly by their specific client families. When using ecosystemic approaches to develop family interventions, clinicians need to be familiar with the resources available in "larger systems," such as the community, mainstream institutions, and society at large. Because these larger systems are culturally determined, it is ever more important for family therapists to have a thorough understanding of the cultural and social environmental contexts of their Asian American client families.

Application of Specific Family Therapy Techniques With Asian American Clients

We will now examine specific family therapy techniques from the three general classes of interventions and apply them to the cultural and social environmental contexts of Asian American families. We will use segments of the L. family case discussed in Chapter 3 to illustrate our points and to clarify important therapeutic concepts and techniques. After discussing the techniques within each class of interventions, we will present a case synopsis that illustrates how these techniques were integrated into therapy with the L. family. In sum, three examples from the L. family case will be used to illustrate, respectively, the here-and-now interventions, the transgenerational interventions, and the ecosystemic interventions.

Here-and-Now Interventions

A number of tasks or strategies are fundamental to here-and-now interventions with families. The major ones include joining, problem identification, problem sequencing, and addressing the organizational structure of the family (Haley, 1976).

Joining

Joining is the initial task of a family therapist (Haley, 1976; Madanes & Haley, 1977). Through the process of joining, a family therapist gains acceptance of a family and is admitted as part of the family's system (Haley, 1976; Minuchin & Fishman, 1981; Umbarger, 1983). In addition to establishing rapport, joining requires a clinician to respect the family's existing hierarchies, values, and norms, as well as to affirm each member's self-worth. To achieve this, family therapists often use the technique of mimesis, a joining behavior where a clinician parallels the mood or behavior of the family members (Minuchin, 1974). In the process of joining with Asian American families, family therapists are not only socializing with a family (Haley, 1976) but also interacting with a culture. The cultural identification of the members of an Asian American family influences the norms and values they follow. However, family therapists need to keep in mind that members of a family may have different cultural and social environmental experiences. They must discern the cultural identification of the family members in formulating strategies for joining a family. In the process of joining family members who are identified with Asian cultures, family therapists need to attend to their clients' cultural expectation that a clinician will be a professional with expert knowledge; they also need to use the referral source as a means of connecting with the family (Hong, 1989, 1993b; Lee, 1996, 1997b; Jung, 1998). For example, in the L. family case, Mr. and Mrs. L. entered family therapy in a manner that is typical of Asian Americans identified with traditional Asian cultures. Their help-seeking behavior indicated to the clinician their Asian cultural identification, and the clinician joined with them by following Asian cultural norms and etiquette. Even though the L. couple had received their higher education in the United States and had been living in the United States for over two decades, they closely followed traditional Asian social networking practices in seeking therapy. Mrs. L. first sought advice from a close friend, Mrs. C., the wife of a medical doctor, and then asked her to approach her husband, Dr. C., for guidance. Because Mrs. L. and Mrs. C. were equal in gender status, this indirect approach was appropriate in the Asian cultural context. When Mrs. C. reported back to Mrs. L. that Dr. C. recommended family therapy, this advice was accepted by the L. couple because of the confidence accorded to physicians as authority figures in Chinese culture. Furthermore, the family therapist was a friend of Dr. and Mrs. C., and this social connection was helpful for initially establishing therapeutic rapport between the clinician and the couple. Being alert to these cultural issues, the family therapist actively used her cultural knowledge in joining with the family: for example, by frequently mentioning Dr. and Mrs. C. in the initial sessions. We will describe more details of cultural joining in the case synopsis at the end of this section.

Problem Identification

This therapeutic task involves identifying clearly and specifically the problems that a family brings to therapy (Haley, 1976). In working with Asian American families, family therapists need to be aware that often families define their problems in concrete terms and expect the clinician to provide a solution (Hong, 1988, 1989; Jung, 1998; Lee, 1982, 1996, 1997b; Shon & Ja, 1982; Sue & Morishima, 1982). Clinicians also have to be aware of the stigma attached to mental disorders, as discussed in previous chapters. Hence, in problem identification, a family therapist needs to walk the fine line of accurately discerning the problem but at the same time presenting the problem to the family in a culturally congruent manner. For instance, in the L. family case, Mr. L. did not identify his problem as an emotional disorder but rather considered the problem to be emanating from events external to his inner being, such as being laid off from his job and not being treated fairly by his boss. He did not want to see a psychiatrist because this action would imply that his problem was socially unacceptable and thus would bring shame to him and his family. This was consistent with Asian cultures' perception of mental disorders as stigmatizing. Yet Mr. L. agreed to participate in family therapy with his wife because she had already expressed responsibility for her husband's behavior. Instead of seeing the problem as a mental disorder, he attributed it to external events, such as his wife's inability to soothe him adequately regarding his work situation. Being sensitive to the cultural issues underlying problem identification, the family therapist accepted Mr. L.'s initial position, while planning to help him gradually examine the problem from different perspectives.

Problem Sequencing

This technique involves interrupting the sequences of problem-generating behaviors of family members through language or verbal interventions, such as relabeling, reframing, and therapeutic paradox (Haley, 1976; Madanes & Haley, 1977; Watzlawick, Bavelas, & Jackson, 1967, 1969; Watzlawick, Weakland, & Fisch, 1974). For example, in the L. family case, one of the tasks of the family therapist was to relabel and reframe Mr. L.'s identification of his problem to reflect more accurately what was happening. The family therapist achieved this by first accepting Mrs. L.'s formulation of the problem. Mrs. L. did not identify Mr. L.'s problem as his work history or his emotional response to it. Rather, she questioned whether her willingness to embrace the new world had been a mistake and the cause of her husband's problem. Her formulation of the sequence of events leading to therapy was consistent with Asian cultural values and norms. Because this reframing of the problem was acceptable for Mr. L., the family therapist began from this position, as an initial sequence of therapy, and gradually added migration and work experiences that expanded the couple's definition of the problems and their sequencing of the problems.

Addressing the Family Organizational Structure

This technique involves observing and listening for information about the family's organizational structure and then addressing its influence on family behaviors (Minuchin, 1974). Family organizational structure is multifaceted and includes the following components: boundaries between a family and community institutions (e.g., social clubs, church or temple congregations) and between subunits within a family (e.g., the coupleship, the children), alliances among family members (e.g., the closeness and distance of individuals from one another), and the hierarchical position of family members (e.g., the identification of the most influential, most powerful, most controlling member of the family) (Minuchin, 1974; Umbarger, 1983).

In working with Asian Americans, family therapists need to be aware of the cultural and social environmental experiences of Asian American families that alter their familiar Asian family structure and organization. In many instances, Asian American families find that the traditional Asian family structure cannot be sustained in a Western cultural context. For example, Asian American children influenced by the values of mainstream American society may demand greater autonomy and egalitarianism than culturally permitted in traditional Asian families (Hong, 1989, 1996). Moreover, many Asian American families are confronted with societal demands that cannot be met by their familiar family organization. At this point of discovery, they are faced with problematic family situations, such as inversion of the family hierarchy. Hierarchical inversion often occurs when immigrant Asian American parents can no longer maintain their position of power as prescribed in Asian cultures. For example, immigrant parents who do not speak English often find themselves isolated from mainstream institutions. In contrast, their children who are educated in the United States and fluent in English usually have easier access to mainstream society. Consequently, these immigrant parents frequently have to depend on their children to translate for them or to help them interact with mainstream institutions (Hong, 1989, 1996; Lee, 1996, 1997b). Their dependency and social isolation contribute to the inversion of a power hierarchy, often regarded as the single most destructive force in a family's structure (Haley, 1980; Umbarger, 1983). In the L. family case, the family therapist actively observed and listened for information concerning the various elements of family organizational structure. The L. couple described a wall (boundary) between the Chinese American community and the institutions of their adopted U.S. society. They were also psychologically separated from their children, who had been born in the United States and had no experience of life in the couple's countries of origin. The alliances or bonds among the members of the L. family were evident. For example, Mr. and Mrs. L. were very much aware of each other's emotions and were dependent upon each other for company and emotional support. They were also bonded to friends from a Chinese American social club as their link to traditional Asian culture. The children formed another subsystem and had a strong, supportive alliance with one another. They often gave each other advice about how to handle school situations and peer relationships. Each child also maintained a network of mainstream American friends. Because of the hierarchical position of Asian fathers, Mr. L. was the most influential member of the family. Mrs. L. performed her role as wife and mother. Relational problems with the children or her husband were her responsibility, and she was expected to attend to them. However, when Mr. L. was no longer able to adjust to his job situation, the family hierarchy inverted and the entire family unit became dysfunctional. Understanding the family's organizational structure was crucial for the clinician in formulating effective intervention strategies acceptable to the family members.

Case Synopsis

The family therapist was alert to the referral process as a demonstration of Mr. and Mrs. L.'s identification with Chinese culture, and accordingly she related to the couple in a culturally syntonic manner. The goal of the first session was to establish therapeutic rapport and to identify what Mr. and Mrs. L. considered to be their problem and their reason for seeking couples therapy. The family therapist put Mr. and Mrs. L. at ease by making references to Dr. and Mrs. C., who were the referral source, and mutual friends of the clinician and the L. couple. She also alluded to members of their social club. This was a culturally syntonic way of establishing a bond and of joining with the couple. Moreover, the family therapist answered questions about her educational qualifications and her treatment approaches with couples. In this way, she established herself as an expert and authority in the Asian cultural context. She was culturally aware that she needed to establish this hierarchical status to gain the couple's confidence in her abilities to help them.

In identifying the problem, the family therapist was mindful of the importance of respecting the couple's own description of the problem. She knew that the definition of their problem would have some similarities with and some differences from traditional Asian perspectives and mainstream American perspectives. Their definition would be based on their ability to set goals and find solutions consistent with their own lifestyle and values (Berg & Jaya, 1993). During the first session and in subsequent sessions, the family therapist labeled or relabeled Mr. and Mrs. L.'s attitudes and behaviors in several different ways. Some were congruent with traditional Asian cultural interpretations of behaviors and attitudes, and others introduced expressions, behaviors, and attitudes from their adopted mainstream American culture. Although the family therapist accommodated to the couple's existing hierarchy, she frequently would change patterns of communication between the couple by giving Mr. and Mrs. L. equal time to speak. By giving her attention equally to each member of the coupleship, the family therapist created a different hierarchy for the couple that in turn led to a stronger alliance between the couple. For example, when the family therapist asked Mr. L. a question, he took responsibility for his own answers rather than, as he had done previously, indirectly controlling his wife by remaining silent and expecting her to speak for him. The family therapist was also able to observe the effect of structural interventions on the couple by taking note of their shifting body positions. Throughout the course of therapy, the family therapist encouraged Mr. L. to speak about his work history in order to help the couple reevaluate their assessment of the ecosystem, the institutions and society outside of their immediate family and network of Chinese American friends. By encouraging the couple to describe their situation in several different ways, she helped Mr. L. to begin examining alternative ways he could have handled the situation. In this way, the here-and-now interventions of family therapy were applied in a manner that was syntonic with the cultural and social environmental contexts of the L. family.

Transgenerational Interventions

There are several key strategies or tasks in transgenerational interventions. These include tracking family patterns, discerning family loyalties, and identifying family life cycle issues (Bowen, 1978; McGoldrick & Gerson, 1985; Seaburn et al., 1995).

Tracking Family Patterns

This therapy method involves tracking family patterns that have been developed by previous generations as solutions to current problems. These patterns can often be found in addressing relationship issues in one's family of origin (Seaburn et al., 1995). A family therapist tracks family patterns by reviewing a family's history and reflecting upon current family interactions. In Asian American families, transgenerational family patterns are often difficult to track because family members may not have shared the same migration experiences. In many families, the circumstances of premigration, migration, and postmigration can be different for each family member. For example, the pattern of family loyalty, an important Asian value, may be experienced as abandonment by a refugee child whose parents, in an act of devotion for their child, gave her to others who could transport her to a safe country. Differences in cultural and social environmental experiences may also exist for family members of different generations. These generational differences often lead to conflicting attitudes toward a family pattern or theme. For example, members of an Asian American family, in response to a family therapist's request to identify a family pattern, may have different answers that depend upon whether a family member was born in the United States or in an Asian country. Family members born and raised in Asia, such as the parents, may identify a family pattern of responsibility and sacrifice, a theme consistent with Asian cultural values. Family members born and raised in the United States, such as the children, may relabel this pattern as stifling restrictions and abusive authority, whereas their parents consider discipline as a demonstration of responsibility. Because of the complex circumstances surrounding migration experiences, family therapists need to be acutely aware of the cultural influences and social environmental stressors that affect Asian American families.

In the L. family case, clear transgenerational patterns emerge that follow Asian cultural prescriptions for the roles that familism and family hierarchy play in coping with family problems. In the context of traditional Asian cultures, Mr. L.'s psychiatric condition might have been perceived by others as possible evidence of a flaw in his family lineage (Hong, 1995; Hsu, 1985) and thus as something that could bring shame on the entire family. In keeping with this Asian cultural perspective, all family members focused on the traditional value of "saving face"—that is, preserving the family name—as well as on helping him recover. Even the children, all of whom were American born, upheld this position. The oldest son expressed confidence in Mr. L.'s competence to make his own decision about returning to work. In this regard, he was respectful of Mr. L.'s status as their father and perhaps hoped to minimize, in his own mind, the severity of Mr. L.'s condition and related stigma. The youngest son simply deferred to other family members who were of higher hierarchical status. The daughter wanted Mrs. L. to discourage Mr. L. from returning to work because she feared that he would bring more shame on himself and the family. Her action also demonstrated her adherence to the Asian family hierarchy. In terms of family hierarchical status, she was aware that it was more appropriate for one parent to advise the other parent than for a child to advise the father. Another observation concerned Mr. L.'s migration and family history. He and his wife were both aware of the differences between his protected life as a child enveloped by Asian cultural traditions and his current American environment, which he found alien. The coping pattern that he had adopted from his own family history was to withdraw from conflict and to isolate himself in a protected environment of family and social networks. In working with the L. family, the family therapist was conscientious in tracking all of these family patterns and in formulating culturally appropriate treatment plans and goals.

Discerning Family Loyalties

In this task, family therapists identify family loyalties, which are the invisible threads holding families together over generations (Boszormenyi-Nagy & Spark, 1973). These loyalties are both to previous generations and to current family members. At the point in therapy when past and present family relationships seem indistinguishable, a family therapist becomes aware that unresolved issues from the family's past are being transmitted through enactment, a process of projection, to current generations (Bowen, 1978). In their work with Asian American families, family therapists need to understand that in the context of Asian cultures, loyalty, as manifested as care and concern, may often be expressed indirectly through action rather than direct verbal statements (Hong, 1989; Shon & Ja, 1982). For example, a mother's favoritism toward a particular child may be expressed by serving the child additional helpings of food during meals or by giving what is perceived as the best portion to the child. A wife, rather than keep telling her husband verbally that she loves him, may express her loyalty and concern for him by attending to all household tasks or even by acts of self-sacrifice. To identify and discuss family loyalties from the numerous family behaviors and emotions, family therapists need to encourage families to tell their stories and to attend to a family's verbal and nonverbal communication.

In the L. family case, Mrs. L.'s description of her role as wife and mother clearly demonstrated her unwavering loyalty to her husband and her children as prescribed by Asian cultures. She saw her primary responsibility as supporting her husband and her children both emotionally and physically. Because Mrs. L. knew that Chinese cultural traditions were important to Mr. L., she remained loyal to her husband and his expression of Chinese cultural values throughout the therapy process. Mrs. L.'s adherence to Chinese cultural values and norms also demonstrated her loyalty to her own family of origin, whom she fondly remembered. She indicated that she had a particularly strong bond with her mother and stated that she often took to heart her mother's advice, "Always be aware of both sides of a situation." Mrs. L. interpreted this advice to mean being flexible and being open to Western ideas. Because of her mother's words, she had sought, over the years, to develop a bicultural orientation by adopting mainstream American culture while maintaining her Chinese cultural heritage. The family therapist also noted that Mr. L.'s expectations for their children, particularly the oldest son, were illustrative of the enduring threads of loyalty holding the two generations together. The oldest son entered medical school on Mr. L.'s advice. He appeared to embody Mr. L.'s life goals by fulfilling his father's dreams for future success. Although the daughter did not accept the educational goals that Mr. L. had set for her, she continued to find ways to express loyalty to her parents and their cultural heritage. As she stated, she was taking Chinese-language and Asian history courses in college to understand her parents' culture and to converse with them in their first language. Indeed, the interface of Western and traditional Asian cultures tested the strength of loyalty bonds. With her bicultural orientation, Mrs. L. was, in a sense, the link between Mr. L., who was primarily identified with Chinese culture, and the children, who, although bicultural, leaned more toward mainstream American culture, as exemplified by their inability to speak Chinese. She often nurtured the loyalty between the two generations. For the L. family, as for many immigrant families, family loyalties were closely intertwined with cultural identification. The family members perceived their allegiance to the family's Chinese cultural heritage as an integral part of loyalty to the family. The family therapist was alert to this connection in her work with the L. family.

Identifying Family Life Cycle Issues

This task entails identifying transitional points in the family life cycle and then noticing whether family problems occur at those times. Although life cycle changes are natural and unavoidable, family patterns, problem-solving strategies, and family rituals all influence the way current family mem bers meet the challenges of life cycle events, such as births, deaths, and marriages (Carter & McGoldrick, 1988, 1999; Steinglass, 1987). Migration histories may heighten a family's awareness of factors that can affect, or even disrupt and transform, family life patterns (Ho, 1987; Hong, 1996; Hong & Ham, 1992; Lee, 1996, 1997b). Because the majority of Asian American families are immigrant families, the impact of migration on the family life cycle, as discussed in Chapter 4, is an important issue to address in family therapy.

In the L. family case, Mr. and Mrs. L.'s family life cycle issues were very different. Because of global political events outside his family's control, Mr. L. experienced disruptions in the normal stages of childhood development. His disrupted childhood led to his disappointment and anger about his life in Hong Kong. In contrast, Mrs. L. had no problems in her childhood transitions. In leaving home to attend college in the United States, she handled her life stage of launching and individuating from her family in a culturally syntonic way. Overall, her family life cycle development was normative and free of unexpected conflicts until she decided to marry Mr. L., remain in the United States, and have children. Without the familiar support of her family of origin and social network, she had little guidance for raising her children in either a Chinese or a mainstream American society. Although she was more familiar with Chinese approaches for coping with life tasks than with mainstream American styles of living, she found she could not rely on her early life experiences in Taiwan. Hence, the normative life cycle stage of raising children became a disruptive stressor. The L. family children were aware of their parents' migration histories and the effects these histories had on their parents, and indirectly on them. Because both Mr. and Mrs. L. experienced disruptions in their life cycle development, they found it difficult to adapt to their children's transitions from one life stage to another. Mrs. L. was continually anxious about her inability to guide her children through the developmental stages experienced in two cultures. In therapy, she often described herself a poor mother and indicated uncertainty about her role as mother of bicultural children. In contrast, Mr. L. reacted with anger to the life cycle transitions of his children. He expected his bicultural children to ignore the alien mainstream American culture and, instead, to follow the path of traditional Chinese culture. He vehemently disapproved of his oldest son's fiancee, who was non-Asian. He viewed their potential marriage as a threat to the L. family's Chinese heritage. In this regard, the son's, or the next generation's, normative life cycle stage of forming a new family through marriage was at risk of being disrupted. In the context of therapy, the family therapist guided Mr. and Mrs. L. to examine their life cycle transitions and the events that disrupted their normal life cycle development.

Case Synopsis

In the first session with Mr. and Mrs. L., the family therapist, mindful of the key tasks of transgenerational interventions, verbally mapped out a family genogram with them. In a sense, gathering information for a genogram was similar to inquiring about family history. However, the focus of the genogram was to track the patterns and themes that emerged from the L. family histories. The genogram themes exposed both traditional Asian values, such as communication patterns organized around a hierarchical family structure, and altered Asian cultural values, such as split loyalties between Asian and mainstream cultural values. Mr. and Mrs. L. identified family themes and patterns and discussed their life experiences. The importance of these themes was evident. As they spoke of their families, Mrs. L. cried softly and expressed her feelings of loss. She described her own family as if they were present and made comments such as "I thank my mother for giving me sound advice." Mr. L. provided details of his family history in a laconic manner, as if he were reading from a newspaper. For both Mr. and Mrs. L., their stories provided a symbolic and representational enactment of their life experiences, as if their ancestors came alive and were bonded to them with the "threads of loyalty."

Descriptions of the L. family life cycle were embedded in the genogram and in the family life stories. The genogram highlighted the family life cycle of both Mr. and Mrs. L. and emphasized the significance of their migration experience. The family therapist needed only to facilitate and encourage the couple to tell their life stories as a way for them to accept and validate their cultural histories. Mrs. L. acknowledged that she benefited from hearing herself describe her Chinese identity. After separating normative life cycle behavior from imposed life crises such as migration, Mrs. L. felt as if she could understand Mr. L. and his relentless exclusion of "foreign" values. By describing her loyalty to Chinese culture, she appeared to overcome her self-doubts and reestablish her cultural identification as a valued member of both the Asian community and her adopted mainstream American culture. Her feelings of inadequacy, for not being as traditionally Chinese as her husband, and of betrayal, for not always behaving or wanting to behave as a traditional Chinese, also appeared to diminish. By reaffirming her own expression of Chinese cultural values, she expressed more confidence in creating a cultural legacy for her children.

Ecosystemic Interventions

Several fundamental therapeutic processes are essential to ecosystemic interventions. They include identifying the problem-determined system, coconstruction of solutions to problems, therapeutic conversation, and using the family therapist's curiosity (Anderson, 1993, 1997; Anderson & Goolishian, 1992; Gergen, 1994; Gergen, Hoffman, & Anderson, 1995; White, 1995; White & Epston, 1990).

Identifying the Problem-Determined System

This therapeutic process involves all family members in a conversation about the presenting problem. Through this process, the family members organize themselves around a problem and become a "problem-determined system" (Anderson & Goolishian, 1988). For a family to be identified as a "problem-determined system," everyone who is meaningfully involved in the presenting problem must experience the stress induced by the problem, although each individual may respond to the challenge with unique and individualistic coping styles and strategies. In working with Asian American families, a family therapist must recognize the varied interactions among family members, all of whom have different perceptions of their acculturation and social environmental experiences. For example, in immigrant families with American-born children who are highly identified with mainstream culture, the children may see the presenting problem as caused by their parents' inability to "let go of their Asian past" or to change their "old-fashioned" way of thinking (Hong, 1989, 1996). They may not perceive the problem to be a family legacy that concerns everyone. In this regard, differences in cultural identification and social environmental experiences may influence family members' perceptions of their involvement with the presenting problem. In applying ecosystemic interventions, a family therapist engages family members in a conversation that encourages each member to explore his or her own meaning of the presenting problem and to acknowledge other family members' descriptions of the problem (Anderson, 1997).

In the L. family case, Mrs. L. was able to identify the migration experiences of Mr. L. as being problematic for him and for their entire family as well. When the oldest son used migration experiences as an explanation for his father's behavior, he also indicated an awareness of acculturation as an organizing factor for family dysfunction. However, Mr. L. seemed to be less aware of the effect of his migration experience and instead blamed his problems on the external social environmental aspects of his job. His psychotic break was the "problem" that brought the family together as a problem-determined system, but through this event, the family, in conversation with the family therapist, was able to focus on acculturation, a more encompassing problem for the family.

Coconstruction of Solutions to Problems

In this therapeutic process, the meaning of a family's experiences, as created and experienced by individual family members who are in conversation with one another, is coconstructed (Anderson & Goolishian, 1992).

Together, the family members, in conversation, come to a mutual understanding of their shared problems and at the same time coconstruct solutions to these problems. The philosophical assumption about this family
therapy approach is that "the reality and meaning we attribute to ourselves
and others, and to the experiences and events of our lives, are interactional
phenomena [that are] created and experienced by individuals in conversation and action [through language] with one another and with themselves"
(Anderson, 1997, p. 3). In the context of working with Asian American
families, a family therapist needs to remember that in traditional Asian
cultures, social hierarchy is emphasized rather than social egalitarianism.
In a family session, family members may feel uneasy participating as
equal partners (Hong, 1989; Jung, 1998; Shon & Ja, 1982). In our clinical
practice, we have often encountered parents who are hesitant to discuss
their problems with their nonadult children, such as adolescents. Children
who are identified with Asian cultures may keep quiet or may indicate
agreement with those who are older, and thus higher in status, simply out
of compliance with cultural norms. In contrast, some children who are
more identified with mainstream culture than their parents may be so outspoken and direct that the parents will feel disrespected and humiliated.
Hence, in seeking to involve all family members in a therapeutic conversation and the coconstruction of solutions to problems, a family therapist
must be sensitive to cultural norms and communication styles (Hong,
1989; Jung, 1998; Lee, 1996, 1997b; Shon & Ja, 1982).

In working with families identified with Asian cultures, a foremost consideration of family therapists, regardless of their theoretical frameworks,
is to be respectful of individual family members and their unique configuration as a family unit. Once a family therapist has metaphorically filled
the therapeutic space with respect, the family members and family therapist can begin a collaborative process. Often the therapy methods of
ecosystemic interventions are mistakenly thought of as a contrived egalitarian format encouraged by the Western perspective of individualism.
Asian American families may perceive the process of coconstruction as an
imposed Western solution to their problems. For example, the word
coconstruction may be interpreted by Asian American families as "Everyone has equal time to say what they want" or "We don't have to agree with
those in authority." In response to these perceptions, a family therapist
must honor the theoretical intent of a coconstructive process by encouraging family members to talk about their lives, their problems, and their
expectations for therapy. The act of encouraging family members to engage in conversation is the beginning of the collaborative process of
coconstructive problem solving. The role of a family therapist in the
coconstructive process is to bring expertise into the area of process,
whereas the role of family members is to be experts on their life experi-

ences (Anderson, 1997). A family therapist's task is to engage and participate with family members in a dialogical process. As experts in process
rather than content, family therapists do not try to revise the life stories of
families but instead facilitate a process where family members can tell and
retell their stories (Anderson, 1997). From our experiences in family therapy with Asian American families, we have found that a coconstructive
problem-solving process can often be promoted when a mutually respectful conversation exists among family members and the family therapist
and when a family therapist professes a respectful interest in Asian cultural values and norms, such as familism, family hierarchy, and family loyalty bonds.

   In the L. family case, the family therapist joined with the couple as a
third member of the couple system. She encouraged each member of the
couple to talk with her and with each other, and then interactively as a
group of three, in order to listen and speak and to learn from and teach each
other. Together, they initiated a "social action, rather than an independent
individual mental process" (Anderson, 1997, p. 3). This "social action"
began a collaborative process in which Mr. and Mrs. L., even with their different cultural values and worldviews, contributed to a coconstruction of
possible solutions for Mr. L.'s emotional distress and for its impact on
the family.

Therapeutic Conversation

   Therapeutic conversation, through a dialogue among individuals, is a
mutual exploration and search for understanding about issues affecting
the family. This process is not aimed at producing change but is useful in
opening relational space for mutual exchanges of communication (Anderson & Goolishian, 1992). With this framework, family therapy becomes a
therapeutic conversation, an exchange of stories, about issues concerning
the family, and then the therapeutic conversation becomes a mechanism
for generating and creating new stories (Anderson & Goolishian, 1992). In
applying this strategy to Asian American families, family therapists must
observe culturally prescribed hierarchical status (Hong, 1989; Jung, 1998;
Lee, 1996, 1997b; Shon & Ja, 1982). As discussed earlier in relation to
coconstruction, family therapists need to acknowledge and respect
Asian cultural norms and values while encouraging family members to
tell their stories. When family members share their stories, they are participating in a conversation, a collaborative enterprise that is more than a series of separate monologues delivered by individual family members (Anderson, 1997; Shotter, 1993). In fact, family members who enter into a
therapeutic conversation bring with them their everyday lives, their life
history and experiences, their emotions and attitudes, and most impor-

tantly their self-identity (Anderson, 1997). Although Asian American family members may not verbally describe specific life experiences, the richness of each family member's life is "sensed" or observed. For example, the importance of Asian values such as hierarchical family structure, family loyalty, and "face saving" is made known by the verbal and nonverbal interactions among all those participating in the conversation. The family therapist must be aware that a therapeutic conversation encompasses multiple life frameworks, which are the self-representations of each family member as well as the shared experiences of the family unit. In their work with Asian American families, family therapists must have the resiliency, ability, flexibility, and willingness to embrace the multiple life frameworks that contribute to the complexity of a therapeutic conversation. In addition, family therapists working with recent immigrant families must also be acutely sensitive to the effects that migration experiences have on their self-identity. Family therapists must "do-what-the-occasion-calls-for" and be "poised for action" (Anderson, 1997, p. 98) because therapeutic conversation is not a logical set of words to say.

In the L. family case, the family therapist encouraged Mrs. L. and the children to use the family session as a vehicle for engaging in conversations where they could begin to understand their relationships with one another. In keeping with Asian values, Mrs. L. frequently declared during the therapy session her allegiance and her responsibility to her children. In turn, the children appreciated and welcomed the opportunity to affirm their bond with their mother. Together as a unit, they established a conversation that was therapeutic for them as individuals and as a family.

Using the Family Therapist's Curiosity

In this therapeutic process, a family therapist expresses to the family a general attitude of curiosity, of needing and wanting to know more about what has been said by a family (Anderson, 1997; Anderson & Goolishian, 1992). With this attitude in mind, family therapists are not experts about a family's life circumstances. Rather, they take an approach where they are always in the process of understanding and changing, and they do not promote their preconceived ideas about how a problem can be solved (Anderson & Goolishian, 1992). They demonstrate their curiosity in a therapeutic and respectful process.

Because the complexities and variations in Asian cultural and subcultural practices can be difficult to master even for an Asian American clinician, a family therapist's curiosity becomes the foundation for therapeutic conversation. To be curious and to act on their curiosity requires family therapists to have the attitude and belief that they can never fully understand an Asian American family. Thus, a family therapist always needs to be in a position of being informed by family members about their individual lives and collective life as a family unit (Gergen, 1988). Family therapists must ask questions to act on their curiosity (Anderson, 1997). However, they need to be cautious about questions that may be perceived by Asian American family members as too intrusive and probing or as serving the clinician's prurient interests (Wu, Enders, & Ham, 1997). These questions are culturally insensitive and will hinder the therapeutic process. Conversely, questions can be one of the most helpful aspects of successful therapy experience when they invite Asian American family members to elaborate upon their life stories and to engage in conversation with each other and the family therapist. As illustrated in the following case synopsis of the L. family, the family therapist was able to use her therapeutic curiosity to engage the family members in conversation about their lives and their ecosystem and, with therapeutic questions, to help the family members gain insights into their family relationships and concerns.

Case Synopsis

Throughout the therapy sessions, the family therapist assessed her position in the L. family system. She saw herself as a part of a larger system in which different parts within the global environment formed a problem-organizing system (Anderson & Goolishian, 1988). She could not be an expert about the larger system, for her understanding about its meaning for the L. family was influenced by her own personal psychosocial experiences and values. Mr. L.'s hospitalization was a crisis that brought all family members together. The involvement of all the family members indicated to the family therapist that the family had truly begun to organize themselves around "a problem." They had become a "problem-determined system" with far-reaching consequences that encompassed the family as well as many social and political institutions. The family therapist found herself, within this more global environment, a coparticipant with the L. family. Her acknowledgment of being a coparticipant in a large interactive environment was an initial step for pursuing an ecosystemic approach to family treatment. Her position as a family therapist was to be a learner about the L. family problem system while maintaining her personal knowledge and expertise about family therapy. With this therapeutic position, she and the L. family were able to engage in a collaborative relationship and a conversation that had a mutual goal of creating new meanings for the L. family's life situation.

Throughout the family therapy, the family therapist was aware of the contribution that each family member made in constructing solutions for situations that in the past had seemed unsolvable. During a conversation about traditional Chinese cultural values and behaviors, the daughter was able to disclose that she had been raped. In this conversation, the daughter emotionally expressed that she did not want to burden her family with her shameful experience of rape. As part of the conversation, Mrs. L. expressed her feelings of exclusion and isolation because she wanted to share her daughter's pain. The conversation ended with both mother and daughter in tears and with both expressing resentment and rage toward the perpetrator. The rape was no longer just an act bringing shame to the victimized daughter or to the family.

Another example of how therapeutic conversation created a safe environment and led to a new meaning for a situation was Mrs. L.'s understanding of her oldest son's engagement to a non-Asian woman. Mrs. L. had assumed that her son's choice of a wife was a rejection of her and of Asian culture. During the session, the son spoke of his mate selection as a way to explain his values to an outsider and, in turn, to clarify and strengthen his own Asian identity. He also described his fiancee as a helpmate who could help him join mainstream American culture. As a prospective physician, he understood the importance of knowing how to behave in mainstream society. Although Mrs. L. remained disappointed with her son's choice of a non-Asian woman to be his wife, she remarked, during the therapeutic conversation with her children, that she would invite the fiancee and her family for dinner as a way to know them better.

Throughout the family therapy sessions, the family therapist remained therapeutically curious about each family member's understanding of family events. Over a period of time, sessions were becoming "meaning generating" (Anderson & Goolishian, 1988) by offering novel unexpected solutions to problems. However, traditional Asian cultural values were always present in the therapy sessions. What became clear to the family therapist and family members, however, was the variation in the meaning and the different ways those traditional values influenced their lives.

Summative Comments

Currently, the field of family therapy is becoming ever more aware of the diverse contributors to our society. All families and individuals are unique yet are connected to others in their humanness (McGoldrick, 1998) and particular culture. Cultural identification and social environmental experiences are definitely crucial considerations in family therapy. Family therapists working with Asian American families must be knowledgeable about these factors, particularly the values and norms governing Asian American families and the migration experience of Asian American families. As the L. family case illustrated, family therapists must approach Asian American families from a particular family's cultural and social environmental contexts rather than from a Western perspective of the ideal family. In particular, family therapists must be respectful of an Asian American family's structure, values, norms, communication style, and migration experience; family members' cultural identification as individuals and as a family unit; and family members' expectations of family therapists and family therapy itself. When applied with cultural sensitivity, family therapy can be an effective modality in providing treatment to Asian Americans.

Group Therapy With Asian American Clients

In group therapy, a clinician is working concurrently with a number of clients, as in family therapy. The clinician's attention is not only on an individual client but also drawn toward relationships and relational issues between or among individuals. A group therapist, together with the group members, develops a uniqueness, not as a sum of the distinctive individuals within the entity, but as its characteristic formation. As such, worldviews, values, norms, and communication styles brought by clients and the clinician into the group session will have a major influence on the group dynamics and process. Group therapists need to be alert to the cultural and social environmental contexts of the group members as individuals and as a collective entity. More specifically, group therapists need to attend to the group members' cultural identification, migration experiences, physical and social environments of daily life, and expectations of the clinician and group therapy. In mental health clinics, members of treatment groups often do not know one another before the initial meeting. The presence of strangers may intensify the Asian cultural norm that discourages discussing personal or family problems with outsiders. Therapy groups may also be composed of individuals from different ethnic groups within the Asian American population or from both Asian American and non-Asian American populations. This ethnic diversity may create a concern for intercultural miscommunication. All of these situations are challenges facing group therapists. We will return to these issues later. First, we will discuss the practical and therapeutic advantages of group therapy with Asian American clients.

Advantages of Group Therapy

Group therapy is often described as a cost-efficient alternative to individual therapy and counseling. Instead of providing services to a single client in a session, a group therapist can provide treatment to a number of clients at the same time. This is a definite advantage in today's cost-conscious mentality of community mental health programs, particularly in the context of managed care and limited public funding and resources in Asian American communities. For Asian American mental clinics that do not have enough bilingual clinicians to provide individual therapy to all clients requiring services in Asian languages, group therapy is often considered as an alternative to putting clients on long waiting lists. However, clinicians need to focus not only on the cost-effectiveness of group therapy but also on the therapeutic advantages that make this treatment modality an important therapeutic method by its own right. The group format provides an interpersonal environment in which participants can learn from one another, receive feedback, and provide mutual support (Ettin, 1992; Merta, 1995; Napier & Gershenfeld, 1993; Yalom, 1985). Groups also offer a number of therapeutic or curative factors, such as instilling of hope, universality, imparting of information, altruism, corrective recapitulation of the primary family unit or family reenactments, development of socialization skills, imitative behavior, interpersonal learning, group cohesiveness, and catharsis (Ettin, 1992; Yalom, 1985). Clinicians may emphasize different combinations of these therapeutic factors in different groups, depending on a group's purposes and composition, as well as on the stages of group development (Ettin, 1992; Yalom, 1985). By guiding and facilitating the process of the group interaction, a clinician can focus on particular therapeutic factors and provide treatment to clients in the group.

All of the therapeutic factors of groups identified in this discussion are relevant for Asian American clients. For example, clients who are new immigrants are often relieved to find out in a group session that they are not the only ones feeling the isolation or lack of social support in their postmigration environment. Parents who are confused about child-rearing practices because of their dilemma in following Asian or mainstream American cultural practices, or parents who are in conflict with their children because of conduct and discipline issues, may find consolation and strength from the support of other parents in similar situations. They can also exchange information and advice with one another in a group. Children and adolescents dealing with the stress of growing up in two different cultures and struggling with their cultural identification may find solidarity with others who have the same life issues. In a group, they can explore together their life issues and develop resolutions to their problems. Catharsis, interpersonal learning, sharing of information and coping strategies, mutual support, and feedback are some of the most prominent therapeutic assets we have observed in group work with Asian Americans. Psychoeducational groups focusing on acculturation and socialization issues are also very useful in Asian American communities. We will provide more clinical examples later in this chapter. We will also discuss the use of group work in primary prevention programs in the next chapter.

Precautions in Applying Group Treatment
to Asian American Clients

In comparison to other topics in psychotherapy and counseling, relatively little literature is available on group work with Asian Americans (Leong, 1992). Overall, many of the concerns for applying group therapy to Asian American clients are similar to those raised for consideration in individual treatment discussed in previous chapters. The most frequent concerns include clients' uncertainty about the therapeutic rationale for group therapy; clients' expectation for clinicians to be directive and informative; the shame and stigma attached to mental health problems; inhibition about disclosing personal and family issues to outsiders; differences between Asian and mainstream American communication styles; and the Asian cultural preference for subtlety and nonconfrontational approaches in expressing disagreement. Unlike individual therapy, where these concerns are manifested in the context of the client-clinician dyad, these issues are played out among a number of persons in group therapy and are often manifested in a more complex or amplified manner. Furthermore, the group therapy process typically encourages group members to speak up and be frank and direct in expressing their personal ideas or feelings. This direct communication style may contradict the collectivistic orientation of Asian cultures that emphasizes modesty, humility, and deference to a group's needs rather than calling attention to an individual's own needs (Leong, 1992). From a different perspective, Tsui (1997) cautioned that Asian American clients from countries with totalitarian governments may have experienced groups being used as instruments of social and political control or may have participated in groups where some of the group members were government informants. These clients' sociopolitical experiences may inhibit them from participating freely in group therapy, even after they have immigrated to the United States.

In light of these cultural and social environmental issues, the existing literature on group work often has noted that Asian Americans are unwilling to accept group therapy and counseling and often drop out prematurely from group treatment (Gladding, 1991; Leong, 1992; Merta, 1995). During a group session, group therapists often notice that Asian American clients are passive in their participation. For example, they do not spontaneously join in a discussion or volunteer to share information (Gladding, 1991; Leong, 1992; Merta, 1995; Tsui, 1997). These observations have led some clinicians to the conclusion that group therapy is not a preferred treatment modality for Asian Americans. However, clinicians need to avoid overemphasizing these difficulties. Like any other mode of therapy discussed in this book, group therapy can be an effective treatment modality if clinicians apply it in a culturally syntonic manner within the Asian

American cultural and social environmental contexts and refrain from imposing Western values and norms, especially those concerning communication and social interaction, on Asian American clients. For example,
when working with Asian American group members who are not acculturated into mainstream American culture, a group therapist cannot expect
them to be at ease with following mainstream cultural norms of communication. Similarly, group therapists cannot evaluate the behaviors of Asian
American group members by using the normative behaviors of groups
composed of mainstream white Americans. To someone who is not familiar with Asian cultures, a group of Asian American clients may appear to
be discussing an issue in a polite and superficial manner. However, to
someone familiar with Asian cultures, these clients may actually be expressing very frank and strong disagreements. Their verbal and nonverbal
communication may seem mild by mainstream American cultural standards, but by Asian cultural standards the members are conveying strong
and clear messages to one another. In this regard, group therapists must be
very careful not to misconstrue what is actually happening in a group and
whether a group is achieving its purpose.

Depending on a group's ethnic composition, cultural norms governing
interpersonal interaction and communication may have different impacts
on the group dynamics and process. Hence, we will examine ethnically homogeneous and ethnically heterogeneous groups separately.

Ethnically Homogeneous Groups

In forming a therapy group, clinicians can select members on the basis
of presenting problems and a variety of demographic factors. Our discussion is focused on the ethnic composition of group members because this
aspect of group composition is directly related to intercultural or
interethnic perceptions, communication, and interactions. In an ethnically
homogeneous group, there are minimal cultural differences among members. This group may be composed of members from the same ethnic background, such as Korean Americans identified with Asian cultures. In this
situation, the group therapist can simply adjust the group process and format to meet the cultural and social environmental contexts of the clients.
For example, as we have noted for individual therapy, group therapy can
provide a more structured and problem-focused approach to meet the expectations of the clients, particularly at the beginning stage of the group.
Group therapists can also follow the Asian cultural style of communication and avoid direct disagreements or confrontations. Because all group
members are Asian Americans with similar cultural identification, they
will understand the underlying meanings of other group members' statements, even when such communication might seem too subtle or indirect

to a person uninformed about Asian cultures. Also, group members are likely to understand each other's reluctance to disclose personal and family problems and are likely to be more patient and tolerant of each other's slow pace of self-disclosure. Actually, when such a group is observed within the clients' Asian cultural and social contexts, the group members are perceived as participating actively and appropriately. In sum, an ethnically homogeneous group can be an effective format to provide group treatment for Asian American clients as long as the group therapist, whether Asian American or non-Asian American, respects and acknowledges the group members' cultural values and norms.

We will use a parenting group that we led for immigrant Chinese American mothers to illustrate the issues discussed. At the beginning stage of this group, we used a problem-focused and structured format with identified topics regarding Chinese versus American child-rearing practices. The group therapist followed a psychoeducational approach and facilitated the first few sessions in a semididactic manner, with little emphasis on members' introducing themselves or describing their problems. The first session started with a simple introduction, similar to a classroom lesson or meeting. Members simply understood that everyone was there to learn about child rearing. They were not asked to disclose their problems or family situation. In subsequent sessions, the group therapist began each session by describing certain child-rearing practices in the United States and then asked the members whether they considered these practices to be practical for them. After a few sessions, the members knew each other better and started to be more spontaneous in bringing up the problems they had with their own children. Eventually, they felt comfortable enough to bring up other family and adjustment problems, particularly those related to their immigration experiences. Slowly the group evolved to a less structured and more open format. The group members began to give each other advice, feedback, and support and to be less reliant on the group therapist for guidance. At the end of 6 months, when the group was ready to terminate, the members clearly felt a sense of solidarity with each other. However, if the group therapist had structured the group after mainstream American norms for group communication and interaction and had tried to speed up the members' self-disclosure and mutuality, the members might have felt threatened or uncomfortable. Eventually, they might have withdrawn from the group discussions and even have dropped out of the group. The group therapist leading this group, however, was culturally informed and accurately perceived the members to be active, open, and spontaneous. By following Asian cultural norms himself, he was able to provide effective group therapy to the group members.

At times, groups composed of Asian American clients from different ethnic backgrounds may also be conceptualized as ethnically homogeneous. For example, a group may be composed of Asian Americans from similar but not identical ethnic backgrounds. Clinicians can use this type of ethnic composition when the relative cultural differences among group members are not a major concern in terms of the clinical issues being addressed in the therapy group. For example, a group may be composed of immigrant Chinese, Korean, and Vietnamese American high school students who are experiencing emotional difficulties related to their migration experiences and cultural identity issues. Although there are differences among their cultures and countries of origin, sufficient commonalities also exist, particularly when their Asian home cultures are contrasted with mainstream American culture. They also share many experiences as Asian Americans growing up as ethnic minorities in mainstream American society. Thus, the group therapist can adjust the group's structure and format to meet their collective expectations, values, and norms in ways similar to those discussed in the context of homogeneous groups composed of members from a single ethnic group.

When a group is composed of members from different Asian ethnic backgrounds, clinicians need to ensure that all members are equally fluent in English or that they speak another common language. Otherwise, verbal communication may become an issue. Differences in English proficiency may affect members' participation in a group therapy session. Some members will be more "open" and "participating," whereas others will be more "inhibited" or "withdrawn." These variations can be very misleading for the group therapist as well as the group members. The members who are less proficient in English may also feel that they are being ignored or deprived of the opportunity to express themselves. In addition, they may feel frustrated by their inability to express themselves freely. These issues can lead to very negative group dynamics. If this type of group composition is unavoidable due to particular circumstances or limited resources, interpreters may be necessary. In this situation, the group therapist needs to ensure that the group members requiring the services of interpreters will not feel belittled. Also, inclusion of interpreters will slow down the group interaction, as well as the spontaneity of member participation. Consequently, this is a less desirable way to provide group therapy and should be used only when there are no other options.

Ethnically Heterogeneous Groups

In the present discussion, the term *ethnically heterogeneous groups* refers to groups composed of members from different ethnic backgrounds, such as Asian American and non-Asian American. In this situation, intercultural communication and intercultural interaction are major con-

cerns. The group dynamics and process will often depend on the actual ethnic composition of the group, such as the number of ethnic groups involved, the number of members from each ethnic group, and the cultural identification of individual group members. The permutations of such group compositions are infinite. Hence, we will offer some general observations that focus particularly on groups composed of mostly mainstream white Americans and very few Asian Americans. Because our discussion concerns intercultural communication and intercultural interaction, our emphasis is on Asian Americans who are primarily identified with Asian cultures and who are not acculturated into mainstream culture. Otherwise, cultural differences and cultural conflicts between Asian American clients and mainstream white American clients in the group will not be significant issues. As Tsui (1997) observed, Asian American clients in ethnically heterogeneous groups typically report gaining less benefit from the group process than Asian American clients in ethnically homogeneous groups. We will examine the factors that contribute to this situation.

In facilitating ethnically heterogeneous groups, a group therapist cannot simply adjust the group format and process to respond to the cultural values and norms of the Asian American clients. The clinician also needs to consider the cultural values and norms of the members from other ethnic backgrounds. This ethnic mix poses a challenge for group therapists. In a sense, group therapists have to be cultural referees who help group members from different ethnic backgrounds communicate with each other. They also need to protect group members by deflecting questions that may be considered too personal or intrusive in different cultural contexts. For example, a mainstream white American may ask a question or make a remark that is appropriate in the mainstream cultural context, but an Asian American group member who is not acculturated into mainstream culture may consider it too intrusive or crude. Clarifying communications, deflecting intrusive questions, and protecting group members are skills that group therapists need for leading any group, regardless of its composition. However, in an ethnically heterogeneous group, a group therapist has to take the extra step of attending to and preventing cultural misunderstanding, miscommunication, and conflict. Indeed, the frequently mentioned observation that Asian American clients do not participate actively in therapy groups is probably more applicable to ethnically heterogeneous groups than homogeneous groups. An Asian American client who is not acculturated into mainstream culture may feel uneasy about, or even threatened by, the mainstream American members' relatively more open and direct style of communication, self-disclosure, and feedback.

In most cases, Asian American clients are likely to have some fluency in English if they participating in an ethnically heterogeneous group. However, if a client is not very fluent in English, the cultural differences in communication style may further complicate the situation and inhibit him or her from speaking out. Moreover, many Asian Americans who speak English as a second language often do not formulate their thoughts in English (Tsui, 1997; Yansen & Shulman, 1996). Rather, they may have to translate their thoughts from their first language into English. This translation process can lead to words, expressions, or sentence structures that may be misunderstood by other group members or the group therapist. Gestures and other body language can also be misperceived. For example, some Asian American clients may seem to be "yelling" when they are simply feeling anxious speaking in English, their second language. In response, mainstream white American group members may misperceive them as rude or angry. Even though a group therapist may be culturally knowledgeable enough to discern the actual situation, one cannot expect all other group members to be equally sensitive. Often the clinician has to walk a fine line. On one hand, a group therapist must avoid impatiently speaking up for an Asian American member or interpreting what the member has said (Tsui, 1997). On the other hand, there are situations when a group therapist needs to intervene and clarify miscommunications or misunderstandings. Thus, cultural knowledge and sensitivity, as well as proficiency in facilitating intercultural communication, are skills that group therapists must possess in leading ethnically heterogeneous groups.

In addition to language, social environmental factors such as ethnic stereotypes and ethnic relationships in the community may affect the overt and covert processes of ethnically heterogeneous groups. In effect, ethnically mixed therapy groups are a microcosm of the larger U.S. society and have the potential to play out the inequities of society and the conflicts between majority and minority populations (Tsui, 1997). These conflicts are not only between group members from majority and minority cultures but also between group members from different minority cultures. These ethnic stereotypes and ethnic relationships can become disruptive elements in the process of a therapy group. This is particularly true in communities with high degrees of distrust or tension among ethnic groups. However, even in situations with no particular tension, ethnic stereotypes may be a source of misunderstanding that can sidetrack the therapeutic process of the group. Also, Asian American clients who are primarily identified with Asian cultures may be unaccustomed to an ethnically heterogeneous group setting. Even if they are outspoken when they are with their ethnic peers, they may feel uncomfortable in speaking out in such a setting. In light of all these concerns, clinicians need to be careful when they consider placing Asian American clients in groups with members from other ethnic backgrounds. They must always assess how ethnic relationships from the larger society and from the group members' personal experiences may af-

fect a group's effectiveness. The focus of a therapy group is to address group members' clinical problems. The group members, whether Asian American or non-Asian American, cannot be expected to spend an inordinate amount of time and effort to address ethnic stereotypes and relationships. This concern, of course, does not apply to groups organized specifically for the purpose of developing intercultural and interethnic sensitivity.

In a study surveying the attitudes of Asian American university students toward group counseling, Leong, Wagner, and Kim (1995) reported that acculturation status was a significant predictor of positive orientation toward group counseling. These authors advised clinicians to take extra care when referring to group therapy Asian Americans with low acculturation into the mainstream culture. Group therapists also need to be aware that other differences exist within an ethnically heterogeneous group, such as the members' level of functioning, as well as their sophistication and sensitivity in intercultural contexts. These attributes apply to Asian American as well as non-Asian American group members. Hence, the appropriateness of placing a particular Asian American client in a specific ethnically heterogeneous group is, ultimately, the clinical judgment of a group therapist, who must take all of the above factors into consideration and decide whether the potential benefit is worth the risk for the client. Clinicians can also facilitate an Asian American client's participation in an ethnically heterogeneous group by preparing the client at the time of referral to group therapy. They need to be sensitive to a client's reaction to the referral and to address any concern the client has. After placing the client in a group, the group therapist should be alert to the group dynamics, particularly to this member's participation and therapeutic gains, and should make interventions as needed.

Examples of Group Treatment
in Asian American Community Clinics

There are many examples of group therapy being used effectively with Asian American clients. For instance, group therapy is a major component of the Community Living Program for Vietnamese American trauma victims at Coastal Asian Pacific Mental Heath Services (Coastal), mentioned in Chapter 6. As described by Richard Kim, the psychologist who led the therapy group in this program, all the participating clients had experienced major traumas that were primarily related to the Vietnam War and the "reeducation camps" after the war. These traumas included torture, rape, injuries, near-death experiences, and witnessing torture or murder of others. Many of the clients had diagnoses of post-traumatic stress disorder. The Community Living Program at Coastal provides group therapy once a week and lasts for 6 months. Each group follows a structured format and covers topics that include psychological aspects of trauma, medication issues, coping skills, and other clinical issues. Group therapy is also used extensively in the Day Treatment Program at Coastal for chronic psychiatric patients. The diagnoses of these patients include schizophrenia and other psychotic disorders, bipolar disorders, and major depressive disorder, as well as other conditions. These groups are primarily pscyhoeducational and address topics that include coping skills for residual symptoms, medication and side-effects management, relapse prevention, social skills, job skills, vocational issues, recreational skills, and time management. The group structure and topics may vary and are dependent on a particular group of clients' level of functioning. The groups are usually composed of members from different Asian American ethnic backgrounds that include Japanese Americans, Korean Americans, Vietnamese Americans, Chinese Americans, and Filipino Americans. English, a language common to many of the members, is most often used in the groups. However, interpreters are used as needed. Groups are used in other programs of Coastal as well. For example, the children's program has an ongoing adolescent group. From time to time, clinicians offer time-limited groups focused on specific concerns. Examples of these groups include women's groups, cultural diversity groups, and adolescent boys' groups. As indicated by the successful application of group therapy at Coastal, this treatment modality can be very effective with Asian American clients if it is provided in a culturally and linguistically appropriate manner.

The Asian Pacific Counseling and Treatment Centers (APCTC), a mental health agency in Los Angeles that we will describe in greater detail in the next chapter, also uses group therapy extensively. According to Stephen Cheung, a psychologist and an administrator at APCTC, about two thirds of the clients at this agency are involved in group therapy. Some clients receiving group therapy also receive individual therapy or medication. The groups are organized according to the cultural and linguistic needs of the clients, as well as their presenting problems. For example, a group for American-born Asian clients who are acculturated into mainstream American culture is conducted in a format like any other therapy group in a mainstream clinic. However, groups for clients who are identified with Asian cultures and who are less acculturated into mainstream culture are organized differently. To meet the expectations of these clients, the group process is typically more structured and directive. These groups are usually conducted in the language of each specific ethnic group, for the clinic serves sufficient clients from each ethnic background to make this arrangement administratively practical. The content of the

groups is related to the clients' presenting problems, such as symptom identification and management, medication and treatment compliance, family-client communication, stress management and relapse prevention, family support, and rehabilitation. Other relevant psychosocial issues are also discussed. These issues may cover areas such as acculturation, immigration, child rearing, access to social services, daily activities and time management, and other topics that may come up. One interesting aspect of these groups is that tea is usually served during the session. This activity is culturally syntonic for a gathering and is an effective ice-breaker that helps to put the clients at ease. The successful use of group therapy at APCTC indicates that, as always, with proper attention to cultural and social environmental concerns, group therapy can be a useful treatment modality with Asian American clients.

Summary

In this chapter, we have examined the application of family therapy and group therapy with Asian American clients. In comparison to individual psychotherapy and counseling, these two relational treatment modalities bring additional dimensions to the therapeutic context because more than one client is involved in the clinical relationship. In both family and group interventions with Asian American clients, clinicians need to be alert to the differences in cultural identification and social environmental experiences of individual members in the family or in the group. Cultural knowledge and sensitivity, empathic skills, and respectful behaviors are crucial skills for family therapists and group therapists. They must be vigilant about imposing mainstream American cultural values, norms, and worldviews, including communication and interaction styles, on Asian American families and group members. Family therapists must be particularly sensitive to and respectful of the ways Asian cultures and social environmental experiences influence crucial areas of functioning in an Asian American family, such as hierarchy, values, norms, communication styles, child-rearing practices, migration experiences, and cultural identification as individuals and as families. Likewise, group therapists must be particularly aware of Asian cultural values and norms governing self-disclosures and social interactions in a group and must attend to the differences in group process for ethnically homogeneous and ethnically heterogeneous groups. When applied with sensitivity to clients' cultural and social environmental contexts, both family and group treatment modalities can be very effective for Asian Americans.

9

Culturally Appropriate Approaches
to Service Delivery

In the last two chapters, we have been focusing on the therapeutic strategies and approaches that individual clinicians can use in providing mental health services for Asian American clients. Yet provision of culturally appropriate services requires professionals to go beyond the level of an individual clinician to consider changes in the mental health service delivery system. Such institutional changes are imperative for overcoming the cultural and social environmental barriers to services for Asian American clients. In this chapter, we will examine the changes and modifications that are needed in the current mainstream service delivery models. We will also provide examples of innovative programs that are tailored to the needs of the Asian American population. Specifically, we will begin the chapter with a review of three basic models for providing culturally appropriate services: the mainstream model, the parallel model, and the nonparallel model. We will illustrate the issues by examining the approaches used by two exemplary clinics serving Asian Americans. We will follow this discussion with an examination of other promising new approaches that are gaining attention in the field: the general family practitioner approach and the school-based family services or school-linked family services approach. This chapter will also highlight the importance of preventive services in Asian American communities and the role of mental health professionals as agents of institutional change.

Three Basic Models of Service Delivery

The literature on Asian American mental health services has identified three basic models or approaches for making institutional changes to improve mental health services for Asian Americans (Sue, 1977; Sue & Morishima, 1982; Takeuchi et al., 1992). As stated originally by Sue (1977), these approaches are (a) making modifications within existing mainstream programs, (b) developing independent but parallel services in Asian American communities, and (c) creating new, nonparallel services. We will examine these three approaches in detail in the following sections.

Description of Service Delivery Models

The first approach or model involves having existing mainstream mental health facilities provide culturally appropriate services by training their staff to provide bilingual/bicultural services or by hiring personnel to provide such services (Sue, 1977). The second approach, often called the parallel model, involves setting up specific mental health programs to meet the needs of Asian Americans (Sue, 1977). These programs can be independent programs that are set up in ways similar to mainstream programs but are targeted specifically to the Asian American client population. These programs can also be extensions of existing mainstream mental health programs that function separately. They may even be located at a different site from their parent agencies. Most typically, these parallel programs are situated in Asian American communities or other locations easily accessible to the client population. Mental health services at these parallel agencies are provided by bicultural/bilingual staff, and the scope of their services is similar to that of the services provided to clients of mainstream agencies (Sue, 1997; Takeuchi et al., 1992). The third approach, the nonparallel services model, involves creating completely new mental health agencies that incorporate culture-specific healing approaches into mental health services (Sue, 1977). These agencies can provide innovative services that are not found in mainstream mental health institutions.

Effectiveness of Service Delivery Models

In recent years, mainstream institutions have demonstrated a greater responsiveness to community needs by hiring bilingual/bicultural providers. The number of parallel agencies established in areas with large Asian communities has also increased. Mental health professionals as well as agency administrators can certainly attest to the effectiveness of these changes. In addition, a number of studies have documented the efficacy of these practices in providing culturally responsive services to Asian American clients (Sue, Fujino, Hu, Takeuchi, & Zane, 1991; Takeuchi et al., 1992; Takeuchi, Sue, & Yeh, 1995; Yeh, Takeuchi, & Sue, 1994; Zane, Hatanaka, Park, & Akutsu, 1994). The results of these studies indicate that the match of ethnicity and language between a client and a clinician is conducive to engaging Asian American clients in treatment. They also show that parallel clinics, operationally defined as mental health agencies specifically targeted to Asian Americans, are, in general, more effective in providing services to Asian American clients than mainstream clinics.

Sue et al. (1991), drawing on a large database from the Los Angeles County Department of Mental Health (LACDMH), examined the clinical data compiled from approximately 3,000 Asian Americans as well as comparable numbers of African Americans, Mexican Americans, and whites, all of whom had entered the outpatient system during a 5-year period ending in 1988. Their study indicated that, for Asian Americans, when socioeconomic and other clinical variables were controlled, ethnic match between clinician and client had significant effects in reducing dropouts (failure to return after one session) and in increasing the number of treatment sessions. For Asian American clients whose primary language was not English, language match alone, ethnic match alone, and a combination of language and ethnic match all produced a lower dropout and more sessions than lack of matching on these variables. Takeuchi et al. (1995) used the same database from LACDMH and analyzed the data of approximately 4,700 adults consisting of comparable numbers of African Americans, Asian Americans, and Mexican Americans, all of whom used services at a mental health facility in Los Angeles County between 1982 and 1988. They concluded that ethnic clients who went to ethnic-specific programs had a higher return rate than those going to mainstream clinics. Their data also showed that, when other variables were controlled, these clients stayed in treatment longer in ethnic programs. In fact, they estimated that Asian Americans who entered ethnic programs were 15 times more likely to return after their first session than Asian Americans in mainstream programs. Their findings offered strong support for the view that parallel clinics are effective in serving Asian Americans adults. Similar results were found for Asian American children by Yeh et al. (1994). These researchers analyzed the same LACDMH database, selecting 912 Asian American children (18 years or younger) who used outpatient services at a Los Angeles County mental health facility between 1983 and 1988. Four Asian American ethnic-specific clinics, or parallel centers, were included in this study. The authors concluded that, when compared to those who went to mainstream centers, Asian American children who received services at the parallel clinics were less likely to drop out of services after the first session, stayed in treatment longer, and had higher functioning scores at discharge. Again, the study controlled for variables including social class and functioning score at admission. Finally, using data from the Asian Pacific Counseling and Treatment Centers in Los Angeles, a parallel center, Zane et al. (1994) again concluded that the parallel model was generally effective in serving Asian American clients. At the same time, following the parallel model did not diminish the center's effectiveness in serving white clients. Their study also suggested that further service modifications might have to be made to further meet the needs of Southeast Asian refugee clients. Their observation is not surprising in light of the traumatic refugee experiences typical of this group. In sum, all of the above studies supported the efficacy of matching ethnicity and language between clinician and client, as well as the effectiveness of parallel or ethnic-specific clinics in serving Asian American clients.

Implementation of Service Delivery Models

Having examined the research studies, we will now examine specific issues in implementing the three service delivery models.

Bilingual/Bicultural Services in Mainstream Agencies

The first approach, proposed by Sue (1977), calls for mainstream mental health facilities to train their staff to provide bilingual/bicultural services or to hire bilingual/bicultural professionals to provide culturally responsive services. This approach may be effective because ethnic and language match between clinician and client often helps to prevent client dropout and to enhance client cooperation in therapy. However, in actual practice, some mainstream agencies use interpreters and bilingual/bicultural paraprofessionals as an alternative to having bilingual/bicultural mental health professionals on staff. This alternative should be considered a short-term rather than a long-term solution. These paraprofessionals and interpreters can help to overcome some of the language and cultural barriers between professional practitioners and Asian American clients. However, unless professional mental health clinicians understand their clients' culture and communicate directly with them, they will not be able to provide the same quality of care to Asian American clients as they will to mainstream clients. In other words, Asian American clients will receive only second-rate service from the institution.

Realistically, we understand that agencies in areas with small Asian American populations may have no alternative to using interpreters. Also, given the diversity of Asian languages, even areas with larger Asian

American populations may not have clinicians who speak all of the Asian languages or dialects. In such situations, as we have discussed in Chapter 5, interpreters should be properly trained and should work as a team with the clinician. In our experience, we have come across agencies where the interpreters have not been trained in interpretation or in mental health. They are simply staff members who hold other positions and are called to serve as ad hoc interpreters. The quality and accuracy of their translations are dependent on the individual and may be very inconsistent. Such a practice poses a risk of miscommunication between the clinician and the client by omitting or misinterpreting critical clinical data. Hence, we want to emphasize the importance of having institutions provide proper training for interpreters, particularly for volunteers and others serving on an ad hoc basis. The same requirements also apply to paraprofessionals. A clinician should work with the paraprofessional in providing services to a client rather than merely providing supervision and expecting the paraprofessional to take on the responsibility of working with the client. If properly trained, interpreters and mental health paraprofessionals can play an important role in helping mainstream institutions meet the needs of Asian American clients. This approach is often necessary for agencies located in communities where the Asian American population is small.

In communities with fairly large Asian American populations, the ideal staffing approach for institutions is to hire professional mental health providers with the skills to work directly with Asian American clients. Minimally, this can be done through a team approach, where at least one professional member of the mental health team has the appropriate cultural and linguistic skills to provide guidance to other members in providing services to Asian Americans. The eventual goal for institutions is to have enough culturally proficient clinicians that are able to provide direct services to their Asian American clientele.

When mainstream agencies expand their capacity to provide bilingual/bicultural services, clinicians need to ensure that the social and physical environments of the institution are user-friendly for Asian American clients. We have already made some recommendations on this issue in Chapter 6. In this chapter, we want to emphasize that, specifically, attention needs to be given to hiring sufficient bilingual/bicultural support staff, such as phone operators, receptionists, and cashiers. Language and cultural barriers in communicating with these personnel can often interfere or can even prevent a client from seeking services. Though Asian Americans may constitute only a portion of the total clientele served by a mainstream institution, agencies can still include Asian languages on their signs and in their clinic literature. A touch of Asian decor in the waiting room, such as a picture or artwork, can also be very useful for making the Asian American client feel welcome. In sum, to be culturally responsive to the Asian American population, mainstream agencies will need to address the numerous institutional barriers that lessen the accessibility of their mental health services.

Parallel Centers

The second approach involves the establishment of parallel centers that are targeted specifically to Asian American clients (Sue, 1977). These mental health clinics need to be located in Asian American communities and staffed by bilingual/bicultural clinicians. On the basis of their review of literature on parallel clinics, Takeuchi et al. (1992) identified three features that are important for the success of these clinics: accessibility, appropriate services, and community involvement.

Accessibility refers to providing services at locations that are convenient for clients. In addition, an agency's hours of operation have to meet the clients' schedules. Factors such as greater flexibility in scheduling appointments and accommodation of walk-in appointments are known to increase the utilization of mental health services by minority clients (Takeuchi et al., 1992). The provision of *appropriate services,* the second feature of parallel clinics, refers to the availability of bilingual and bicultural mental health services. This feature also includes an agency's capacity to refer clients to other adjunct services, such as social, financial, medical, educational, and legal services. In addition, parallel clinics may use the support system of their clientele, including family members and relatives, pastors and other religious personnel, indigenous healers, or respected community leaders, all of whom can help reduce a client's resistance to seek or to cooperate with mental health treatment (Takeuchi et al., 1992). The third feature of parallel programs is *community involvement* in the planning and evaluation of services. This participation can be achieved by inviting community members to serve on policy and advisory boards of the clinic. Their participation can help ensure that the program is providing culturally appropriate services that meet the needs of the community. To promote utilization, the list of services provided by a clinic also needs to be publicized in community and ethnic media (Takeuchi et al., 1992). In addition, administrators and clinicians in policy-making positions need to participate actively on community policy or planning boards and committees. Their involvement is a valuable opportunity for them to learn about the emerging needs of the community, as well as to coordinate their clinics' services with other community agencies. This networking is a good way to obtain feedback and suggestions for ensuring the quality of services provided by their clinics.

As the research studies have demonstrated, parallel clinics are very effective in engaging Asian American clients in mental health services

(Takeuchi et al., 1992, 1995; Yeh et al., 1994; Zane et al., 1994). Currently, a number of parallel clinics have been established on both the East and the West Coasts in regions with large Asian American populations, particularly in southern California. Although parallel clinics provide an effective model for serving Asian Americans, they are less feasible in regions where the Asian American population is small or spread out. In these areas, the first model, improving the cultural responsiveness of mainstream agencies, may be more practical to implement. However, the mainstream model and the parallel-clinics model are not mutually exclusive. For example, even in regions with large Asian American populations, not all Asian Americans live in ethnic communities. Some of these individuals will need to seek mental health services from mainstream agencies because they can reach these clinics more conveniently in terms of transportation or commuting time. Thus, a comprehensive network of mental health services for the region should include parallel centers as well as mainstream agencies with bilingual/bicultural capability. In fact, a system of having the two models complement each other may be an ideal approach as the United States becomes more ethnically diverse with the anticipated growth of Asian Americans and other minority populations.

Nonparallel Programs

The third model goes beyond parallel clinics by establishing new, nonparallel mental health programs that can provide services unavailable in mainstream agencies (Sue, 1977). This model takes a culturally specific approach that seeks innovations in the organization and in the services of a clinic. A clinic may offer treatment modalities that are different from those offered by mainstream communities. For example, nonparallel clinics may incorporate traditional healing practices based on the specific cultures of their client population into Western-based mainstream mental health treatment modalities (Takeuchi et al., 1992).

Although nonparallel programs may be an ideal way to meet the mental health needs of Asian Americans, such programs are not easy to establish. In fact, nonparallel programs present special challenges to mental health administrators in terms of funding and third-party reimbursement (Takeuchi et al., 1992). Truly innovative culture-specific programs and services, by their very nature, often do not fit neatly into established mainstream bureaucratic procedures for attaining agency certification and professional licensure and for receiving funding or reimbursement. Further, the use of traditional Asian healing practices for mental health problems is not a subject taught or widely researched in accredited clinical programs in the United States. Hence, clinicians need to exercise caution in integrating these practices or offering them alongside conventional mainstream mental health services. The inclusion of traditional Asian healing practices may increase liability concerns and even affect malpractice insurance for a clinic. These "unconventional" services may also fall into a gray area in terms of legal and business codes that govern services permissible at mental health clinics. Although these obstacles are not insurmountable, they are important concerns that mental health professionals must anticipate when planning to establish nonparallel programs.

From a different perspective, mental health clinicians and administrators designing nonparallel programs need to remember that Asian Americans differ in their identification with Asian and mainstream American cultures. Thus, a nonparallel clinic should offer treatment choices rather than imposing traditional Asian healing practices across the board. Moreover, as discussed in previous chapters, some Asian American clients may have already tried traditional Asian remedies before accepting a referral for mental health services. These clients are ready to try something different and may be disappointed if a clinician emphasizes traditional Asian healing approaches. At the same time, unbeknownst to these clients, conventional mainstream treatment approaches may be too foreign to them. What they really need may perhaps be described as conventional psychotherapy and counseling adapted to their cultural and social environmental contexts, as in the examples given in previous chapters. Thus, nonparallel programs need to be flexible and responsive to the expectations of each individual Asian American client.

In actual practice, the distinction between the second model of parallel services and the third model of nonparallel services is not necessarily discrete or dichotomous. Parallel clinics, depending on their level of autonomy or independence from their parent organization (if there is one), can develop additional services as they are needed. For example, advocacy, social, and legal services, which are frequently needed by immigrant Asian Americans of lower socioeconomic status, can be provided concurrently with medical and mental health services in a multiservice center (Lee, 1980). This concept is innovative but can also be redefined to fit within the framework of mainstream administrative, funding, and legal guidelines. Programs within a parallel agency can also develop different approaches for delivering their services. For example, part of their services can be "conventional," while other parts can be "innovative" and nonparallel. In this regard, the ideal parallel and nonparallel programs can be considered to be at either end of a continuum, with the numerous culture-specific Asian American agencies placed somewhere along this continuum.

Examples of Culturally Congruent Mental Health Programs

Currently, a number of clinics in the United States are providing effective mental health services to Asian Americans. We have chosen two of these clinics, South Cove Community Health Center and Asian Pacific Counseling and Treatment Centers, to illustrate our discussion of culturally appropriate mental health services.

South Cove Community Health Center

The South Cove Community Health Center (SCCHC) in Boston exemplifies an innovative program that provides comprehensive services to Asian Americans. This agency is nonprofit and funded mainly by governmental grants and contracts. It started in 1972 as a small storefront clinic in Boston's Chinatown to provide culturally and linguistically appropriate services that would be accessible and affordable for the community. In a few years, it grew into a major health center providing comprehensive medical, mental health, and social services. Currently, SCCHC operates on a multi-million-dollar annual budget and provides services to Asian Americans throughout the Greater Boston area as well as the other New England states and to the diverse ethnic populations in the South Cove area of Boston. Its client population is primarily Chinese Americans, Vietnamese Americans, and Cambodian Americans, the groups that constitute the vast majority of the Asian American population in the Greater Boston area.

SCCHC offers a full range of outpatient services, including adult medicine, pediatrics, obstetrics/gynecology, dentistry, optometry, podiatry, health education, mental health, and social services. Acupuncture, a traditional Asian medical practice, is also included in its services. The clientele of the center ranges from infants, toddlers, and children to adults and the elderly. Mental health services are provided by the Family and Behavioral Health Division. Specific services of the division include psychiatric evaluation and medication, individual, family, and group therapy, psychological testing/evaluation, infant/toddler early intervention, case management for chronic psychiatric patients, services for clients with mental retardation and developmental delays, and school-based counseling. In addition to services provided at two buildings closely located in Chinatown, SCCHC operates an off-site extension clinic and an off-site after-school program. Both of these services are located in regions of Greater Boston with large concentrations of Asian Americans. In addition, two other off-site programs specialize in serving Southeast Asian Americans: the Vietnamese Youth and Family Center in Dorchester (an area of Boston) and the Khmer Youth and Family Center in Lynn (a nearby city). Both programs are located in areas with significant concentrations of the respective populations. Services provided by these programs include adjustment counseling, adolescent tracking, educational support services, middle school support, hospital diversion, runaway youth, teen pregnancy prevention, and summer programs. The Chinatown main center also offers a variety of youth programs for Asian Americans.

SCCHC maintains a close relationship with area hospitals and psychiatric hospitals to ensure appropriate inpatient care for medical as well as for psychiatric patients. The center also works closely with public school districts and other service agencies in the Greater Boston area and provides consultation and technical assistance to them. SCCHC itself is an integral part of the Chinatown community. The main clinic is located in a building complex containing a public school, a neighborhood center that provides a variety of adult and children/youth programs, and a senior housing building with a senior day center. Another office is located in a nearby building. Both offices are within convenient walking distance from the public housing complexes in the area, as well as other community agencies and organizations that offer a variety of services, such as after-school programs and senior services. SCCHC actively networks with these community agencies and organizations in the development, coordination, and delivery of services to the Asian American community.

As discussed in Chapter 6, one way to engage Asian American clients in mental health services is to streamline the referral process. Medical professionals are a common source of referral for Asian American clients to mental health programs. Instead of going from one agency to another, medical clients at SCCHC can simply go from one department for medical services to another department for mental health services. The medical staff can easily check whether a client has followed through with a mental health referral and can collaborate with the mental health staff to engage the client. Medical staff members are also in a position to reinforce the importance of mental health services when clients see them for medical appointments. In addition, community residents go to SCCHC for health care, social services, or other non-mental health services. This familiarity with the center makes it less inhibiting or stigmatizing when clients are referred to the mental health division for services. Providers of different disciplines can work together to encourage client compliance with treatment and to coordinate services for clients.

SCCHC, as a multiservice agency, is an illustration of an "one-stop shopping center" that provides a full range of culturally responsive services to Asian American clients. Some of its programs may be considered parallel services, but overall, its comprehensive approach, its integration of cultural elements, and its close linkage with community organizations are illustrative of a nonparallel approach. The center is clearly an effective model for mental health service delivery in Asian American communities.

Asian Pacific Counseling and Treatment Centers

The Asian Pacific Counseling and Treatment Centers (APCTC) started in 1977 as a program of the Los Angeles County Department of Mental

Health. The main center was the first mental health clinic in Los Angeles County specifically developed to serve Asian Pacific Americans. In 1990, APCTC privatized and became a county-contract agency. Most of its mental health professionals are bilingual and bicultural. Languages and dialects spoken by the providers include Cambodian, Cantonese, Mandarin, Taiwanese, Japanese, Korean, Laotian, Cebuano, Ilocano, Tagalog, Thai, and Vietnamese. Services are provided at the main center close to downtown Los Angeles and at five other centers located in areas of Greater Los Angeles with large concentrations of Asian Americans. Among these five centers, the Indochinese Center is designated to serve Southeast Asian Americans, including Cambodian, Laotian, Thai, and Vietnamese Americans.

APCTC operates a variety of programs. Two of these programs provide outpatient mental health services: the Adult Program and the Children and Family Services Program. Another program, the Day Rehabilitation Program, provides services to clients with chronic mental disorders, such as bipolar disorders and schizophrenia. It also provides placement in government housing for chronic mental health patients. The Vocational Rehabilitation Program provides job placement for clients with mental or physical disabilities. Besides providing services at the various centers, the Children and Family Services Program sends clinicians to schools in various areas of Los Angeles to provide on-site mental health services to their students. In addition, the centers work closely with Metropolitan State Hospital and other psychiatric hospitals in the area for clients who need inpatient services.

The services described above can be considered "parallel programs" in that they are similar to services provided by mainstream agencies. However, APCTC can also be considered a "nonparallel" clinic that offers services at a "one-stop shopping center." Furthermore, some of the services provided by the center's programs are uniquely suited to Asian Americans and are seldom found in mainstream mental health clinics. For example, the Children and Family Services Program operates a computer literacy program for Asian American children from low-income families. It runs as an after-school program, 4 days a week. This program actually serves as a respite program for parents as well as a preventive program for the children. This creative way of featuring computer literacy is an effective way of attracting participants and of introducing and destigmatizing mental health services.

In addition to providing bilingual and bicultural mental health services, APCTC incorporates Asian cultural practices into treatment strategies. As mentioned in the last chapter, tea is usually served in the group therapy sessions. Another noteworthy example is a therapy group designed to engage Chinese American clients with chronic mental disorders who were initially resistant to being seen for medication or psychotherapy. This group was led by Stephen Cheung, and its focus was psychoeducation as well as socialization. Dr. Cheung arranged for these clients to be seen for medication on the same day as the group therapy. This procedure made it possible for the clients to receive both medical and psychological services with one visit to the clinic, rather than having to go on different days for different services. It helped to promote compliance with treatment. Clients began each visit to the clinic with their medication appointments. Then the therapy group would start with a simple lunch. When lunch was over, the clinician would lead the group to practice *Liu Tong Quan,* a form of slow-motion Chinese martial art exercise similar to the *Tai Ji Quan (Tai Chi Chuan)* discussed in Chapter 2. This activity would take about 15 minutes. Then the group would sit down and discuss clinical issues. Overall, the agenda of this group has been found to be very successful in engaging these clients, who previously were very reluctant to attend group or individual sessions. Several unique cultural elements contribute to this group's success. The lunch is a cultural expression of hospitality and is also a stimulus for social interaction. As some of the clients expressed, they really appreciated this caring gesture. Later, the clinic changed to serving tea instead of lunch. This is also a cultural expression of hospitality that can serve as an ice-breaker for the group interaction. The inclusion of martial arts exercise is particularly helpful for engaging the clients in treatment. This type of exercise is a traditional Asian health practice and is congruent with the clients' cultural perspective. Initially, they probably saw this activity as more helpful for their problems than group therapy or "chatting with others in a group." In fact, the appeal of this activity to clients in this group has led to the introduction of *Tai Ji Quan (Tai Chi Chuan)* to another group at APCTC. The second group was equally successful.

There are many other ways in which clinicians at APCTC incorporate culturally syntonic features into their services and outreach efforts. Those we have mentioned are sufficient to illustrate that APCTC uses both theparallel and the non-parallel approaches to serving its Asian Pacific American clientele. The agency provides a broad spectrum of mental health and related services that parallel mainstream approaches, and, concurrently, offer culturally responsive programs and treatment strategies. This kind of adaptability and innovativeness is a major key to success in designing effective mental health programs for Asian Americans.

Overall Observations

These brief descriptions of SCCHC and APCTC illustrate effective models for providing mental health services to Asian Americans. These programs are closely in tune with the needs of the community, and they maintain a flexible approach in developing services to meet the community's changing trends and demands. Moreover, in addition to their culturally appropriate services for the overall Asian American population, both of these clinics provide programs to meet the specific needs of Southeast Asian Americans whose traumatic refugee experiences interfere with their adjustment to life in the United States. The programs provided by these two agencies serve as a model for addressing the needs of both the general Asian American population and its specific subgroups.

We want to emphasize that in addition to SCCHC and APCTC, other programs in the United States provide exemplary parallel and non-parallel mental health services for Asian Americans. From our personal observations and discussions with colleagues working in the Asian American communities, we have noticed that many programs, in varying degrees, are incorporating cultural components into their services. Their efforts include adaptations or modifications of traditional mainstream treatment strategies, as well as institutional practices and regulations. However, only a few descriptions of these culturally responsive treatment strategies and institutional practices have appeared in the professional literature. Thus, we encourage clinicians to learn more about these adaptations and innovations by visiting community programs and talking to clinicians working on the front line in the communities.

Promising New Service Delivery Approaches

We will now examine two promising new approaches to mental health service delivery that are gaining attention in the field: the general family practitioner approach and the school-based family services or school-linked family services approach. These new approaches can be incorporated into any of the three previously discussed models. Both approaches share a common concern: to provide coordinated or integrated services in order to prevent the fragmentation of services, found in many mainstream agencies, that so often confuses clients and alienates them from mental health services.

General Family Practitioner Approach

The general family practitioner approach calls for the mental health professional to function as a primary care provider similar to the traditional "family doctor" who provides treatment for clients and their family members for different reasons over a period of time (Fritzsimmons, 1986; Griswold, 1980, 1986; Hong, 1988; Vane, 1986). For example, a clinician may initially see a child for counseling for a school-related problem and later see the child's parents, who are seeking help for another child or for other family problems (Hong, 1988; Vane, 1986). In this manner, the clinician has an ongoing interaction with the family and serves as a resource for the family. This approach is not the same as family therapy, which treats family members concurrently as a unit to address a problem. In contrast, the general family practitioner approach is concerned with seeing members of a family sequentially, often individually over different periods of time, for different problems. Over time, the practitioner may use both individual and family therapy as needed.

As Hong (1988) observed, the general family practitioner approach is a culturally syntonic method for providing mental health services in the Asian American communities. It helps to minimize the cultural inhibition against revealing family problems to outsiders. By staying with a family over time and serving as its primary provider and resource person, the clinician, in a sense, has joined with the family as an insider. Disclosures to this clinician will be preferable to "spreading family secrets" to other clinicians who are total strangers. Moreover, other family members, knowing that the clinician has previously helped one family member, will be inclined to have confidence in the clinician and seek his or her services when the need arises. In fact, given the family orientation in Asian cultures, we find that quite often Asian American clients actually assume that the same clinician will be the primary provider for their family. They do not expect different clinicians to see different members of the family. No doubt, clinicians need to assess their own biases toward individual family members whom they have not met but have heard about in previous therapeutic work with other family members. However, if a clinician's prior knowledge of a family situation is used judiciously and ethically, this knowledge can be helpful in assisting other family members with their problems.

The general family practitioner approach is consistent with the expectation of many Asian American clients that the clinician will take on multiple roles as healer/doctor, expert, teacher, consultant, advocate, and resource person (Gaw, 1993; Hong, 1988, 1989; Lee, 1982, 1997b; Lorenzo & Adler, 1984; Shon & Ja, 1982; Sue & Morishima, 1982; Uba, 1994). This approach calls for clinicians to embrace these multiple roles (Griswold, 1980, 1986; Hong, 1988) and expects clinicians to be knowledgeable about the family, community, and social environment of their clients (Fritzsimmons, 1986; Griswold, 1980, 1986; Hong, 1988). Furthermore, as discussed in previous chapters, Asian American clients who are identified with Asian cultures often seek quick relief from their symptoms or distress and typically request termination once these immediate goals are achieved (Gaw, 1993; Hong, 1988, 1993a; Lee, 1980, 1982, 1997c; Shon & Ja, 1982; Sue & Morishima, 1982; Uba, 1994). The general family practitioner approach is well suited to meet this expectation and behavior by accepting "interruption of treatment" after the client has achieved certain therapeutic goals, with the understanding that the client will return in the future when the need arises (Hong, 1988). Unlike the socially awkward situation where a client has to terminate unilaterally and drop out of treatment, the interruption at this point is a mutual decision that preserves the therapeutic relationship and makes it more likely that the client will return in the future. In this sense, the general family practitioner approach is actually focused on extended, long-term relationships with clients. Also, this approach does not exclude long-term treatment as a modality for clients who can benefit from it and are willing to pursue it.

In applying the general family practitioner approach, clinicians need to assess each case carefully and decide whether it is appropriate for them to see a client or a family (Hong, 1988). This approach simply suggests that it is often clinically effective for members of a family to be seen by a clinician who serves as both a primary provider and a resource person. A clinician should refer family members to other clinicians if the clients' problems are not within the clinician's expertise. Also, there are times when a client may prefer to see another clinician. For example, a client may have concerns about confidentiality regarding a personal secret that he or she does not want other family members to know, or a client may associate the clinician with a strongly disliked family member who has previously seen the clinician for treatment. In these cases, a client's preference must be respected. Indeed, clinicians need to be clear about confidentiality and be vigilant against making unintended revelations. They must also be careful about maintaining objectivity when working with different family members over time and must be particularly alert to the issues of transference, countertransference, and alliances with different family members (Hong, 1988). All of these are issues to be addressed through clinical training, supervision, or peer consultation. Referrals to other clinicians should be made when these issues pose a problem for the clinician.

In sum, the general family practitioner approach is a basic orientation. A clinician needs to take the specific situation of a client into consideration when applying this approach. Because this approach is particularly congruent with Asian cultures, we encourage clinicians working in Asian American communities to take an active role in its development and refinement.

School-Based Family Services

School-based family services (SBFS), also known as school-linked family services, is another emerging approach that has been gaining popularity and attention in recent years (Adelman & Taylor, 1993; Dryfoos,

1994; Soriano & Hong, 1997). Basically, the SBFS approach involves providing an integrated set of services in a school setting for children and their families, such as mental health, social services, and preventive medical care (Dryfoos, 1994; Fine & Carlson, 1992; Melaville & Blank, 1991, 1993; Simeonsson, 1994; Soriano & Hong, 1997). These services are typically offered in a school located in the community. In situations where the physical environment, such as space, is limited, the integrated services are provided at another community location in close collaboration with a community-based school. These programs are known as *school-linked family services.*

The SBFS approach embraces a "one-stop shopping" concept that encourages providers from different agencies to collaborate closely as a team. Again, the intent is to eliminate the confusing and frustrating situation where families or individuals are referred from agency to agency for different services. The providers also work together to address the possible gaps in services and to avoid duplication of services (Soriano & Hong, 1997). The specific components of a SBFS program will depend on the needs of a particular community and the available funding. Currently, there are a number of model programs nationwide, each with its own emphasis, such as California's Healthy Start, New Jersey's School-Based Youth Services Program, and Georgia's New Futures Initiative (Melaville & Blank, 1991, 1993; Soriano & Hong, 1997). These programs all share a core purpose: to provide integrated services located or linked to schools. The creation of a SBFS program does not necessitate an institutional merger of service agencies and schools (Soriano & Hong, 1997). The process simply requires the various agencies to send one or more providers to work in collaboration as a team in the school. This does not mean that all services have to be provided in schools. For instance, medical services (as distinct from preventive medical care) and mental health services for clients with major psychiatric problems can be provided at the participating agencies' home clinics, with the SBFS team helping as a resource and facilitating referrals. In a sense, the entire SBFS team functions in a general family practitioner approach and takes the role of a primary service provider, a resource, and an advocate for children and their families.

Although the SBFS approach was not developed specifically for Asian American communities, the model is particularly relevant for providing mental health services to immigrant Asian Americans who are not familiar with mental health services and service delivery systems in the United States. Many immigrant Asian Americans are confused and frustrated by being referred from provider to provider and from agency to agency (Hong, 1988; Hong et al., 1995; Soriano & Hong, 1997). This array of referrals is typical given the fragmented way in which mental health services and the closely related fields of social, educational, and medical services are being provided in many mainstream settings. Integrated services provided by a SBFS approach clarify this confusion and encourage service utilization. Moreover, teachers in schools have daily interactions with children and are in a position to notice if the children or their families are in need of mental health or other services (California Wellness Foundation, 1993; Fine & Carlson, 1992; Melaville & Blank, 1991, 1993; Simeonsson, 1994; Soriano & Hong, 1997). Because of the high cultural value placed on education and the traditional respect for educators, Asian Americans are more likely to follow through on a referral from a school personnel member to a mental health clinician conveniently located at the same school. Also, when a clinician works with other school personnel as a member of a school-based or school-linked team, the image of a mental health provider is seemingly enhanced as a result of being associated with familiar and respected educators, rather than with unfamiliar psychiatric professionals who work with "crazy" people. This association helps to destigmatize mental health services and reinforces service utilization.

The advantages of working in collaboration with the school system are widely recognized by mental health agencies in Asian American communities. Many of these agencies have already placed mental health clinicians in schools to provide services. For example, as discussed previously, clinicians from APCTC are providing services in a number of schools throughout the Los Angeles area. SCCHC in Boston is, in effect, a school-linked program. Before SCCHC outgrew the capacity of its physical space and moved some of its offices to a nearby building, all of its services in Chinatown were provided in a building complex shared with a public school and other agencies. Parents and children could simply walk from the school to the clinic or to other community programs without getting onto the street. Currently, many services are still being provided at this convenient site, with the rest provided at another building within walking distance. SCCHC also places mental health clinicians in other public schools in the Greater Boston area to provide services to Asian American students.

Clearly, schools are the best base of operations for reaching out to Asian American children and their families, and particularly to immigrants. Thus, clinicians serving Asian American communities have to take the lead in promoting and establishing school-based or school-linked programs.

Primary Prevention

A comprehensive service delivery model always includes a primary prevention component. The intent of primary prevention models is to prevent problems before they occur and to target individuals or groups at risk of developing the problems. Asian American communities face many of the same problems encountered by other communities, such as the risk factors associated with the social environmental conditions of contemporary urban living, particularly in inner-city or lower socioeconomic neighborhoods. In addition, many Asian American families, especially immigrant families, experience a "cultural gap," which is a major issue that deserves special attention in preventive work (Hong, 1989, 1996).

Hong (1996) has identified two aspects of this cultural gap. The first aspect pertains to the discrepancies between the culture practiced within Asian American homes and the culture of mainstream American society. Often mainstream institutions, such as the mass media, wittingly or unwittingly accentuate these cultural discrepancies in a manner that is insensitive to Asian American cultural practices. For example, television programs and newspaper articles may stereotype Asian practices as exotic oddities. Similarly, while emphasizing the importance of English proficiency, schools and other institutions may be sending the additional message that Asian languages, and hence Asian cultures, are "unacceptable," "uneducated," and "inferior" (Hong, 1996). This cultural gap between the home and mainstream society is often a major obstacle in the development of Asian American children's self-esteem and ethnic identity (Hong, 1989, 1996; Sue, 1989; Sue & Sue, 1993, 1999). It also challenges the self-efficacy of many parents, particularly those who are less acculturated into mainstream culture, when they try to offer guidance to their children (Hong, 1989, 1996; Lee, 1982). This aspect of the cultural gap is a major threat to the psychoemotional welfare of many Asian Americans, especially immigrants, and to the stability of their families. The second aspect of the cultural gap pertains to the differences in cultural identification between Asian American parents and their children (Hong, 1996). As discussed in previous chapters, in Asian American families, especially immigrant families, parents are often more identified with Asian cultures than their children, who become more identified with mainstream American culture as they grow up. This cultural gap within the family is another risk factor for Asian American families and may become a major source of tension and conflict (Hong, 1989, 1996).

A number of primary prevention services may be used to address these two aspects of the cultural gap. One effective approach is to provide preventive counseling groups and workshops for children and parents (Hong, 1996). These services can be offered in any setting, including mental health centers, community agencies, and particularly public schools, which are strategic locations for reaching out to children and parents. For example, preventive counseling groups can be offered in a school to children at different grade levels to address issues specific to their developmental stage. Special attention needs to be directed toward recruiting new immigrants to these groups. Discussion topics for the groups can include issues related to cultural identity, cultural practices at home and in mainstream society, and the potential for friction between children and parents because of differences in their cultural identification. Similarly, groups or workshops can be offered for parents to address parenting in the context of Asian and mainstream American cultures. Topics can include, for example, differences between appropriate discipline for children and abuse, the trends and fads followed by mainstream youths, the extent to which these trends and fads are considered acceptable by mainstream standards (e.g., punk hair style, body piercing, smoking, drug use, dating practices, or sex), and methods for addressing these concerns within the context of Asian cultures. Even though clinicians cannot provide definitive answers to all of these questions, a discussion about them will keep parents informed and empowered. Clinicians can also direct parents to necessary resources when they need help in the future. In sum, preventive services can be focused on helping Asian American children and parents gain a mutual understanding of each party's cultural underpinnings and thereby helping to close the cultural gap between home and mainstream society, as well as between parents and children. In addition to family work, acculturation training groups or workshops and newcomers' support groups are helpful primary prevention services that clinicians can offer to help new immigrants and refugees adjust to life in the United States.

Another type of primary intervention takes place on the institutional level rather than on the clinician-client level (Hong, 1996). For example, mental health clinicians can provide cultural proficiency training and consultation to mainstream providers and institutions. These educational services can help minimize situations where providers or institutions inadvertently undermine Asian cultures and affront the self-image of Asian Americans. In this regard, advocacy, consultation, and provision of in-service training for other agencies are important components of primary prevention services.

Clinicians as Agents of Institutional Change

Mental health clinicians are bound by institutional rules and procedures when they provide services. These institutional guidelines may be specific to a particular agency or may involve broader systemic policies. To provide culturally responsive services, clinicians need to make sure that these regulations are appropriate for their target client population.

In reviewing the policies of a specific agency, mental health professionals need to examine areas such as hours of operation, fee schedules, range of services, and administrative and service procedures. Many of these policies are within an agency's own control. But because these rules and procedures are often based on mainstream institutions, clinicians and administrators need to evaluate them carefully before applying them to service programs targeting Asian Americans. Broader systemic considerations involve examining the practice of mental health services as an institution or as a system. Significant issues include third-party reimbursement policies, target populations, and service catchment areas. For example, restrictions to services may be imposed by third-party reimbursement such as insurance companies, health maintenance organizations, Medicaid, Medicare, and other governmental funding, such as grants and contracts. Also, third-party reimbursement and governmental funding policies play a major role in shaping mental health agencies and their services through defining the frequency, duration, and type of services allowable. Grants and contracts may determine the target population for a clinic by defining characteristics of its clientele, such as diagnostic or problem categories, socioeconomic group, geographical neighborhood, or ethnic/language group. Often, these specifications are obstacles for mental health agencies seeking maximum flexibility in providing culturally responsive services to Asian Americans. Therefore, clinicians and administrators need to advocate for systemic changes and, at the same time, creatively seek funding that will allow them to develop their services to meet the needs of their clientele. They must constantly be on the lookout for institutional barriers to the delivery of culturally responsive services and actively take on the role of agents for institutional change (Arredondo, 1998; Arredondo et al., 1996).

Summary

In this chapter, we have examined three basic models of providing culturally responsive mental health services to Asian Americans: modification of mainstream programs, establishment of parallel programs, and creation of new, non-parallel programs. We have also considered two emerging approaches: the general family practitioner approach and the school-based or school-linked services approach, both seeking to minimize the confusion often caused by the fragmented delivery of services in many mainstream settings.

A comprehensive mental health program always includes a primary prevention component. For Asian Americans, the cultural gap between the home and the mainstream society and the cultural gap between parents and children within the family are major risk factors that need to be addressed through preventive work. Besides direct services to clients, preventive services need to include advocacy for clients and their community, as well as consultation and training to other agencies. In addition, delivery of culturally responsive services requires mental health professionals to be constantly on the alert to recognize institutional barriers to effective services and to be prepared to take on a role as agents for institutional change.

10

Onward Into the New Millennium

As discussed in the beginning of this book, the Asian and Pacific Islander American population is projected to increase from the existing 3.9% of the total U.S. population in 1997 to about 8.7% of the total population by the year 2050 (U.S. Bureau of the Census, 1998d). In other words, about 1 in every 11 Americans will be Asian and Pacific Islander by the middle of this millennium. This demographic trend means that in the coming years mental health professionals, regardless of their ethnicity, will be increasingly likely to encounter Asian American clients. Given this situation, it is crucial for all mental health clinicians to learn more about the cultural and social environmental contexts of the Asian American population, to develop clinical skills that are culturally and social environmentally responsive, and to design service delivery models that meet the cultural and social environmental needs of this population. With this imperative in mind, we will conclude this book with a discussion of the critical issues in the curriculum and training of mental health professionals who will be working with Asian Americans. This chapter ends with a synopsis of the major issues covered in this book and summarizes these issues with the acronym *ASIAN AMERICAN*.

Curriculum and Training

In training mental health professionals to work with Asian Americans, the primary concern for an educational or training program is to provide culturally informed curricular content and skill training. We have selected two pedagogical areas that we consider critical in the development of curriculum and training programs to prepare clinicians to work proficiently with Asian American clients. The first area concerns the challenges that educators and trainers face as they balance information about Asian Americans as a general group with information about the many distinct Asian American subgroups. The second area concerns the range of competencies that need to be covered in an educational or training program.

Curriculum Considerations

In the process of developing a curriculum relevant to mental health services for Asian Americans, educators and trainers often find that their first step is to resolve the dilemma of whether they should discuss Asian Americans as a general group with shared characteristics or emphasize the unique differences among Asian ethnic groups.

As discussed in Chapter 2, Asian Americans, despite their interethnic and intraethnic differences, have enough common cultural characteristics as well as common life experiences in the United States to have a pan-Asian identity (Min, 1995c). This is particularly true in the context of mental health services, where Asian Americans, as a group, have been noted to share certain cultural characteristics that warrant specific therapeutic techniques and service delivery models different from established Western practices (Hong, 1988, 1993a; Lee, 1980, 1997c; Shon, 1980; Sue & McKinney, 1975; Sue & Morishima, 1982; Uba, 1994; Wong, 1985). Consequently, a curriculum can address content about mental health services for Asian Americans in general while acknowledging the differences among Asian American groups. We are aware of concerns about overgeneralization when Asian Americans are discussed as a group. Although this is a valid issue, educators and trainers must be careful not to take the misleading position that because differences exist among Asian Americans, a curriculum can never or should never focus on the common identity and experience of Asian Americans (Hong, 2000; Hong et al., 2000). The situation is analogous to other areas of psychology. For example, even though most clinicians agree with the importance of attending to the unique personal characteristics and experiences of each individual client, clinical literature still discusses general theories of psychotherapy and counseling. Likewise, while keeping in mind that differences exist in the cultures and social environmental experiences of distinct Asian ethnic groups, a curriculum can discuss the characteristics shared by Asian Americans as a general group.

Besides theoretical and conceptual concerns, our perspective also takes the practical situation into consideration. Because there are many Asian

American ethnic groups, an inconceivable amount of time would be required for a curriculum to cover each specific group in detail, even if the curriculum simply included the three or four largest groups (Hong & Ham, 1994; Hong et al., 2000). In addition, we must not forget that trainees would also be required to learn about other American minority groups and their subgroups. This would be an overwhelming task for most trainees. Hence, we have found it more practical for a curriculum to focus on the commonalities among Asian Americans and on detailed examinations of how these commonalities affect mental health service delivery and utilization. This basic curriculum can provide trainees a general orientation and the fundamental skills for working with most Asian American groups. This general approach to curriculum design, of course, should include discussions of the cultural and social environmental differences among Asian American subgroups—the between-groups differences as well as the within-group differences. After achieving this foundation, trainees should be encouraged to go beyond the basic curriculum and acquire additional information about one or more groups, such as East Asians, Southeast Asians, or South Asians, that they are most likely to work with in actual clinical practice. Based on our experience as clinicians in community agencies and as educators in university training programs, this approach is a viable way to prepare clinicians to work in the Asian American community clinics, as well as to serve Asian American clients in other settings.

Multicultural Competencies

In recent years, considerable attention has been devoted to identifying and describing the goals, objectives, and competencies that need to be addressed in multicultural clinical training (Arredondo, 1998; Arredondo et al., 1996; Pedersen, 1988; Sue et al., 1982; Sue, Arredondo, & McDavis, 1992). These goals, objectives, and competencies can be classified into three dimensions: awareness, knowledge, and skills (Arredondo et al., 1996; Pedersen, 1988; Sue et al., 1982, 1992). These three dimensions have also been conceptualized as levels of professional development through which clinicians or trainees progress. The competency levels have been further elaborated and operationalized by Arredondo and members of the Professional Standards and Certification Committee of the Association of Multicultural Counseling and Development (Arredondo et al., 1996). These authors have also offered many excellent and specific suggestions for implementing these competencies in multicultural training. Because cultural competence training is an entire content area that goes beyond the scope of this book, we will not elaborate upon the details here. Instead, we will highlight the major issues within the context of training mental health clinicians to work with Asian American clients.

The dimension of awareness is the first of the three competency levels. At this level, trainees develop sensitivity to their own cultural heritage, a respect for other cultures, and a positive orientation toward multiculturalism (Arredondo et al., 1996; Sue et al., 1992). On the basis of our own experiences in providing cultural competency training, we find that self-exploration and reflective exercises, as well as open and frank discussions of these issues during classroom instruction, are very helpful at this level (Hong & Ham, 1994; Hong et al., 2000). For example, we would encourage trainees to examine their own experiences for cultural differences that they may have encountered during their interactions with other people or to explore their own cultural heritage through genograms (Hong & Ham, 1994). In addition, through discussions and self-reflection, we can facilitate a process in which trainees are able to explore their feelings, opinions, assumptions, and generalized stereotypes or biases toward Asian Americans, specific Asian American groups, and Asian immigrants and refugees. This self-reflective exploration applies to all trainees, including Asian American trainees. In particular, Asian American trainees need to examine their attitudes and feelings toward Asian Americans whose countries of origin are different from theirs (e.g., Korean versus Vietnamese or Filipino Americans) and toward Asian Americans whose migration status (e.g., foreign born versus American born) and cultural identification are different from their own.

The second dimension of cultural competency is knowledge. At this level, trainees seek knowledge of specific cultural issues, including the life experiences, cultural heritage, and historical background of their client populations. They also learn the appropriateness of specific intervention approaches, strategies, and services for their target client populations (Arredondo et al., 1996; Sue et al., 1992). Besides lectures and reading assignments, we find direct exposure to minority cultures to be very helpful at this level (Hong & Ham, 1994; Hong et al., 2000). For example, we may ask trainees to visit ethnic communities or community agencies, individually or in groups, and to relate their observations to the literature. For training programs located in areas without easy access to Asian American communities or agencies, a possible alternative experience is to have trainees interview Asian American students on campus or perhaps visit their homes or even attend an Asian American social event. Another option is to invite Asian American individuals, including students and faculty, to share their own cultural, social environmental, and family experiences with the class. Movies and videotapes can also be used to complement personal observations and direct contact. Besides training videotapes depicting psychotherapy and counseling sessions, trainers can select movies and videotapes that portray the cultures, family interactions, migration issues, or life experiences in Asian American communities. For example, *The Joy Luck Club* (1993, directed by W. Wang), a film based on a novel of the same title by Amy Tan (1989), presents a touching portrayal of family interactions in four Chinese American families, particularly mother-daughter relationships. This film highlights cultural and generational issues by contrasting the life experiences of immigrant mothers and their American-born daughters, as well as the premigration and postmigration social environmental contexts and historical circumstances in which they lived. Another example, the film *Heaven and Earth* (1993, directed by Oliver Stone), presents a heart-rending story of a young Vietnamese woman's traumatic experience of growing up in her war-torn homeland, her adjustment to life in the United States as the wife of an American serviceman, and an emotional return visit to Vietnam with her children years later. Even a comedy like *The Wedding Banquet* (1993, directed by Ang Lee), which portrays a gay Chinese American's effort to appease his parents by arranging a marriage of convenience, can inform trainees about Asian American family values, norms, rituals, communication style, and family interactions, among other issues. These three films are just some examples of movies that are easily available from video rental stores or public libraries. They can be assigned to trainees for viewing at home and can be followed up with reflective papers or class discussions. Such assignments can be very useful for developing a trainee's empathic understanding of Asian American cultural and social environmental issues and of the impact of these issues on individuals and families.

The third dimension of cultural competency, the skills level, involves mastery of intercultural communication skills, as well as specific clinical skills, strategies, and assessment methods needed in working with particular client populations (Arredondo et al., 1996; Sue et al., 1992). At this level, trainees learn to modify their clinical approaches or to select different treatment methods as necessary. They also learn to consult other professionals, including traditional healers or helpers in the culture, when appropriate. In addition, trainees learn to advocate for their clients and to promote institutional changes to ensure adequate, fair, and quality care for their client populations (Arredondo et al., 1996). At the skills level, there is no substitute for direct experience through practica and internships where trainees actually provide clinical services to Asian American clients (Hong & Ham, 1994; Hong et al., 2000). Community agencies are preferred placement sites as compared to agencies located in mainstream settings, for working in the community gives trainees the opportunity to experience its culture and its way of functioning. In our experience, language is often a deterrent for trainees seeking placement in community clinics because the clientele of these agencies typically require services in Asian languages. If the trainees are not fluent in particular Asian languages or dialects, their caseload may be minimal. Even though this situation may apply to trainees of any ethnicity, it is particularly frustrating for many second-, third-, or further-generation Asian Americans who are eager to serve the community but are not fluent in the required languages or dialects. In this case, trainees with limited or no Asian language skills can seek placement in mainstream institutions, such as college counseling centers and public schools, where there are often more English-speaking Asian American clients. We also encourage Asian American trainees to refine their skills in particular Asian languages by building on what they have learned at home in their childhood. In our experience, a trainee's success in developing Asian language skills is often dependent on each individual's determination, as well as personal and professional goals (Hong, & Ham, 1994). We want to emphasize that trainees who are not fluent in an Asian language should not feel discouraged from developing their cultural competence and from providing services to Asian American clients. They can always start by working with English-speaking Asian American clients, while seeking to acquire language proficiency, which, like any other element of cultural competency, is a skill that takes time and effort to develop.

In sum, cultural proficiency in mental health services for Asian Americans, as well as for any other ethnic groups, is a comprehensive curriculum that needs to be covered throughout a trainee's education and training, rather than addressed in a few lectures or workshops (Hong et al., 2000). We hope that faculty in university training programs and clinicians in community clinics will collaborate closely to ensure that our future mental health professionals will develop the cultural awareness, cultural knowledge, and cultural skills to serve the growing Asian American population.

Concluding Remarks

In this book, we have examined the major cultural and social environmental issues relevant to the provision of effective counseling and psychotherapeutic services for Asian American clients. Knowledge of these issues is essential for mental health professionals to develop their cultural competency in working with Asian Americans.

In providing psychotherapy and counseling to Asian American clients, clinicians need to understand the cultural orientation of Asian Americans as a group and at the same time be aware that individual clients may differ in their identification with Asian and mainstream American cultures. Clinicians also have to be aware of the social environmental issues faced by Asian Americans as an ethnic minority group in the United States and of the specific problems experienced by individual clients. Because the majority of Asian Americans are foreign born, it is crucial for clinicians to appreciate the complexities of acculturation and cultural identification for immigrant Asian Americans; the cultural gap within immigrant families and between immigrant families and mainstream society; the social environmental stressors of migration; and the long-lasting effects of refugee ordeals. Culturally proficient clinicians are knowledgeable about these cultural and social environmental issues and choose their clinical approaches and strategies according to the needs and expectations of each individual client or family. On a systemic level, clinicians need to be vigilant about institutional practices and policies that are incongruent with the cultural or social environmental contexts of Asian American communities. These institutional barriers may inhibit Asian American clients from seeking mental health services or limit the ability of clinicians to design and provide appropriate services to the community. Thus, mental health professionals concerned with the delivery of effective services for Asian American clients must be ready to advocate for institutional change.

Here we will conclude with the acronym *ASIAN AMERICAN,* which summarizes the issues we have discussed in this book:

A: Acculturation issues. When applying cultural issues to mental health services, clinicians must be sensitive to the differences in cultural identification among different Asian American clients and even among members of the same family.

S: Social environmental issues. These issues are the life problems and physical problems encountered by clients in daily living. At times they are closely intertwined with cultural issues. Social environmental issues include personal problems such as financial hardship, educational problems, occupational problems, and migration stress, as well as systemic issues such as racism and socioeconomic disadvantages of inner-city communities. These issues are important variables to consider in mental health services.

I: Immigration and refugee issues. This set of issues warrants special attention because the majority of Asian Americans are immigrants or from immigrant families. Clinicians need to appreciate the dynamics of migration and the stress of relocation and acculturation experienced by immigrants. They also need to understand the lasting effects of refugee trauma and the hardships experienced by refugee Asian Americans in their adjustment to life in the United States.

A: Acknowledgment of and respect for cultural differences. Clinicians need to take a positive approach toward cultural differences and acknowledge rather than ignore them. If clinicians are unsure of particular cultural issues, they need to ask their clients for clarification. They must always respect the cultural position of their clients.

N: Norms. In a diagnostic assessment, clinicians need to examine a client's thoughts and behaviors in the context of the norms and values of the client's culture and social environmental experiences. When standardized psychological tests are used, clinicians must be cautious of culturally biased test contents and statistical norms that are based on samples unrepresentative of Asian Americans.

A: *Approaches.* Theoretical approaches and strategies of clinical intervention, as well as the modality of services, must be relevant to the cultural and social environmental contexts of the client. Clinicians need to accommodate their clients by adapting their approach, strategies, or treatment modality rather than imposing a particular approach or modality on clients and expecting clients to adjust to it.

M: *Medical issues.* Clinicians need to respect their clients' use of traditional Asian medicine and healing practices. These practices can be viewed as adjuncts to psychotherapy and counseling as long as they are not contraindicative. Clinicians must also be careful about the issue of somatization in Asian American clients. They need to explore the possible underlying causes of somatic symptoms and at the same time guard against callously dismissing all physical symptoms as somatization without a thorough medical examination.

E: *Expectations.* Regardless of what theoretical approach clinicians follow, they must engage their Asian American clients by attending to these clients' expectations regarding mental health services and treatment goals. Otherwise, clients may not return for further sessions.

R: *Reorganization.* Clinicians must be alert to institutional barriers that impede the utilization of mental health services by Asian Americans or hinder providers from delivering culturally and social environmentally responsive services. They must be proactive in reorganizing and changing an agency to meet the needs of their client population.

I: *Innovative services.* Clinicians must be responsive to the Asian American communities and be proactive in looking at new paradigms of service delivery. They need to be innovative in designing services as well as intervention strategies that are congruent with the cultural and social environmental contexts of the communities.

C: *Comprehensive services.* Some promising new approaches to service delivery involve the provision of comprehensive services that minimize confusion caused by multiple referrals. These include the general family practitioner approach, which is applicable on the level of individual clinicians, and the school-based or school-linked family services approach, which is applicable on the level of agencies. Primary prevention services that focus on acculturation issues need to be a component of a comprehensive mental health program.

A: *Advocacy.* Culturally responsive clinicians must be active in advocating for their clients to access appropriate mental health services as well as adjunct or support services. This includes advocacy on the systemic or societal level to improve the availability of mental health resources in the Asian American communities, particularly those in the inner cities.

N: Networking. No single professional knows everything about the cultural or social environmental issues concerning Asian Americans. It is important for mental health clinicians to network and consult with one another, with professionals in related fields, with community workers, and with others who are knowledgeable about the culture and the community. Mental health programs need to network and collaborate with other community agencies and organizations to perform needs assessment and program evaluation, as well as to develop services that are responsive to the cultural and social environmental contexts of their clients.

References

Abu-Rabia, S. (1996). Attitudes of Arab minority students in Israel and Canada toward learning a second language. *Journal of Social Psychology, 136,* 541-544.

Adelman, H. S., & Taylor, L. (1993). School-based mental health: Toward a comprehensive approach. *Journal of Mental Health Administration, 20*(1), 32-45.

Agbayani-Siewert, P., & Revilla, L. (1995). Filipino Americans. In P. G. Min (Ed.), *Asian Americans: Contemporary trends and issues* (pp. 134-198). Thousand Oaks, CA: Sage.

Alba, R. (1990). *Ethnic identity: The transformation of white America.* New Haven, CT: Yale University Press.

American Psychological Association. (1994). *Publication manual of the American Psychological Association* (4th ed.). Washington, DC: Author.

American Psychiatric Association. (1994). *Diagnostic and statistical manual of mental disorders* (4th ed.). Washington, DC: Author.

Anderson, H. (1993). On a roller coaster: A collaborative language systems approach to therapy. In S. Friedman (Ed.), *The new language of change: Constructive collaboration in therapy* (pp. 323-344). New York: Guilford.

Anderson, H. (1995). Collaborative language systems: Toward a postmodern therapy. In R. Mikesell, D. D. Lusterman, & S. McDaniel (Eds.), *Integrating family therapy: Family psychology and systems theory* (pp. 27-44). Washington, DC: American Psychological Association.

Anderson, H. (1997). *Conversation, language, and possibilities: A postmodern approach to therapy.* New York: Basic Books.

Anderson, H., & Goolishian, H. A. (1988). Human systems as linguistic systems: Preliminary and evolving ideas about the implications for clinical theory. *Family Process, 27,* 371-393.

Anderson, H., & Goolishian, H. A. (1992). The client is the expert: A not-knowing approach to therapy. In S. McNamee & K. J. Gergen (Eds.), *Therapy as social construction* (pp. 25-39). Newbury Park, CA: Sage.

231

Aponte, J. F., Rivers, R. Y., & Wohl, J. (Eds.). (1995). *Psychological interventions and cultural diversity.* Boston: Allyn & Bacon.

Araneta, E. G., Jr. (1993). Psychiatric care of Pilipino Americans. In A. C. Gaw (Ed.), *Culture, ethnicity, and mental illness* (pp. 377-412). Washington, DC: American Psychiatric Press.

Arredondo, P. (1985). Cross-cultural counselor education and training. In P. B. Pedersen (Ed.), *Handbook of cross-cultural counseling and therapy* (pp. 281-290). Westport, CT: Greenwood.

Arredondo, P. (1998). Integrating multicultural counseling competencies and universal helping conditions in culture-specific contexts. *Counseling Psychologist, 26,* 592-601.

Arredondo, P., Toporek, R., Brown, S. P., Jones, J., Locke, D. C., Sanchez, J., & Stadler, H. (1996). Operationalization of the multicultural counseling competencies. *Journal of Multicultural Counseling and Development, 24,* 42-78.

Atkinson, D. R., Morten, G., & Sue, D. W. (Eds.). (1993). *Counseling American minorities: A cross-cultural perspective* (4th ed.). Madison, WI: Brown & Benchmark.

Atkinson, D. R., Morten, G., & Sue, D. W. (Eds.). (1998). *Counseling American minorities: A cross-cultural perspective* (5th ed.). Boston: McGraw-Hill.

Auerswald, E. H. (1968). Interdisciplinary versus ecological approach. *Family Process, 7,* 202-215.

Axelson, J. A. (1993). *Counseling and development in a multicultural society* (2nd ed.). Pacific Grove, CA: Brooks/Cole.

Bankart, C. P. (1997). *Talking cures: A history of Western and Eastern psychotherapies.* Pacific Grove, CA: Brooks/Cole.

Baron, D. G., & Gall, S. B. (1996). *Asian American chronology.* New York: UXL.

Bateson, G. (1972). *Steps to an ecology of mind: Collected essays in anthropology, psychiatry, evolution, and epistemology.* Northvale, NJ: Jason Aronson.

Beck, A. T. (1976). *Cognitive therapy and emotional disorders.* New York: International Universities Press.

Beck, J. S. (1995). *Cognitive therapy: Basics and beyond.* New York: International Universities Press.

Becvar, D. S., & Becvar, R. (1996). *Family therapy: A systemic integration* (3rd ed.). Boston: Allyn & Bacon.

Beiser, M. (1996). Adjustment disorder in DSM-IV: Cultural considerations. In J. E. Mezzich, A. Kleinman, H. Fabrega, Jr., & D. L. Parron (Eds.), *Culture and psychiatric diagnosis: A DSM-IV perspective* (pp. 215-226). Washington, DC: American Psychiatric Press.

Berg, I. K., & Jaya, A. (1993). Different and same: Family therapy with Asian-American families. *Journal of Marital and Family Therapy, 19*(1), 31-38.

Berg, I. K., & Miller, S. D. (1992). Working with Asian American clients: One person at a time. *Families in Society, 73,* 356-363.

Berry, J. W. (1992). Acculturation and adaptation in a new society. *International Migration, 30,* 69-85.

Berry, J. W. (1994). Acculturation and psychological adaptation: An overview. In A. M. Bouvy, F. J. R. van de Vijver, P. Boski, & P. Schmitz (Eds.), *Journeys into cross-cultural psychology: Selected papers from the Eleventh International Conference of the International Association for Cross-Cultural Psychology* (pp. 129-141). Amsterdam: Swets & Zeitlinger.

Berry, J. W. (1995). Psychology of acculturation. In N. R. Goldberger & J. B. Veroff (Eds.), *The culture and psychology reader* (pp. 457-488). New York: New York University Press.

Berry, J. W., & Sam, D. L. (1997). Acculturation and adaptation. In J. W. Berry, M. H. Segall, & C. Kagitcibasi (Eds.), *Handbook of cross-cultural psychology* (2nd ed., Vol. 3, pp. 291-326). Needham Heights, MA: Allyn & Bacon.

Bertalanffy, L. von (1968). *General system theory.* New York: George Braziller.

Boszormenyi-Nagy, I., & Spark, G. M. (1973). *Invisible loyalties: Reciprocity in intergenerational family therapy.* Hagerstown, MD: Harper & Row.

Bowen, M. (1978). *Family therapy in clincal practice.* New York: Jason Aronson.

Brammer, L. M. (1973). *The helping relationship: Process and skills.* Englewood Cliffs, NJ: Prentice Hall.

Brand, D. (1987, August 31). The new whiz kids: Why Asian-Americans are doing so well, and what it costs them. *Time, 130,* 42-51.

Bronfenbrenner, U. (1977). Toward an experimental ecology of human development. *American Psychologist, 32,* 513-531.

Broom, L., & Selznick, P. (1963). *Sociology: A text with adapted readings* (3rd ed.). New York: Harper & Row.

Bruch, H. (1974). *Learning psychotherapy: Rationale and ground rules.* Cambridge, MA: Harvard University Press.

Buie, D. (1981). Empathy: Its nature and limitations. *Journal of the American Psychoanalytic Association, 29,* 281-307.

Butcher, J. N., Dahlstrom, W. G., Graham, J. R., Tellegen, A., & Kaemmer, B. (1989). *Minnesota Multi-Phasic Personality Inventory II (MMPI-II): Manual for administration and scoring.* Minneapolis: University of Minnesota Press.

California Wellness Foundation. (1993). *First annual report.* Woodland Hills, CA: Author.

Cao, L., & Novas, H. (1996). *Everything you need to know about Asian American history.* New York: Plume.

Carlson, E., & Rosser-Hogan, R. (1991). Trauma experiences, posttraumatic stress, dissociation, and depression in Cambodian refugees. *American Journal of Psychiatry, 148,* 1548-1551.

Carter, B., & McGoldrick, M. (Eds.). (1988). *The changing family life cycle: A framework for family therapy* (2nd ed.). New York: Gardner.

Carter, B., & McGoldrick, M. (Eds.). (1999). *The expanded family life cycle: Individual, family, and social perspectives* (3rd ed.). Boston, Allyn & Bacon.

Chan, S. (1986). Parents of exceptional Asian children. In M. K. Kitano & P. C. Chinn (Eds.), *Exceptional Asian children and youth* (pp. 36-53). Reston, VA: Council for Exceptional Children.

Chataway, C., & Berry, J. W. (1989). Acculturation experiences, appraisal, coping and adaptation. *Canadian Journal of Behavioural Sciences, 21,* 295-309.

Chen, P. (1996). Modern Chinese, dialects, and regional identity. *Language Problems and Language Planning, 20,* 223-243.

Chin, J. L. (1993). Transference. In J. L. Chin, J. H. Liem, M. D. Ham, & G. K. Hong, *Transference and empathy in Asian American psychotherapy* (pp. 15-29). Westport, CT: Praeger.

Chin, J. L. (1998). Mental health services and treatment. In L. C. Lee & N. W. S. Zane (Eds.), *Handbook of Asian American psychology* (pp. 485-504). Thousand Oaks, CA: Sage.

Chin, J. L., Liem, J. H., Ham, M. D., & Hong, G. K. (1993). *Transference and empathy in Asian American psychotherapy: Cultural values and treatment needs.* Westport, CT: Praeger.

China develops indigenous psychotherapy [Chinese newspaper article]. (1998, July 9). *Wen Wei Po* (American edition), p. 4.

Chua-Eoan, H. G. (1990, April 9). Strangers in paradise: Even as they stake claims to the American West, Asians experience the ambivalence of assimilation and the perils of prosperity. *Time, 135,* 32-35.

Chung, R., & Kagawa-Singer, M. (1993). Predictors of psychological distress among Southeast Asian refugees. *Social Science and Medicine, 36,* 631-639.

Cohen, M. L. (1991). Being Chinese: The peripheralization of traditional identity. *Daedalus: Journal of the American Academy of Arts and Sciences, 120*(2), 113-134.

Comas-Diaz, L., & Minrath, M. (1985). Psychotherapy with ethnic minority borderline clients. *Psychotherapy, 22,* 418-426.

Corey, G. (1996). *Theory and practice of counseling and psychotherapy* (5th ed.). Pacific Grove, CA: Brooks/Cole Publishing.

Cotterell, A. (1993). *East Asia: From Chinese predominance to the rise of the Pacific Rim.* New York: Oxford University Press.

De Shazer, S. (1985). *Keys to solution in brief therapy.* New York: W. W. Norton.

Dryfoos, J. G. (1994). *Full service schools: A revolution in health and social services for children, youth, and families.* San Francisco: Jossey-Bass.

Egan, G. (1997). *The skilled helper: A problem-management approach to helping* (6th ed.). Pacific Grove, CA: Brooks/Cole.

Ellis, A., & Dryden, W. (1997). *The practice of rational emotive behavior therapy* (2nd ed.) New York: Springer.

Encyclopedia Britannica Online. (1999). "Bimbisara." Encyclopedia Britannica Online. http://search.eb.com/bol/topic?eu=1793&sctn=1&pm=1 [Accessed 12 August, 1999].

Engel, G. L. (1980). The clinical application of the biopsychosocial model. *American Journal of Psychiatry, 137,* 535-544.

Epstein, N. B., Bishop, D. S., & Levin, S. (1978). The McMaster model of family functioning. *Journal of Marriage and Family Counseling, 4,* 19-21.

Espiritu, Y. L. (1992). *Asian American panethnicity: Bridging institutions and identities.* Philadelphia: Temple University Press.

Ettin, M. F. (1992). *Foundations and applications of group psychotherapy: A sphere of influence.* Boston: Allyn & Bacon.

Fairbank, J. K., Reischauer, E. O., & Craig, A. M. (1973). *East Asia: Tradition and transformation.* Boston: Houghton Mifflin.

Falicov, C. (1988). Learning to think culturally. In H. A. Liddle & D. C. Breunlin (Eds.), *Handbook of family therapy training and supervision* (pp. 335-357). New York: Guilford.

Falicov, C. (1995). Training to think culturally: A multidimensional comparative framework. *Family Process, 34,* 373-388.

Farley, R. (1996). *Increasing interracial marriage: Trends revealed by the census and Census Bureau surveys.* Unpublished report, University of Michigan Populations Studies Center, Ann Arbor.

Fine, M. J., & Carlson, C. (Eds.). (1992). *The handbook of family-school intervention: A systems perspective.* Needham Heights, MA: Allyn & Bacon.

Florsheim, P. (1997). Chinese adolescent immigrants: Factors related to psychosocial adjustment. *Journal of Youth and Adolescence, 26*(2), 143-163.

Ford, D., & Urban, H. (1963). *Systems of psychotherapy.* New York: John Wiley.

Freud, S. (1958a). A note on the unconscious in psychoanalysis. In J. Strachey (Ed. & Trans.), *The standard edition of the complete psychological works of Sigmund Freud* (Vol. 12, pp. 255-266). London: Hogarth. (Original work published 1912)

Freud, S. (1958b). Papers on technique. In J. Strachey (Ed. & Trans.), *The standard edition of the complete psychological works of Sigmund Freud* (Vol. 12, pp. 97-171). London: Hogarth. (Original work published 1911-1915)

Friedman, L. (1985). Toward a comprehensive theory of treatment. *Psychoanalytic Inquiry, 5,* 589-599.

Fritzsimmons, B. L. (1986). The need to train psychologists as family practitioners. *Psychotherapy in Private Practice, 4*(4), 35-37.

Gall, S. B., & Gall, T. L. (Eds.). (1993). *Statistical record of Asian Americans.* Detroit, MI: Gale Research Inc.

Gall, S. B., & Natividad, I. (Eds.). (1995). *The Asian-American almanac: A reference work on Asians in the United States.* Detroit, MI: Gale Research Inc.

Gardner, R. W., Robey, B., & Smith, P.C. (1985). Asian Americans: Growth, change, and diversity. *Population Bulletin, 40*(4). Washington, DC: Population Reference Bureau.

Gaw, A. C. (Ed.). (1993). *Culture, ethnicity, and mental illness.* Washington, DC: American Psychiatric Press.

Gergen, K. J. (1988). If persons are texts. In S. B. Messer, L. A. Sass, & R. L. Woolfolk (Eds.), *Hermeneutics and psychological theory* (pp. 28-51). New Brunswick, NJ: Rutgers University Press.

Gergen, K. J. (1994). *Realities and relationships: Soundings in social construction.* Cambridge, MA: Harvard University Press.

Gergen, K. J., Hoffman, L., & Anderson, H. (1995). Is diagnosis a disaster: A constructionist trialogue. In F. Kaslow (Ed.), *Handbook of relational diagnosis* (pp. 102-118). New York: John Wiley.

Giordano, J., & Carini-Giordano, M. A. (1995). Ethnic dimensions in family therapy. In R. Mikesell, D. Lusterman, & S. McDaniel (Eds.), *Integrating family therapy* (pp. 190-206). Washington, DC: American Psychological Association.

Gladding, S. T. (1991). Counselor self-abuse. *Journal of Mental Health Counseling, 13,* 414-419.

Gonzalez, C. A., & Griffith, E. H. (1996). Culture and the diagnosis of somatoform and dissociative disorders. In J. E. Mezzich, A. Kleinman, H. Fabrega, Jr., & D. L. Parron (Eds.), *Culture and psychiatric diagnosis: A DSM-IV perspective* (pp. 137-150). Washington, DC: American Psychiatric Press.

Goolishian, H. A., & Anderson, H. (1987). Language systems and therapy: An evolving idea. *Psychotherapy, 24*(Suppl.), 529-538.

Gordon, M. H. (1964). *Assimilation in American life: The role of race, religion, and national origins.* New York: Oxford University Press.

Graves, T. (1967). Psychological acculturation in a tri-ethnic community. *South-Western Journal of Anthropology, 23,* 337-350.

Gray, P. (1994). *The ego and analysis of defense.* Northvale, NJ: Jason Aronson.

Grieger, I., & Ponterotto, J. (1995). A framework for assessment in multicultural counseling. In J. G. Ponterotto, J. M. Casas, L. A. Suzuki, & C. M. Alexander (Eds.), *Handbook of multicultural counseling* (pp. 357-374). Thousand Oaks, CA: Sage.

Griswold, P. M. (1980). A family practice model for clinical psychology. *Professional Psychology, 11,* 628-636.

Griswold, P. M. (1986). Functioning as a family or general practitioner of psychology. *Psychotherapy in Private Practice, 4*(4), 23-28.

Haley, J. (1976). *Problem-solving therapy.* San Francisco: Jossey-Bass.

Haley, J. (1980). *Leaving home: The therapy of disturbed young people.* New York: McGraw-Hill.

Ham, M. D. (Ed.). (1989). Immigrant families and family therapy [Special issue]. *Journal of Strategic and Systemic Therapies, 8*(2).

Ham, M. D. (1993). Empathy. In J. L. Chin, J. L. Liem, M. D. Ham, & G. K. Hong, *Transference and empathy in Asian American psychotherapy* (pp. 35-58). Westport, CT: Praeger.

Ham, M. D. (1999). Oriental. In J. S. Mio, J. E. Trimble, P. Arredondo, H. E. Cheatham, & D. Sue (Eds.), *Key words in multicultural interventions: A dictionary* (pp. 205-206). Westport, CT: Greenwood.

Hamilton, D. (1993a, July 29). Chinese-American leaders class for action on "parachute kids." *Los Angeles Times,* p. B3.

Hamilton, D. (1993b, June 27). Home alone—Up-market L.A. style. *Los Angeles Times,* p. M4.

Hamilton, D. (1993c, June 24). A house, cash, and no parents. *Los Angeles Times,* p. A1.

Harris, A. M., Reynolds, M. A., & Koegel, H. M. (1996). Nonverbal assessment: Multicultural perspectives. In L. A. Suzuki, P. J. Meller, & J. G. Ponterotto (Eds.), *Handbook of multicultural assessment: Clinical, psychological, and educational applications* (pp. 223-252). San Francisco: Jossey-Bass.

Harwood, J. (1981). The sociology of science: Problems, approaches and research. *British Journal of Sociology, 32,* 292-293.

Hedstrom, J. (1994). Morita and Naikan therapies: American applications. *Psychotherapy, 31*(1), 154-160.

Hing, B. O. (1993). *Making and remaking Asian America through immigration policy: 1850-1990.* Stanford, CA: Stanford University Press.

Ho, M. K. (1987). *Family therapy with ethnic minorities.* Newbury Park, CA: Sage.

Ho, M. K. (1990). *Intermarried couples in therapy.* Springfield, IL: Charles C Thomas.

Hoffman, L. (1981). *Foundations of family therapy: A conceptual framework for systems change.* New York: Basic Books.

Hoffman, L. (1990). *Constructing realities: An art of lenses.* Family Process, 29, 1-12.

Hong, G. K. (1988). A general family practitioner approach for Asian American mental health services. *Professional Psychology: Research and Practice, 19,* 600-605.

Hong, G. K. (1989). Application of cultural and environmental issues in family therapy with immigrant Chinese Americans. *Journal of Strategic and Systemic Therapies, 8,* 14-21.

Hong, G. K. (1993a). Contextual factors in psychotherapy with Asian Americans. In J. L. Chin, J. L. Liem, M. D. Ham, & G. K. Hong, *Transference and empathy in Asian American psychotherapy: Cultural values and treatment needs* (pp. 3-13). Westport, CT: Praeger.

Hong, G. K. (1993b). Synthesizing Eastern and Western psychotherapeutic approaches: Contextual factors in psychotherapy with Asian Americans. In J. L. Chin, J. L. Liem, M. D. Ham, & G. K. Hong, *Transference and empathy in Asian American psychotherapy: Cultural values and treatment needs* (pp. 77-90). Westport, CT: Praeger.

Hong, G. K. (1995). Cultural considerations in rehabilitation counseling for Asian Americans. *National Association of Rehabilitation Professionals in the Private Sector Journal, 10*(2), 59-65.

Hong, G. K. (1996). Culture and empowerment: Counseling services for Chinese American families. *Journal for the Professional Counselor, 11*(1), 69-80.

Hong, G. K. (2000, February). Some reflections on multiculturalism for Asian American psychologists. *Newsletter of the Asian American Psychological Association,* p. 10.

Hong, G. K., & Friedman, M. M. (1998). The Asian American family. In M. M. Friedman (Ed.), *Family nursing: Theory and practice* (4th ed.) (pp. 547-566). Norwalk, CT: Appleton & Lange.

Hong, G. K., Garcia, M., & Soriano, M. (2000). Responding to the challenge: Preparing mental health professionals for the new millennium. In I. Cuellar & F. A. Paniagua (Eds.), *Handbook of multicultural mental health: Assessment and treatment of diverse populations* (pp. 455-476). San Diego, CA: Academic Press.

Hong, G. K., & Ham, M. D. (1992). Impact of immigration of the family life cycle: Clinical implications for Chinese Americans. *Journal of Family Psychotherapy, 3*(3), 27-40.

Hong, G. K., & Ham, M. D. (1994). Psychotherapy and counseling for Chinese Americans: Curriculum and training issues. *Bulletin of the Hong Kong Psychological Society, 32/33,* 5-19.

Hong, G. K., & Hong, L. K. (1991). Comparative perspectives on child abuse and neglect: Chinese versus Hispanics and whites. *Child Welfare, 70,* 463-475.

Hong, G. K., Lee, B. S., & Lorenzo, M. K. (1995). Somatization in Chinese American clients: Implications for psychotherapeutic services. *Journal of Contemporary Psychotherapy, 25,* 89-104.

Hsu, J. (1985). The Chinese family: Relations, problems and therapy. In W. Tseng & D. Y. Wu (Eds.), *Chinese culture and mental health* (pp. 95-110). Orlando, FL: Academic Press.

Huang, L. J. (1976). The Chinese American family. In C. H. Mindel & R. W. Habenstein (Eds.), *Ethnic families in America: Patterns and variations* (pp. 124-147). New York: Elsevier Scientific Press.

Hudson, B. (1990, March 25). They juggle business, family ties at jet speed. *Los Angeles Times*, p. B1.

Imber-Black, E. (1988). *Families in larger systems.* New York: Guilford.

Imber-Black, E., Roberts, J., & Whiting, R. A. (Eds.). (1988). *Rituals in families and family therapy.* New York: W. W. Norton.

Ishiyama, F. I. (1986). Morita therapy: Its basic features and cognitive intervention for anxiety treatment. *Psychotherapy, 23,* 375-381.

Ishiyama, F. I. (1991a). A Japanese reframing technique for brief social anxiety treatment: An exploratory study of cognitive and therapeutic effects of Morita therapy. *Journal of Cognitive Psychotherapy: An International Quarterly, 5*(1), 55-70.

Ishiyama, F. I. (1991b). Limitations and problems of directive outpatient Morita therapy: Necessity for modifications and process-related sensitivities. *International Bulletin of Morita Therapy, 4*(1/2), 15-31.

Ishiyama, F. I. (1995). Use of validationgram in counselling: Exploring sources of self-validation and impact of personal transition. *Canadian Journal of Counselling/Revue canadienne de counseling, 29*(2), 134-146.

Ishiyama, F. I., & Westwood, M. J. (1992). Enhancing client-validating communication: Helping discouraged clients in cross-cultural adjustment. *Journal of Multicultural Counseling and Development, 20,* 50-63.

Jacobs, J. H. (1992). Identity development in biracial children. In M. P. Root (Ed.), *Racially mixed people in America* (pp. 190-206). Newbury Park, CA: Sage.

Jenkins, A. H. (1997). The empathic context in psychotherapy with people of color. In A. C. Bohart & L. S. Greenberg (Eds.), *Empathy reconsidered: New directions in psychotherapy* (pp. 321-342). Washington, DC: American Psychological Association.

Joiner, G. W., & Kashubeck, S. (1996). Acculturation, body image, self-esteem, and eating-disorder symptomatology in adolescent Mexican American women. *Psychology of Women Quarterly, 20,* 419-435.

Jung, C. G. (1971). The concept of the collective unconscious (R. F. C. Hull, Trans.). In J. Campbell (Ed.), *The portable Jung* (pp. 59-69). New York: Viking. (Original work published 1936)

Jung, M. (1998). *Chinese American family therapy: A new model for clinicians.* San Francisco: Jossey-Bass.

Keefe, T. (1976). Empathy: The critical skill. *Social Work, 21*(1), 10-14.

Keitel, M. A., Kopala, M., & Adamson, W. S. (1996). Ethical issues in multicultural assessment. In L. A. Suzuki, P. J. Meller, & J. G. Ponterotto (Eds.), *Handbook of multicultural assessment: Clinical, psychological, and educational applications* (pp. 29-48). San Francisco: Jossey-Bass.

Kerwin, C., & Ponterotto, J. (1995). Biracial identity development: Theory and research. In J. Ponterotto, J. Casas, L. Suzuki, & C. Alexander (Eds.), *Handbook of multicultural counseling* (pp. 199-217). Thousand Oaks, CA: Sage.

Kich, G. (1992). The developmental process of asserting a biracial, bicultural identity. In M. Root (Ed.), *Racially mixed people in America* (pp. 304-317). Newbury Park, CA: Sage.

Kim, H. C. (1986). *Dictionary of Asian American history.* Westport, CT: Greenwood.

Kim, S. C. (1985). Family therapy for Asian Americans: A strategic structural framework. *Psychotherapy, 22,* 342-348.

Kim, Y. Y. (1991). Intercultural communication competence: A systems-theoretic view. In S. Ting-Toomey & F. Korzenny (Eds.), *International and intercultural communication annual: Vol. 15. Cross-cultural interpersonal communication* (pp. 259-275). Newbury Park, CA: Sage.

King, A. Y. C., & Bond, M. H. (1985). The Confucian paradigm of man: A sociological view. In W. S. Tseng & D. Y. H. Wu (Eds.), *Chinese culture and mental health*. Orlando, FL: Academic Press.

Kinzie, J. D. (1996). Cultural comments on adjustment disorders. In J. E. Mezzich, A. Kleinman, H. Fabrega, Jr., & D. L. Parron (Eds.), *Culture and psychiatric diagnosis: A DSM-IV perspective* (pp. 233-236). Washington, DC: American Psychiatric Press.

Kitano, H. H. L., & Daniels, R. (1988). *Asian Americans: Emerging minorities*. Englewood-Cliffs, NJ: Prentice Hall.

Kleinman, A. M. (1977). Depression, somatization and the new cross-cultural psychiatry. *Social Science and Medicine, 11,* 3-10.

Kleinman, A. M. (1982). Neurasthenia and depression: A study of somatization and culture in China. *Culture, Medicine and Psychiatry, 6,* 117-190.

Knight, G. P., Bernal, M. E., Garza, C. A., & Cota, M. K. (1993). A social cognitive model of the development of ethnic identity and ethnically based behaviors. In M. E. Bernal & G. P. Knight (Eds.), *Ethnic identity: Formation and transmission among Hispanics and other minorities* (pp. 213-234). Albany: State University of New York Press.

Kohatsu, E. L., & Richardson, T. Q. (1996). Racial and ethnic identity assessment. In L. A. Suzuki, P. J. Meller, & J. G. Ponterotto (Eds.), *Handbook of multicultural assessment: Clinical, psychological, and educational applications* (pp. 611-650). San Francisco: Jossey-Bass.

Kohut, H. (1984). *How does analysis cure?* Chicago: University of Chicago Press.

La Fromboise, T., Coleman, H. L. K., & Gerton, J. (1993). Psychological impact of biculturalism: Evidence and theory. *Psychological Bulletin, 114,* 395-412.

Langs, R. (1974). *The technique of psychoanalytic psychotherapy* (Vols. 1 & 2). New York: Jason Aronson.

Langs, R. (1988). *Primer of psychotherapy*. New York: Gardner.

Lazarus, R. S., & Folkman, S. (1984). *Stress, appraisal, and coping*. New York: Springer.

Lee, D. (1998, July 15). Asian Americans finding cracks in the glass ceiling. *Los Angeles Times,* pp. A1, A12-A13.

Lee, E. (1980). Mental health services for the Asian Americans: Problems and alternatives. In U.S. Commission on Civil Rights (Ed.), *Civil rights issues of Asian and Pacific Americans: Myths and realities. A consultation sponsored by the U.S. Commission on Civil Rights* (pp. 734-756) (GPO: 1980 624-865/1772). Washington, DC: Government Printing Office.

Lee, E. (1982). A social systems approach to assessment and treatment for Chinese American families. In M. McGoldrick, J. K. Pearce, & J. Giordano (Eds.), *Ethnicity and family therapy* (pp. 527-551). New York: Guilford.

Lee, E. (1996). Asian American families: An overview. In M. McGoldrick, J. K. Pierce, & J. Giordano (Eds.), *Ethnicity and family therapy* (2nd ed., pp. 227-248). New York: Guilford.

Lee, E. (1997a). Cross cultural communication: Therapeutic use of interpreters. In E. Lee (Ed.), *Working with Asian Americans: A guide for clinicians* (pp. 464-476). New York: Guilford.

Lee, E. (1997b). Overview: The assessment and treatment of Asian American families. In E. Lee (Ed.), *Working with Asian Americans: A guide for clinicians* (pp. 3-36). New York: Guilford.

Lee, E. (Ed.). (1997c). *Working with Asian Americans: A guide for clinicians*. New York: Guilford.

Lee, L. C., & Zane, N. W. S. (Eds.). (1998). *Handbook of Asian American psychology.* Thousand Oaks, CA: Sage.

Lee, S., & Yamanaka, K. (1990). Patterns of Asian American intermarriage and marital assimilation. *Journal of Comparative Family Studies, 21,* 287-305.

Leong, F. T. L. (1992). Guidelines for minimizing premature termination among Asian American clients in group counseling. *Journal for Specialists in Group Work, 17,* 218-228.

Leong, F. T. L. (1998). Special issue on acculturation and ethnic identity among Asian Americans [Guest editorial]. *Asian American and Pacific Islander Journal of Health, 6*(1), 3-4.

Leong, F. T. L., & Chou, E. L. (1998). Developing brief versions of the Suinn-Lew Asian Self-Identity Acculturation (SL-ASIA) Scale for counseling research. *Asian American and Pacific Islander Journal of Health, 6*(1), 15-24.

Leong, F. T. L., Wagner, N. S., & Kim, H. H. (1995). Group counseling expectations among Asian American students: The role of culture-specific factors. *Journal of Counseling Psychology, 42,* 217-222.

LeVine, P. (1993a). Morita-based therapy and its use across cultures in the treatment of bulimia nervosa. *Journal of Counseling and Development, 72,* 82-93.

LeVine, P. (1993b). Morita therapy and its divergence from existential psychotherapy: A proposal for adopting a Morita-based philosophy for use in counseling and psychotherapy. *International Bulletin of Morita Therapy, 6*(1-2), 47-58.

Lietaer, G., Rombauts, J., & VanBalen, R. (1990). *Client-centered and experiential psychotherapy in the nineties.* Leuven, Belgium: Leuven University Press.

Lin, J. C. H. (1992). *Fan yang de hai tze* [Children who go abroad]. Taipei, Taiwan: Teacher Chang.

Lin, J. C. H. (1998). *In pursuit of education: Young Asian students in the United States.* El Monte, CA: Pacific Asian Press.

Lin, K. M. (1996). Asian American perspectives. In J. E. Mezzich, A. Kleinman, H. Fabrega, Jr., & D. L. Parron (Eds.), *Culture and psychiatric diagnosis: A DSM-IV perspective* (pp. 35-38). Washington, DC: American Psychiatric Press.

Lin, K. M., Tazuma, L., & Masuda, M. (1979). Adaptational problems of Vietnamese refugees: Health and mental status. *Archives of General Psychiatry, 36,* 955-961.

Lin, N. (1973). *The study of human communication.* New York: Bobbs-Merrill.

Lin, T. Y. (1985). Mental disorders and psychiatry in Chinese culture: Characteristic features and major issues. In W. S. Tseng & D. Y. H. Wu (Eds.), *Chinese culture and mental health* (pp. 369-394). New York: Academic Press.

Lin, T. Y. (1989). Neurasthenia revisited: Its place in modern psychiatry. *Culture, Medicine and Psychiatry, 13,* 105-130.

Liu, W. T. (1979). *Transition to nowhere: Vietnamese refugees in America.* Nashville, TN: Charter House.

Liu, W. T., & Fernandez, M. (1987). Asian immigrant households and strategies for family reunification. *The Pacific/Asian American Mental Health Research Center: A Decade Review of Mental Health Research, Training, and Services (Chicago),* pp. 115-119.

Lorenzo, M. K., & Adler, D. A. (1984). Mental health services for Chinese in a community health center. *Social Casework, 65,* 600-609.

Lu, F. G., Lim, R. F., & Mezzich, J. E. (1995). Issues in the assessment and diagnosis of culturally diverse individuals. *Review of Psychiatry, 14,* 477-510.

Lyman, S. (1974). *Chinese Americans.* New York: Random House.

Madanes, C., & Haley, J. (1977). Dimensions of family therapy. *Journal of Nervous and Mental Disease, 165*(2), 88-98.

Masters, J. C., Burish, T. G., Hollon, S. D., & Rimm, D. C. (1987). *Behavior therapy: Techniques and empirical findings* (3rd ed.). Orlando, FL: Harcourt Brace Jovanovich.

Matarazzo, J. D. (1990). Psychological assessment versus psychological testing. *American Psychologist, 45,* 999-1017.

McCasland, S. V., Cairns, G. E., & Yu, D. C. (1969). *Religions of the world.* New York: Random House.

McGoldrick, M. (1982). Normal families: An ethnic perspective. In F. Walsh (Ed.), *Normal family processes* (pp. 329-424). New York: Guilford.

McGoldrick, M. (Ed.). (1998). *Re-visioning family therapy: Race, culture, and gender in clinical practice.* New York: Guilford.

McGoldrick, M., & Gerson, R. (1985). *Genograms in family assessment.* New York: W. W. Norton.

McGrath, E. (1983, March 28). Confucian work ethic: Asian-born students head for the head of the class. *Time, 121,* 52.

Meissner, W. W. (1974). Correlative aspects of introjective and projective mechanisms. *American Journal of Psychiatry, 131,* 176-180.

Melaville, A. I., & Blank, M. J. (1991). *What it takes: Structuring interagency partnerships to connect children and families with comprehensive services.* Washington, DC: Education and Human Services Consortium.

Melaville, A. I., & Blank, M. J. (1993). *Together we can: A guide for crafting a profamily system of education and human services.* Washington, DC: U.S. Department of Education Research and Improvement.

Merta, R. J. (1995). Group work: Multicultural perspectives. In J. G. Ponterotto, J. M. Casas, L. A. Suzuki, & C. M. Alexander (Eds.), *Handbook of multicultural counseling* (pp. 567-585). Thousand Oaks, CA: Sage.

Min, P. G. (Ed.). (1995a). *Asian Americans: Contemporary trends and issues.* Thousand Oaks, CA: Sage.

Min, P. G. (1995b). Korean Americans. In P. G. Min (Ed.), *Asian Americans: Contemporary trends and issues* (pp. 199-231). Thousand Oaks, CA: Sage.

Min, P. G. (1995c). An overview of Asian Americans. In P. G. Min (Ed.), *Asian Americans: Contemporary trends and issues* (pp. 10-37). Thousand Oaks, CA: Sage.

Min, P. G. (1997). The Korean American family. In C. H. Mindel, R. W. Habenstein, & R. Wright, Jr. (Eds.), *Ethnic families in America: Patterns and variations* (4th ed., pp. 223-253). Upper Saddle River, NJ: Prentice Hall.

Ming-Yuan, Z. (1989). The diagnosis and phenomenology of neurasthenia: A Shanghai study. *Culture, Medicine and Psychiatry, 13,* 147-161.

Minuchin, S. (1974). *Families and family therapy.* Cambridge, MA: Harvard University Press.

Minuchin, S., & Fishman, H. C. (1981). *Family therapy techniques.* Cambridge, MA: Harvard University Press.

Mokuau, N., & Matsuoka, J. (1992). The appropriateness of personality theories for social work with Asian Americans. In S. M. Furuto, R. Biswas, D. K. Chung, K. Murase, & F. Ross-Sheriff (Eds.), *Social work practice with Asian Americans* (pp. 67-84). Newbury Park, CA: Sage.

Napier, R. W., & Gershenfeld, M. K. (1993). *Groups: Theory and experience* (5th ed.). Boston: Houghton Mifflin.

Ng, F. (1995). Introduction. In F. Ng (Ed.), *The Asian American encyclopedia* (Vol. 1, pp. xi-xv). North Bellmore, NY: Marshall Cavendish.

Nishi, S. M. (1995). Japanese Americans. In P. G. Min (Ed.), *Asian Americans: Contemporary trends and issues* (pp. 95-133). Thousand Oaks, CA: Sage.

Oberg, K. (1960). Culture shock: Adjustment to new cultural environments. *Practical Anthropology, 7,* 177-182.

O'Hara, M. (1997). Relational empathy: Beyond modernist ethnocentrism to postmodern holistic contextualism. In A. C. Bohart & L. S. Greenberg (Eds.), *Empathy reconsidered:*

New directions in psychotherapy (pp. 321-342). Washington, DC: American Psychological Association.

Okonogi, K. (1978). The Ajase complex of the Japanese (1): The depth psychology of the Moratorium people. *Japan Echo, 5*(4), 88-105.

Okonogi, K. (1979). The Ajase complex of the Japanese (2): The depth psychology of the Moratorium people. *Japan Echo, 6*(1), 104-118.

Owen, T. C. (1985). *Southeast Asian mental health: Treatment, prevention, services, training, and research* (DHHS Pub. No. (ADM) 85-1399). Rockville, MD: National Institute of Mental Health.

Padilla, A. M., & Medina, A. (1996). Cross cultural sensitivity in assessment. In L. A. Suzuki, P. J. Meller, & J. G. Ponterotto (Eds.), *Handbook of multicultural assessment: Clinical, psychological, and educational applications* (pp. 3-37). San Francisco: Jossey-Bass.

Palinkas, L., & Pickwell, S. (1995). Acculturation as a risk factor for chronic disease among Cambodian refugees in the United States. *Social Science and Medicine, 40,* 1643-1653.

Pan, L. (1990). *Sons of the Yellow Emperor: A history of the Chinese diaspora.* Boston: Little, Brown.

Patel, N., Power, T., & Bhavnagri, N. P. (1996). Socialization values and practices of Indian immigrant parents: Correlates of modernity and acculturation. *Child Development, 67,* 302-313.

Pedersen, P. (1988). *A handbook for developing multicultural awareness.* Alexandria, VA: American Association for Counseling and Development.

Pedersen, P. (1994). *Handbook for developing multicultural awareness* (2nd ed.). Alexandria, VA: American Counseling Association.

Phinney, J. S. (1992). The Multi-Group Ethnic Identity Measure: A new scale for use with diverse groups. *Journal of Adolescent Research, 7,* 156-176.

Raskin, N. J., & Rogers, C. R. (1995). Person-centered therapy. In R. Corsini & D. Wedding (Eds.), *Current psychotherapies* (5th ed.). Itasca, IL: F. E. Peacock.

Redfield, R., Linton, R., & Herskovits, M. (1936). Memorandum on the study of acculturation. *American Anthropologist, 38,* 149-152.

Reynolds, D. K. (1976). *Morita psychotherapy.* Berkeley: University of California Press.

Reynolds, D. K. (1983). *Naikan psychotherapy.* Chicago: University of Chicago Press.

Reynolds, D. K. (1989a). *Flowing bridges, quiet waters: Japanese psychotherapies, Morita and Naikan.* Albany: State University of New York Press.

Reynolds, D. K. (1989b). On being natural: Two Japanese approaches to healing. In A. A. Sheikh & K. S. Sheikh (Eds.), *Healing East and West: Ancient wisdom and modern psychology* (pp. 180-194). New York: John Wiley.

Ritzler, B. A. (1996). Projective methods for multicultural personality assessment: Rorschach, TEMAS, and the Early Memories Procedure. In L. A. Suzuki, P. J. Meller, & J. G. Ponterotto (Eds.), *Handbook of multicultural assessment: Clinical, psychological, and educational applications* (pp. 115-136). San Francisco: Jossey-Bass.

Rogers, C. (1957). The necessary and sufficient conditions of therapeutic personality change. *Journal of Consulting Psychology, 21,* 95-103.

Rogers, C. (1975). Empathic: An unappreciated way of being. *Counseling Psychologist, 5*(2), 2-10.

Roid, G. H., & Miller, L. J. (1997). Leiter International Performance Scale-Revised: Examiner's manual. In G. H. Roid & L. J. Miller, *Leiter International Performance Scale-Revised.* Wood Dale, IL: Stoelting.

Roland, A. (1988). *In search of self in India and Japan: Toward a cross-cultural psychology.* Princeton, NJ: Princeton University Press.

Root, M. P. P. (Ed.). (1992). *Racially mixed people in America.* Newbury Park, CA: Sage.

Root, M. P. P. (1995). Resolving "other" status: Identity development of biracial individuals. In N. R. Goldberger & J. B. Veroff (Eds.), *The culture and psychology reader* (pp. 575-595). New York: New York University Press.

Root, M. P. P. (Ed.). (1997). *Filipino Americans: Transformation and identity.* Thousand Oaks, CA: Sage.

Rumbaut, R. G. (1995). Vietnamese, Laotian, and Cambodian Americans. In P. G. Min (Ed.), *Asian Americans: Contemporary trends and issues* (pp. 232-270). Thousand Oaks, CA: Sage.

Russell, J. G. (1989). Anxiety disorders in Japan: A review of the Japanese literature on Shinkeishitsu and taijinkyofusho. *Culture, Medicine and Psychiatry, 13,* 391-403.

Ryan, A. S., & Smith, M. J. (1989). Parental reactions to developmental disabilities in Chinese American families. *Child and Adolescent Social Work, 6,* 283-299.

Sabnani, H. B., & Ponterotto, J. G. (1992). Racial/ethnic minority-specific instrumentation in counseling research: A review, critique, and recommendations. *Measurement and Evaluation in Counseling and Development, 24,* 161-187.

Schmitz, P. G. (1994). Acculturation and adaptation process among immigrants in Germany. In A.-M. Bouvy, F. J. R. van de Vijver, & P. Schmitz (Eds.), *Journeys into cross-cultural psychology* (pp. 142-157). Amsterdam: Swets & Zeitlinger.

Seaburn, D., Landau-Stanton, J., & Horwitz, S. (1995). Core techniques in family therapy. In R. H. Mikesell & D. D. Lusterman (Eds.), *Integrating family therapy: Handbook of family psychology and systems theory* (pp. 5-26). Washington, DC: American Psychological Association.

Searle, W., & Ward, C. (1990). The prediction of psychological and sociocultural adjustment during cross-cultural transitions. *International Journal of Intercultural Relations, 14,* 449-464.

Sheth, M. (1995). Asian Indian Americans. In P. G. Min (Ed.), *Asian Americans: Contemporary trends and issues* (pp. 169-198). Thousand Oaks, CA: Sage.

Shon, S. P. (1980). The delivery of mental health services to Asian Americans. In U.S. Commission on Civil Rights (Ed.), *Civil rights issues of Asian and Pacific Americans: Myths and realities. A consultation sponsored by the U.S. Commission on Civil Rights* (pp. 724-733) (GPO: 1980 624-865/1772). Washington, DC: Government Printing Office.

Shon, S. P., & Ja, D. Y. (1982). Asian families. In M. McGoldrick, J. K. Pierce, & J. Giordano (Eds.), *Ethnicity and family therapy* (pp. 208-228). New York: Guilford.

Shotter, J. (1993). *Conversational realities: Constructing life through language.* Newbury Park, CA: Sage.

Simeonsson, R. J. (Ed.). (1994). *Risk, resilience and prevention: Promoting the well-being of all children.* Baltimore, MD: Brookes.

Simon, F. B., Stierlin, H., & Wynne, L. C. (1985). *The language of family therapy: A systemic vocabulary and source book.* New York: Family Process Press.

Smith, H. (1991). *The world's religions: Our great wisdom traditions.* San Francisco: Harper.

Sodowsky, G., Kwan, K., & Pannu, R. (1995). Ethnic identity of Asians in the United States. In J. G. Ponterotto, J. M. Casas, L. A. Suzuki, & C. M. Alexander (Eds.), *Handbook of multicultural counseling* (pp. 123-154). Thousand Oaks, CA: Sage.

Soo-Hoo, T. (1999). Brief strategic family therapy with Chinese Americans. *American Journal of Family Therapy, 27,* 163-179.

Soriano, M., & Hong, G. K. (1997). School-based family services: Administrative leadership for a caring model of effective education. *Journal for a Just and Caring Education, 3*(2), 180-191.

Soriano, M., Soriano, F. I., & Jimenez, E. (1994). School violence among culturally diverse populations: Sociocultural and institutional considerations. *School Psychology Review, 23,* 216-235.

Spector, R. E. (1996). *Cultural diversity in health and illness* (4th ed.). Stamford, CT: Appleton & Lange.

Spickard, P. R. (1989). Mixed blood: Intermarriage and ethnic identity in twentieth-century America. Madison: University of Wisconsin Press.

Stark, M. (1999). *Modes of therapeutic action: Enhancement of knowledge, provision of experience, and engagement in relationship.* Northvale, NJ: Jason Aronson.

Steinglass, P. (1985). Family systems approaches to alcoholism. *Journal of Substance Abuse Treatment, 2,* 161-167.

Steinglass, P. (1987). A systems view of family interaction and psychopathology. In T. Jacob (Ed.), *Family interaction and psychopathology: Theories, methods, and findings* (pp. 25-65). New York: Plenum.

Steinglass, P., Bennett, L. A., Wolin, S. J., & Reiss, D. (1987). *The alcoholic family.* New York: Basic Books.

Sue, D., & Sue, D. W. (1993). Ethnic identity: Cultural factors in the psychological development of Asians in America. In D. R. Atkinson, G. Morten, & D. W. Sue (Eds.), *Counseling American minorities* (pp. 199-210). Madison, WI: William C. Brown.

Sue, D. W. (1989). Racial/cultural identity development among Asian-Americans: Counseling/therapy implications. *AAPA Journal, 13*(1), 80-86.

Sue, D. W., Arredondo, P., & McDavis, R. J. (1992). Multicultural competencies/standards: A pressing need. *Journal of Counseling and Development, 70,* 477-486.

Sue, D. W., Bernier, Y., Durran, A., Feinberg, L., Pedersen, P., Smith, E. J., & Vasquez-Nuttal, E. (1982). Cross-cultural counseling competencies [Position paper]. *Counseling Psychologist, 10,* 45-52.

Sue, D. W., Ivey, W., & Pedersen, P. (Eds.). (1996). *A theory of multicultural counseling and therapy.* Pacific Grove, CA: Brooks/Cole.

Sue, D. W., & Sue, D. (1999). *Counseling the culturally different: Theory and practice* (3rd ed.). New York: John Wiley.

Sue, D. W., & Zane, N. (1987). The role of culture and cultural techniques in psychotherapy: A critique and reformulation. *American Psychologist, 42,* 37-45.

Sue, S. (1977). Community mental health services to minority groups: Some optimism, some pessimism. *American Psychologist, 32,* 616-624.

Sue, S., Fujino, D. C., Hu, L. T., Takeuchi, D., & Zane, N. (1991). Community mental health services for ethnic minority groups: A test of the cultural responsiveness hypothesis. *Journal of Consulting and Counseling Psychology, 59,* 533-540.

Sue, S., & McKinney, H. (1975). Asian Americans in the community mental health care system. *American Journal of Orthopsychiatry, 45*(1), 111-118.

Sue, S., & Morishima, J. K. (1982). *The mental health of Asian Americans.* San Francisco: Jossey-Bass.

Suinn, R. M. (1998). Measurement of acculturation of Asian Americans. *Asian American and Pacific Islander Journal of Health, 6*(1), 7-13.

Suinn, R. M., Richardson-Figueroa, K., Lew, S., & Vigil, P. (1987). The Suinn-Lew Asian Self-Identity Acculturation Scale: An initial report. *Educational and Psychological Measurement, 47,* 401-407.

Suzuki, L. A., Meller, P. J., & Ponterotto, J. G. (1996). Multicultural assessment: Present trends and future directions. In L. A. Suzuki, P. J. Meller, & J. G. Ponterotto (Eds.), *Handbook of multicultural assessment: Clinical, psychological, and educational applications* (pp. 672-684). San Francisco: Jossey-Bass.

Suzuki, T. (1989). The concept of neurasthenia and its treatment in Japan. *Culture, Medicine and Psychiatry, 13,* 187-202.

Takeuchi, D. T., Mokuau, N., & Chun, C. A. (1992). Mental health services for Asian - Americans and Pacific Islanders. *Journal of Mental Health Administration, 19,* 237-245.

Takeuchi, D. T., Sue. S., & Yeh, M. (1995). Return rates and outcomes from ethnicity-specific mental health programs in Los Angeles. *American Journal of Public Health, 85,* 638-643.

Tan, A. (1989). *The Joy Luck Club.* New York: Putnam.

Tang, N. M. (1997). Psychoanalytic psychotherapy with Chinese Americans. In E. Lee (Ed.), *Working with Asian Americans: A guide for clinicians.* New York: Guilford.

Tayabas, T., & Pok, T. (1983). The Southeast Asian refugee's arrival in America: An overview. In Special Service for Groups (Ed.), *Bridging cultures: Southeast Asian refugees in America* (pp. 3-14). Los Angeles: Asian American Community Mental Health Training Center, Special Service for Groups.

Tien, S. S. (1989). The phases of renewal: Steps to integration of the self in psychotherapy. *Journal of Contemporary Psychotherapy, 19,* 171-181.

Tran, T. V. (1988). The Vietnamese American family. In C. H. Mindel, R. W. Habenstein, & R. Wright, Jr. (Eds.), *Ethnic families in America: Patterns and variations* (3rd ed., pp. 276-299). New York: Elsevier Science.

Triandis, H. C. (1995). Individualism and collectivism. Boulder, CO: Westview.

Truax, C. B., & Carkhuff, R. R. (1967). *Toward effective counseling and psychotherapy.* Chicago: Aldine.

Tsai, S. S. H. (1986). Chinese in the United States. In H. C. Kim (Ed.), *Dictionary of Asian American history* (pp. 3-6). Westport, CT: Greenwood.

Tseng, W. S. (1975). The nature of somatic complaints among psychiatric patients: The Chinese case. *Comprehensive Psychiatry, 16,* 237-243.

Tseng, W. S. (1996). Cultural comments on mood and anxiety disorders: I. In J. E. Mezzich, A. Kleinman, H. Fabrega, Jr., & D. L. Parron (Eds.), *Culture and psychiatric diagnosis: A DSM-IV perspective* (pp. 115-121). Washington, DC: American Psychiatric Press.

Tseng, W. S., & McDermott, J. F., Jr. (1981). *Culture, mind and therapy: An introduction to cultural psychiatry.* New York: Spectrum.

Tsui, P. (1997). The dynamics of cultural and power relations in group therapy. In E. Lee (Ed.), *Working with Asian Americans: A guide for clinicians* (pp. 354-363). NY: Guilford.

Tu, W. M. (1991). Cultural China: The periphery as the center. *Daedalus: Journal of the American Academy of Arts and Sciences, 120*(2), 1-32.

Umbarger, C. C. (1983). *Structural family therapy.* New York: Grune & Stratton.

U.S. Bureau of the Census. (1983). *1980 census of population: General population characteristics summary* (PC80-1-D1). Washington, DC: Government Printing Office.

U.S. Bureau of the Census. (1988). *Statistical abstract of the United States* (108th ed.). Washington, DC: Government Printing Office.

U.S. Bureau of the Census. (1992). *1990 census of population: General population characteristics* (CP-1-1). Washington, DC: Government Printing Office.

U.S. Bureau of the Census. (1993a). *1990 census of population: Asian and Pacific Islanders in the United States* (CP-3-5). Washington, DC: Government Printing Office.

U.S. Bureau of the Census. (1993b). *1990 census of population and housing—guide: Part B, glossary series* (CPH-R-1B). Washington, DC: Government Printing Office.

U.S. Bureau of the Census. (1994). *1990 census of population: General social and economic characteristics* (CP-2-1). Washington, DC: Government Printing Office.

U.S. Bureau of the Census. (1998a). *Asians and Pacific Islanders have nation's highest median household income in 1997, Census Bureau reports* (CB98-177). Available: http://www.census.gov/Press-Release/cb98-177.html

U.S. Bureau of the Census. (1998b). *California leads states and Los Angeles County, Calif., tops counties in Asian and Pacific Islander population increase, Census Bureau reports* (CB98-161). Available: http://www.census.gov/Press-Release/cb98-161.html

U.S. Bureau of the Census. (1998c). *Selected characteristics of the population by citizenship: March 1997* (Internet release date: April 9, 1998). Available: http://www.census.gov/population/socdemo/foreign/97/ppltab1.txt

U.S. Bureau of the Census. (1998d). *Statistical abstract of the United States: 1997* (118th ed.). Washington, DC: Government Printing Office.

U.S. Bureau of the Census. (1999). *Asian and Pacific Islander American Heritage Month: May 1-31* (CB99-FF.06). Available: http://www.census.gov/Press-Release/www/1999/cb99ff06.html

Uba, L. (1994). *Asian Americans: Personality patterns, identity, and mental health.* New York: Guilford.

Umbarger, C. C. (1983). *Structural family therapy.* New York: Grune & Stratton.

Valencia, R. R., & Guadarrama, I. (1996). High stakes testing and its impact on racial and ethnic minority students. In L. A. Suzuki, P. J. Meller, & J. G. Ponterotto (Eds.), *Handbook of multicultural assessment: Clinical, psychological, and educational applications* (pp. 561-610). San Francisco: Jossey-Bass.

Vane, J. R. (1986). The need to train psychologists as family practitioners [Symposium]. *Psychotherapy in Private Practice, 4*(4), 17-18.

Wallace, R. K., & Benson, H. (1972, February). The physiology of meditation. *Scientific American, 226,* 85-90.

Wang, L. L. (1991). Roots and changing identity of the Chinese in the United States. *Daedalus: Journal of the American Academy of Arts and Sciences, 120*(2), 181-206.

Ward, C. (1996). Acculturation. In D. Landis & R. S. Bhagat (Eds.), *Handbook of intercultural training* (2nd ed., pp. 124-125). Thousand Oaks, CA: Sage.

Watson, G., & Seiler, R. (Eds.). (1992). *Text in context: Contributions to ethnomethodology.* Newbury Park, CA: Sage.

Watson, J. L. (1988). The structure of Chinese funerary rites: Elementary forms, ritual sequence, and the primacy of performance. In J. L. Watson & E. S. Rawski (Eds.), *Death ritual in late imperial and modern China* (pp. 3-19). Berkeley: University of California Press.

Watson, R. (1992). The understanding of language use in everyday life: Is there a common ground? In G. Watson & R. M. Seiler (Eds.), *Text in context: Contributions to ethnomethodology* (pp. 1-19). Newbury Park, CA: Sage.

Watzlawick, P., Bavelas, J. B., & Jackson, D. D. (1967). *Pragmatics of human communication: A study of interactional patterns, pathologies, and paradoxes.* New York: W. W. Norton.

Watzlawick, P., Bavelas, J. B., & Jackson, D. D. (1969). *Human communication: Forms, disturbances, paradoxes.* Bern, Switzerland: Hans Huber.

Watzlawick, P., Weakland, J. H., & Fisch, R. (1974). *Change: Principles of problem formation and problem resolution.* New York: W. W. Norton.

Wechsler, D. (1991). *Manual for the Wechsler Intelligence Scale for Children-Third Edition (WISC-III).* San Antonio, TX: Psychological Corporation.

Wechsler, D. (1997). *Manual for the Wechsler Adult Intelligence Scale-Third Edition (WAIS-III).* San Antonio, TX: Psychological Corporation.

Weil, S. (1983). The effect of ethnic origin on children's perceptions of their families. *Journal of Comparative Family Studies, 14,* 347-366.

Westwood, M. J., & Ishiyama, F. I. (1990). The communication process as a critical intervention for client change in cross-cultural counseling. *Journal of Multicultural Counseling and Development, 18,* 163-171.

White, M. (1995). *Re-authoring lives.* Adelaide, Australia: Dulwich Centre.

White, M., & Epston, D. (1990). *Narrative means to therapeutic ends.* New York: W. W. Norton.

Wickberg, E. (1965). *The Chinese in Philippine life: 1850-1898.* New Haven, CT: Yale University Press.

Williams, D. A., McDonald, D. H., Howard, L., Mittlebach, M., & Kyle, C. (1984, April 23). A formula for success: Asian-American students win academic honors—and cope with the mixed blessings of achievement. *Newsweek, 103,* 77-80.

Wong, H. Z. (1985). Training for mental health service providers to Southeast Asian refugees: Models, strategies, and curricula. In T. C. Owen (Ed.), *Southeast Asian mental health: Treatment, prevention, services, and research* (pp. 345-390, DHHS Publication No. ADM 85-1399). Washington, DC: National Institute of Mental Health.

Wong, M. G. (1995). Chinese Americans. In P. G. Min (Ed.), *Asian Americans: Contemporary trends and issues* (pp. 58-94). Thousand Oaks, CA: Sage.

Wong, M. G. (1998). The Chinese American family. In C. H. Mindel, R. W. Habenstein, & R. Wright, Jr. (Eds.), *Ethnic families in America: Patterns and variations* (4th ed., pp. 284-310). Upper Saddle River, NJ: Prentice Hall.

Wu, D. Y. H. (1987, August). *Achieving intra-cultural and inter-cultural understanding in psychotherapy with Asian Americans.* Paper presented at the Interactive Forum on Transference and Empathy in Psychotherapy with Asian Americans, South Cove Community Health Center and University of Massachusetts, Boston.

Wu, S. J., Enders, L., & Ham, M. D. (1997). Cross-cultural practice with couples and families: Social constructionist inquiry in family therapy with Chinese Americans. *Journal of Family Social Work, 2,* 111-128.

Yalom, I. D. (1985). *The theory and practice of group psychotherapy* (3rd ed.). New York: Basic Books.

Yamamoto, J. (1982). *Psychotherapy for Asian Americans.* Paper presented at the Second Pacific Congress of Psychiatry, Korea Extension Meeting, Korean Neuropsychiatric Association, Seoul, Korea.

Yamamoto, J., & Chang, C. (1987, August). *Empathy for the family and the individual in the social context.* Paper presented at the Interactive Forum on Transference and Empathy in Psychotherapy with Asian Americans, South Cove Community Health Center and University of Massachusetts, Boston.

Yansen, E. A., & Shulman, E. L. (1996). Language assessment: Multicultural considerations. In L. A. Suzuki, P. J. Meller, & J. G. Ponterotto (Eds.), *Handbook of multicultural assessment: Clinical, psychological, and educational applications* (pp. 353-393). San Francisco: Jossey-Bass.

Yee, J. (1997). Psychological testing for monolingual Asian American clients. In E. Lee (Ed.), *Working with Asian Americans: A guide for clinicians* (pp. 365-387). New York: Guilford.

Yeh, C. J., & Huang, K. (1996). The collectivistic nature of ethnic identity development among Asian-American college students. *Adolescence, 31*(123), 645-661.

Yeh, M., Takeuchi, D. T., & Sue, S. (1994). Asian-American children treated in the mental health system: A comparison of parallel and mainstream outpatient service centers. *Journal of Clinical Child Psychology, 23,* 5-12.

Yi, K. (1995). Psychoanalytic psychotherapy with Asian clients: Transference and therapeutic considerations. *Psychotherapy, 32,* 308-316.

Young, K., & Takeuchi, D. T. (1998). Racism. In L. C. Lee & N. W. S. Zane (Eds.), *Handbook of Asian American psychology* (pp. 401-432). Thousand Oaks, CA: Sage.

Zane, N., Hatanaka, H., Park, S., & Akutsu, P. D. (1994). Ethnic-specific mental health services: Evaluation of the parallel approach for Asian-American clients. *Journal of Community Psychology, 22,* 68-81.

Index

About the Authors

George K. Hong, PhD, is Professor in the Division of Administration and Counseling at California State University, Los Angeles. He is a clinical psychologist with extensive experience in providing mental health services to Asian Americans. He has worked for many years at the South Cove Community Health Center, a comprehensive medical and mental health clinic serving the Asian American communities of Greater Boston. He is active in many professional organizations and has recently served as a board member of the Asian American Psychological Association. He is a core member of the Consortium on Asian American Mental Health Training, a group of mental health professionals from major Asian Pacific clinics and related institutions in the Greater Los Angeles area, which offers annual training conferences on Asian American mental health issues.

MaryAnna Domokos-Cheng Ham, EdD, is Associate Professor in the Department of Counseling and School Psychology, University of Massachusetts Boston. In 1985, she established the department's Marriage and Family Therapy Track and developed its curriculum and courses, which emphasize a multicultural and urban perspective. She has been the director of the track since its inception and teaches courses in family therapy and ethics. She is a family psychologist with extensive experience in providing therapy to individuals, couples, and families, particularly mixed racial and ethnic couples and families. She is designated as an Approved Supervisor by the American Association of Marriage and Family Therapy. She is active in many professional organizations, including the Asian American Psychological Association, and is currently on the Board of the Massachusetts Association of Marriage and Family Therapy.